Vintage Radios

CROWOOD COLLECTORS' SERIES

Vintage Radios

TONY THOMPSON

THE CROWOOD PRESS

First published in 2007 by
The Crowood Press Ltd
Ramsbury, Marlborough
Wiltshire SN8 2HR

www.crowood.com

© R A Thompson 2007

British Library Cataloguing-in-Publication Data
A catalogue record for this book is available from the British Library.

ISBN 978 1 86126 949 2

DEDICATION

This book is dedicated to the memory
of Edward Laing Thompson.

ACKNOWLEDGEMENTS

To augment the author's own photographic collection, many people generously provided photographs and other graphic material for use in this book. In particular, the author wishes to thank Jools Zauscinski, Andy Mills, John P. Blagburn, George Bichard, John Northall, Mike Fulton, Eleanor Fulton, John Clappison, Jon Evans, Howard Craven, Mike Izycky, Frank Goddard, Neil Breward, Michael Horne, John Rickmansworth, Peter Hughes, Neil Purling, Joe Foreman, Neil Deacon and Trevor White.

Special thanks must go to Andy Mills for his invaluable assistance in checking the manuscript, to Mike Izycky for his help with the '1930s Germany' feature in Chapter Three, and to Jools Zauscinski, Mike Fulton and Jon Evans for their help and support in this project. Finally, thanks to the many enthusiasts who freely offered their assistance during the development of this book.

With graphic material of great age it is almost impossible to track ownership; apologies to anyone not credited in this first edition.

Typeset and designed by
D & N Publishing
Lambourn Woodlands, Hungerford, Berkshire.

Printed and bound in Singapore by Craft Print International Ltd.

INTRODUCTION

Vintage radios are fascinating as an echo of the technology of a bygone era, in much the same way as are vintage cars, motorcycles and steam-powered vehicles; but unlike the latter, it isn't essential to spend a fortune to obtain the majority of receivers. Although it is the case that certain vintage radios, popular with collectors, are now rare and consequently expensive to purchase, the sheer volume of sets produced between the years 1930–75 ensures that a good general supply remains available for the present. It is inevitable that numbers will dwindle in future times, and growing scarcity may well gradually create an all-round increase in average value, as it already has with the relatively few receivers presently in high demand and so commanding commensurately high selling prices; but this must only be speculation, and for the moment, there is a lot out there for the beginning collector and restorer.

There are several reasons why radios have become collectable. The technology itself is interesting, as intimated above; but also and importantly, the external design elements reflect the era in which they were manufactured. The Art Deco influence can be seen in 1930s receivers, with their sleek Bakelite and elegant veneered wood cabinets. Post-war radio design continued to reflect the decade, from the austerely 'modern' 1940s to the 'high tech' of the 1970s. Then there is the unique nostalgia associated with the warm sound of a vintage radio; perhaps a journey in memory back to childhood, or an echo of days long past. To listen to a working radio that can be seventy or more years old is something very special, the fact that it is still living when those who created it, paid for it and listened avidly to it have long departed.

Here, then, is the story of how radio was invented and developed, where to obtain and what to look for when purchasing vintage receivers, plus ways to improve the appearance of sets that have suffered the twin ravages of time and neglect. Technical and visual design points are described in straightforward terms. Throughout, a wide range of makes and models are identified, and details provided wherever possible, ranging from the commonplace offerings available at moderate cost, to the esoteric and expensive, so as to ensure something of interest for every reader, regardless of experience or knowledge. Sections on safety and cabinet restoration have been included, although this is not a technical restoration manual. Further suggestions for reading, sources for sets and radio-related items, magazines, web sites and organizations are listed in the appendix.

Collecting for Pleasure or Investment

Notwithstanding the above comments regarding the scarcity of certain receivers, buying any set to keep in the hope that it will accrue value over a period of time is fraught with risks: tastes change, and what is popular one year may not be the next. The best advice must be to collect the sets you like the look of and enjoy them for what they are, regardless of trends. After all, in doing so you become the keeper of an important technical heritage, preserving and protecting it not only for your own pleasure and satisfaction in owning something rather amazing, but also in the hope that they will endure for future generations to see and to admire. The whole world over, there are people of all ages, all nationalities, all walks of life and with budgets large and small who find great pleasure and interest in this activity. Why not join them? Whether you wish to specialize in a particular make or type, or in documentation, leaflets, advertising matter, or perhaps receivers from a particular period in time, with the information and the facts to hand in this book as a guide, the choice is yours to make.

Abbreviations

To keep the photograph captions to a manageable length, the following abbreviations are used:

L,M,S = long-, medium- and short-wave coverage
SH = superheterodyne receiver (superhet)
TRF = tuned radio frequency receiver
c. = circa, meaning 'around' when referring to the
    maker's release date
AC = receiver power supply must be alternating
    current mains
DC = receiver power supply must be DC mains
AC/DC = receiver will operate from AC or DC mains
B = battery operated
A/D = all-dry battery operated
B/M = battery or mains operated
HT = high tension
LT= low tension

Note that 'tension' in this context equals 'voltage'. Power supplies were generally abbreviated to initial form. American schematics use 'A' voltage for HT and 'B' voltage for LT. Information is provided where available, and has been checked for accuracy wherever possible – however, note 'c.' (for circa) regarding the year of production. There is more information about terminology in the glossary.

Radio Size Guide

The following terms are used to give an approximate indication of the physical size and shape of a receiver:

Miniature table model: up to 8in (20cm) length
Small table model: up to 12in (30cm) length
Medium table model: up to 16in (40cm) length
Large table model: up to 20in (50cm) length (or height)
Cathedral/tombstone shape: cabinet in upright, rather than long form
Console: floor-standing, either directly, or with legs (consolette)
Photographs are not to scale; approximations of size are provided in the captions.

Star Rating: What's it Worth?

To provide guidance as to the value and rarity of a given receiver, a star rating system from 1 to 4 has been used for many – but not all – radios in this book:

*   Both plentiful and requiring only a modest outlay to purchase
**   The lower middle range for cost and availability
***   Less easily obtained and/or more desirable receivers
****   Rare and/or expensive: these sets are prized by collectors

Do not assume that where no star rating is given the radio in question has no value; it actually means that insufficient evidence is available upon which to base a value. **The rating system should be seen as only a very approximate guide,** for the following reasons:

Vintage and antique artefacts are by their nature intrinsically valueless unless and until someone is prepared to pay the asking price, or to barter (the latter is strongly recommended in most cases).

General auctions are at best something of a lottery, dependent upon the interests of those attending, where a receiver up for auction on a favourable day may attract an inordinately high price, yet on another day, the same receiver may fail to reach even a modest reserve. Dedicated vintage radio auctions provide a more consistent source.

As in all collecting fields, certain models or styles come into vogue – and consequently attract high prices at sale – then drift out of popularity, to be replaced by others.

It is impossible to apply an accurate monetary figure to any particular make or model, because such factors as condition and originality (for example, the presence or absence of original control knobs, dial, back cover, components, wiring, grille cloth and so on) vary enormously. The star ratings assume auction-level pricing of a receiver in good original condition. The sets adorning the shelves of antique shops will generally be more costly.

Generally speaking, although sets built prior to World War II still tend to sell at higher prices than those of post-war manufacture, more recently smaller 'shelf-sized' sets have become popular. Generally these are from the post-World War II period. In modern homes where space is at a premium, it is easier to display these smaller radios; it may be one reason, among others, why transistor sets are now gaining in popularity as collectables.

Bakelite, that amazing plastic material, has a fan base of its own, and Bakelite receivers often sell on appearance as much as functionality.

Added Value

Like most vintage items, any radio receiver is inherently more collectable and therefore likely to attract a higher selling price if it is accompanied by provenance in the form of original documentation such as sales receipts, service or repair bills, owner's instruction leaflets, or even complete with its original packing box.

Ekco RS3, c. 1931. An odd mix of Art Deco and Art Nouveau makes this Ekco RS3 a popular collectable. Four valves plus rectifier valve AC TRF, L/M. ME moving-coil loudspeaker with output transformer tapped on the primary and forming part of the tone-control circuit. Unusual scale-drive mechanism. ***/****

HOW IT ALL BEGAN

The Need to Communicate

Communication in one form or another could be seen as one of the foundations of society. Over centuries, philosophers and men of science and technology speculated about mass communication in both visual and aural terms. By the nineteenth century the postal system and the printed word in book form had already created their own revolution in communication, but although a valuable development in the progress of mankind, the key element of immediacy was lacking, and books in particular are best seen as an accessible long-term storage system.

Early Recording Methods

In 1877 Edison demonstrated his phonograph, and proved that sound could be recorded and was no longer ephemeral; the audible storage equivalent of the book had been invented. With recorded sound placed alongside Fox Talbot's somewhat earlier invention of photography, mankind now held the means for creating an archive in sounds and pictures of the great and the good, and, of course, music. All these early recording methods were essentially mechanical, printing via the press, with wooden or metal type, on to paper: in sound, at first, by means of the physical indentations in a rotating wax cylinder caused by the sound waves created by the artiste speaking or singing loudly enough to vibrate a cutting stylus; and photographic images created by light focused by a lens upon a thin layer of sensitized silver halides.

Radio Waves Discovered

Meanwhile, as the nineteenth century progressed, the first practical system using electricity as a means of communication had been developed. The telegraph, useful as it was, still needed code. The invention of the telephone created another leap forward in one-to-one communication, and was the first truly instant speech-based communication system. Others searched for a new and at that time undiscovered technology to free communication from the constraints of linking wires. The foundations of this can be traced back to 1820, when the Danish physicist Hans Christian Oersted (1777–1851, Denmark) made observations on the link between electricity and magnetism. This was followed by the practical experiments of Michael Faraday (1791–1867, Great Britain) in 1831.

The Genius of Maxwell

Using the work of Oersted and Faraday as his starting point, James Clerk Maxwell (1831–79, Scotland), a brilliant Scottish mathematician working in Cambridge in 1864, was able to calculate the virtual inevitability of the existence of 'radio' waves. A further step forward occurred in 1888 when the German scientist Heinrich Hertz (1857–94) finally proved Maxwell's assumptions correct.

Arguably, Maxwell's most important achievement was the mathematical formulation of Michael Faraday's theories of electricity and magnetic lines of force. He predicted that electromagnetism moved through space in waves that could be generated in the laboratory. His

RIGHT: **James Clerk Maxwell,** who formulated the first mathematical theory indicating the existence of radio waves.

FAR RIGHT: **Heinrich Rudolf Hertz,** the first person to demonstrate electromagnetic radiation (radio waves).

calculations indicated that their velocity was the same as the speed of light, therefore proving, at least to his own satisfaction, that light was an electromagnetic phenomenon, stating 'We can scarcely avoid the conclusion that light consists in the transverse undulations of the same medium which is the cause of electric and magnetic phenomena'. The medium in question was thought to be the 'ether', the existence – or non-existence – of which became an issue of considerable debate.

Maxwell's paper on Faraday's lines of force was read to the Cambridge Philosophical Society in two parts, 1855 and 1856. He also showed how complex was the interaction of electric and magnetic fields. Maxwell died in Cambridge on 5 November 1879, before his theorizing was successfully tested and proven by practical means. Although not our main concern here, it is interesting to note that the outstanding mind of Maxwell contributed also to the study of colour blindness and colour vision, and from his studies of colour theory came the first colour photograph, which was produced by photographing one subject through filters of the three primary colours of light and then recombining the images.

Hertz turned Maxwell's theorizing on electromagnetic waves – radio waves – into practical reality in Berlin in 1888 when he created an apparatus to generate and detect electromagnetic waves, proving Maxwell's theories to be accurate – including the fact that the speed of radio waves was indeed equal to the speed of light – and showed that such waves could be radiated (transmitted) into the atmosphere without the need for conducting wires. In hindsight it seems almost incredible that at the

time, he and other scientists of high standing foresaw no practical use for his discoveries.

Radio Transmission Becomes a Reality

So it was that as the last decade of the nineteenth century began, the discovery of 'radio waves' remained unused and undeveloped, firmly fixed in the realm of theoretical physics and untainted by technological intervention or commercial enterprise. What was needed was someone far-sighted enough to see the possibilities, and then to prove that electromagnetic waves could be harnessed for communication purposes; that someone is generally accepted to have been Guglielmo Marconi (1874–1937, Italy). After reading an article by Hertz about his discoveries, the young Italian with a genius for invention demonstrated genuine radio transmission in the closing years of the nineteenth century, successfully transmitting and receiving a coded signal over several kilometres on Salisbury Plain,

The young Guglielmo Marconi.

England, in 1896. At about the same time, Alexander Stepanovitch Popov (1859–1905), working in Russia, also succeeded in transmitting radio signals. Popov wasn't gifted with Marconi's enthusiasm for promotion, nor possessed his business acumen, which perhaps goes some way towards explaining why his name is absent from many historic radio reference sources.

Someone else who missed out on recognition was David Hughes (1831–1900), a professor of music who was a keen experimenter and prolific inventor. It seems that he actually demonstrated radio transmission in 1879, only to be told by the scientists of the Royal Society that his 'invention' was merely a facet of already observed electrical induction – something it clearly was not. The discouraged Hughes decided not to publish his experiments.

Radio or Wireless?

Marconi called his system a 'wireless telegraph' – that is, a telegraph with no interconnecting wires – which was an accurate description of his invention, the name later being shortened to 'wireless'. These very early pioneering transmissions were by 'spark gap' and were not frequency-selective – or, to put it another way, they were untunable. If two transmissions were made at the same time within range of each other, interference would result. The spark system also suffered from a limited range. But despite the severe limitations of the primitive system, Marconi succeeded in transmitting signals from England to Newfoundland in 1901; these were in code, and in one direction only.

WHO REALLY INVENTED RADIO?

This is an argument that has continued for many years without reaching an answer satisfactory to all. It seems likely that there never will be a definitive name credited with the invention, despite Marconi's sterling work and the fact that there is a widespread perception that it was he, and he alone, who invented the first electric communication system that worked without the need for linking wires; for the truth is, Marconi was far from the only inventor and experimenter involved with radio at the outset. He himself freely 'borrowed' ideas and devices for his system, in time-honoured fashion.

Among the many names connected with wireless communication around the turn of the century was Nicola Tesla (1856–1943), the brilliant Croatian experimenter, who demonstrated wireless communication in 1893. Then again, there is good evidence to suggest that a British scientist, David Hughes, first transmitted by radio a decade or more earlier, but was persuaded that what he claimed wasn't possible and that it was simply an effect of electromagnetic induction. Whatever the rights and wrongs of the unfortunate Hughes case, ahead of other experimenters such as Oliver Lodge, Jagdish Chandra Bose and Alexander Popov, it is Marconi who is popularly credited with being the first to make radio transmission a reality.

Marconi was an astute businessman and an effective self-publicist as well as being inventive, strong-minded and quick-witted, possessed of the innate certainty that he would succeed; all useful qualities that others may not have held to the same degree. Having succeeded, as he knew he would, he was the first to publicize the fact, and he certainly deserves credit for that and also for his undoubted far-sightedness regarding the revolution in communication that radio was to bring about.

Guglielmo Marconi.

Oliver Lodge (1851–1940, later Sir Oliver Lodge) made a great advance when he came up with a system using an inductance in the form of a coil, together with a capacitor. Together, these two components form a tuned circuit, and he was able to transmit and receive on selected frequencies with his invention, which used a continuous wave modulated by an audible tone when controlled by a morse key. The advantages of the system were a far greater transmission range compared to the spark transmitter, and the selective tuning, which prevented one transmission from interfering with another.

More importantly, if a coded tone could be transmitted, so for the first time could speech and music. On Christmas Eve, 1906, Reginald Fessenden (1866–1932, Canada) used a continuous wave generator made to his specification to transmit the first audio radio broadcast from Massachusetts, USA. Ships off the coast were treated to Fessenden himself playing on his violin and reading a bible passage. Sadly, despite the advances he achieved, Fessenden could not find financial backing and his progress stalled.

The terms 'wireless' and 'radio' are interchangeable, the former being superseded by the latter over a period of many years.

Caught by wireless message, Dr Crippen and Miss LeNeve face Bow Street police court committal proceedings.

Practical Uses for Radio

Marconi was convinced, and correctly so, that his 'wireless telegraph' system would be of great benefit to shipping, and with an aim to commercial development, he held a successful demonstration in 1898 in the presence of officials from Trinity House, the British organization in charge of the maintenance of lighthouses and lightships. The Marconi system saved lives for the first time when it was used to summon the assistance of the Ramsgate lifeboat to the aid of the German ship *Elbe*, aground on the Goodwin Sands. Marconi even transmitted news to ships at sea, proving that radio might have other uses than simply emergency contacts: it could provide information.

The Italian inventor's fame spread even further when in 1910 his wireless telegraph helped the apprehension of the fleeing murderer Dr Crippen, who was aboard the SS *Montrose* hoping to make good his escape, together with his disguised accomplice Ethel LeNeve. The captain thought they looked suspicious, especially LeNeve who was poorly disguised as a man, so he had a message transmitted to the effect that he believed he had the murderers aboard. His message was relayed to the police and the press as British police gave chase across the Atlantic, to arrest Crippen whilst still aboard. Famously – and tragically – in 1912, despite radio warnings received by the *Titanic* about the likelihood of icebergs, the great ship foundered on its maiden voyage after its fatal collision, with a resultant tragic loss of so very many lives. The distress signals from the doomed vessel were received until it sank.

Developments in Radio Technology

As far as entertainment value went, the Marconi wireless telegraph with its coded signal was ultimately limited in scope. The biggest problem in those early years was the innate weakness of signal. That, together with the lack of any satisfactory means of amplification, meant that although Morse code transmitted quite well, the signals from continuous wave broadcasting were too feeble, and despite experiments, could not be adapted to carry intelligible speech or music, at least to any worthwhile degree. Some way had to be found to increase their strength.

John Ambrose Fleming (1849–1945, Great Britain) invented the diode valve by adding an anode (plate) to an Edison electric lamp. This important development, which he named the 'thermionic valve', could not amplify, but it could detect (convert signals from their AC form to DC – it rectified in a manner similar to the 'cat's whisker' crystal diodes, although its action was very different). It was, however, an important step in the right direction. A breakthrough occurred when Lee DeForest (1873–1961, USA) invented the so-called 'triode' or three-electrode valve by fitting a grid of fine wires between the anode and cathode of Fleming's diode. He named his invention 'the Audion' and it opened the floodgates. Rapid development of practical amplifying valves began, and with it, radio for the masses.

But before that could come about, broadcasting stations had to be put into operation. At first these

RIGHT: **John Ambrose Fleming, the inventor of the diode valve.**

BELOW: **Fleming's thermionic diode, 1905.**

BELOW RIGHT: **DeForest 'Audion' valve, c. 1906.**

were semi-commercial ventures, aimed at creating public interest in radio and promoting the sales of radio receivers. Before these went on air there was little for the British radio enthusiast, armed with his receiving licence, to tune into other than time signals and Morse code transmissions.

LODGE AND THE MYSTERY OF TRANSMISSION

Once radio had been proven to work, a theory was needed to explain how such waves could radiate through seemingly empty space. Oliver Lodge (1851–1940, later Sir Oliver Lodge) actually demonstrated radio transmission two years before Marconi did. Assuming, reasonably, that some 'medium' had to exist to carry the radio waves – and yet being unable to discover one – he, along with others, postulated the existence of something they called the luminiferous aether, or ether, an invisible and undetectable medium assumed to permeate the universe. It was thought to conduct radio waves in a manner similar to the way an expanding wave ripples through a body of water when a stone is dropped into it. Post-Victorian scientists, however, discredited the whole 'ether' concept.

Sir Oliver Lodge.

Many, if not all of those arguing the need for the existence of the ether, were to a greater or lesser extent religious and, like Lodge, held a profound belief in the survival of the spirit for which the medium of the ether seemed to be an essential requirement. Sir Oliver's belief was formed through his many investigations into the claims of spiritualism. He explained that he believed the 'realm of spirit' was contained within the ether, itself, surely, the essence of the universe, condensing here and there to create the physical world – and consequently life. He was far from alone in his support for spiritualism; numerous other eminent scientists and acclaimed philosophers also believed as he did, notable among their number being Sherlock Holmes' creator, Sir Arthur Conan Doyle, and also Lord Balfour (1848–1910) who was the British Prime Minister from 1902–1905 and the chairman of the Society for Psychic Research in 1894. Lodge even promised to return after his demise to prove that life went on after death. To date, no sightings of his spirit form have been recorded.

Because of the scientific advances made by Einstein and his like, the ether theory was discredited, and nowadays it is no longer thought to exist. Lodge was in error when he allowed his personal beliefs to colour his scientific judgement, though it has to be allowed that in those Victorian times, the scientific understanding of electromagnetic fluctuations was very limited. Knowledge is gained, progress is made. Today's physicists no longer think of space as empty in the way that Lodge and his peers did; rather, it is thought by some to be a foaming sea of virtual sub-atomic particles, which constantly come into and go out of existence. This is academic, however, as it seems that radio waves do not actually need a medium to travel through. Radio waves and light waves differ only in their assigned wavelengths. Light spans across a submicroscopic range between 4,000 to 8,000 atoms wide, or 4 to 8 nanometres (a nanometre is a billionth of a metre), whereas radio waves can be anything from a tiny fraction of a metre to several kilometres. Furthermore, all radio and light waves are part of the electromagnetic spectrum and move at ultimate speed through space, not like ripples in water. Analogies, however useful, have their limits.

THE 1920s –
RADIO FOR ALL

By the end of World War I, the technology was in place to make true 'speech'-based wireless communication a commercial reality. A notable first for this occurred in Britain in 1920 when Dame Nellie Melba, the famous Australian soprano, sang in a broadcast from Marconi's own transmitter at the Chelmsford works.

Impressive as this was, it failed to kick-start a full-time radio service in Britain. America was first off the starting blocks when, in 1920, Westinghouse, already by then a major radio manufacturer, decided to open a transmitter for entertainment purposes – and, of course, to help boost interest in sales. Station KDKA in Pittsburgh made the first broadcast on 2 November 1920. America went radio crazy; over the following four years, KDKA was joined by hundreds of commercially sponsored transmitting stations spreading across the USA – all effectively unregulated until, in 1927, the jammed airwaves forced the establishment of the Federal Radio Commission, a body designed to control and assign broadcasting frequencies.

Dame Nellie Melba
sings for Marconi.

Chelmsford. The station call sign was 'Two Emma Toc' (2MT). Soon after this, the company was granted a licence to set up a 100-watt transmitter at Marconi House, The Strand, London, using the now famous call-sign 2LO. Transmissions were limited to hour-long programmes, and reception was in the London area only. Not long afterwards, meetings between the Postmaster General and interested parties – set makers – outlined the PMG's plan for a single broadcasting company for Britain, in contrast to the situation in America where the multitude of stations was seen to be causing havoc with frequency allocation. The BBC (British Broadcasting Company) was formed in May 1922 at the behest of the government by the creation of a cartel of interested radio makers, with the directors of the largest companies becoming board members, and one smaller radio manufacturing concern, Burndept, co-opted on to the board. The personable Captain Eckersley was highly technically proficient, and in 1923 he became the BBC's first chief engineer. His brother, Roger, also worked for the company in a variety of non-technical posts.

The First British Radio Station

In Britain, the Marconi Company was licensed in 1922 to broadcast an experimental weekly half-hour programme. This was to be set up by Marconi subsidiary 'The Marconi Scientific Instrument Company Ltd'. Peter Eckersley wrote, produced and presented these transmissions from an ex-army hut in Writtle, a village near

Wireless Licences

In November 1922 the broadcast receiving licence was introduced by the Postmaster General. At the same time, all commercial receivers bought for use with the licence had to be manufactured in Britain by one of the BBC's member companies. This included crystal radios and 'add-on' valve amplifiers. All equipment was required to carry the BBC-PMG stamp with a unique GPO registration number for each item, which itself was subject to a royalty surcharge. Radio was truly the province of the rich in those times. In addition, before production could begin on any receiver, a sample set had to be submitted for approval to the Post Office. This was to check that no interference was caused by the set to other receivers in the vicinity. In effect this ruled out the use of variable reaction in the aerial circuits of the early TRF receivers, although reaction was allowed to be fitted to subsequent stages. Lack of aerial stage reaction must have severely limited the sensitivity of those primitive radios, and would have been very unpopular with both makers and the public. The ruling was withdrawn in 1923, the only stipulation being that purchasers were provided with instructions on the correct operation of the reaction control.

By 1924 the royalties payable on BBC-PMG stamped receivers were abolished, and receivers and valved amplifiers could be purchased from any British manufacturer, not just those belonging to the BBC – although, oddly, the latter were still required to display the stamp on their products even though it no longer carried any actual approval from the PMG. In order of date, the first circular stamps showing the BBC initials across the centre with the wording 'type approved by postmaster general' around the edge were issued from November 1922 to September 1924. From September 1924 to 1927, the wording around the edge was changed to 'entirely British manufacture'. A few wording-free 'BBC' badges were seen in the same period.

BBC-PMG stamp, 1922–24. The first of two stamps that signified technical approval by the Postmaster General, and also confirmed that the receiver had been manufactured by members of the BBC. In addition to these there was another stamp that simply held the BBC letters as a logo with no peripheral wording, but its use seems to have been limited.

the end of 1926, at which time the company was succeeded by the corporation. By the end of 1922 the BBC, together with its first director general, the dour John Reith, had a new and prestigious home. Broadcasting House is an Art Deco extravaganza of a building, which remains at the heart of the corporation. The BBC was both witness to, and cause of, a phenomenal growth of sales in licences to receive (British radio receiving licences, issued by the Postmaster General): from virtually zero in 1922, almost two and a quarter million licences were applied for in 1926.

Exclusivity

Radio, expensive to make and to purchase, remained a rich man's toy, but by 1922 there were hundreds of small firms producing component parts and self-build kits for a market probably at first not exceeding a few thousand enthusiasts. But by 1926, major league players had come on the scene and ousted lots of the small fry. Large scale 'wireless' manufacturing had begun in earnest, but kits of every level of complexity continued to be marketed, from simple crystal receivers with their 'cat's whisker' metallic crystal diodes, through to complex multi-valve designs.

The Stated Aim of the British Broadcasting Company

The BBC's brief was to set up a nationwide network of transmitters and to provide regular broadcast entertainment. To this end, the licence to transmit was limited to

Crystal Radio Receivers

In the early 1920s there were two ways for any listener to receive the fledgling BBC's transmissions: the first and by far the cheapest and, therefore, unsurprisingly most popular being the crystal set, while expensive valved receivers were very much for the more affluent minority. The great advantage of the crystal receiver was that no external power source was required – the transmission alone provided that. Unfortunately that advantage was also a major limitation because reception was in the main available only within a certain radius of the transmitting station, due to the fall-off in signal strength over distance. Anything over 30 miles (50km) was the exception – and exceptions there were, with some experimenters even receiving continental stations on fortuitous occasions when weather conditions were favourable for the propagation of radio waves.

Despite this handicap, for many listeners the crystal radio proved to be a very popular way into radio reception, so much so that in those early years, sales of them far exceeded sales of expensive valve receivers. This is readily understandable from the purchaser's point of view. The crystal receiver was relatively cheap to purchase (a commercially made example could be purchased for £2 to £3, compared with a typical valve radio at around £15 upwards) and even cheaper to build at home – and, importantly, it cost nothing to run and it could, when reception was at an optimum, reputedly power more than one set of headphones. Also, crystal 'front ends' were often used in conjunction with valved 'note magnifiers' (amplifiers): with this combination, the crystal 'cat's whisker' acted as detector, converting the high frequency radio signal to low frequency audio, and the valve or valves boosted the audio signal sufficiently to allow either more than one set of headphones or a horn loudspeaker to be used.

Advantages and Disadvantages

Along with its obvious advantages, the crystal receiver suffered serious drawbacks. Loudspeakers were out, although as mentioned above, a valve amplifier could be connected to any crystal set to provide power sufficient to drive a horn loudspeaker, so in that sense it was possible to upgrade when finances allowed. Furthermore, at audio frequencies, the initially ubiquitous 'R'

valve performed well, but exhibited instability at radio frequencies, where a crystal tuner did not – but what proved to be an utterly intractable problem with the typical crystal receiver was the lack of selectivity (sharpness of tuning) that was a function of all crystal sets.

It was a case of selectivity versus sensitivity, and it applied just as much to valve radio as it did to crystal receivers – but the crucial difference was amplification. A valve radio could, through the amplifying power of valves and the somewhat problematic use of reaction,* be designed to make up for losses in sensitivity in a way that crystal receivers could not. This wasn't too important until the later 1920s, at which time the expanding number of BBC relay stations made it difficult for crystal receivers to avoid the audible jumble of multi-station reception. From this point onwards the popularity of crystal radios lost out to the rapidly advancing valved equipment. The technological principle behind the crystal diode was to reappear in a new form in later years to challenge and ultimately prove, in many ways, superior to the valve. That form was the crystal 'triode', better known as the transistor.

---

* A way of increasing sensitivity by taking the output of a valve and feeding it back into the input.

**Radio instruments (RI)
V4A, 1922. Four-valve battery receiver covering 300–4,000m without plug-in coils. BBC/PMG stamp, reg. no. 2100. The mahogany cabinet features a black ebonite panel. *****

BELOW: R.I. V1M amplifier, 1922. A single-valve 'distortionless magnifier', this unit is mounted in a mahogany case with brass fittings and a black ebonite panel. ***

RIGHT: Marconiphone V2 01, 1922. Two-valve battery receiver by Marconi's Wireless Telegraph Co. Ltd. 185–3,200m using plug-in regeneration unit and slot-in range blocks. Tuned by means of sliding copper spades over the range block. ***

ABOVE: Mitchel crystal receiver, c. 1923. With BBC/PMG stamp, GPO reg. no. 475. Sliding-contact tuning coil and cat's whisker detector. ***

LEFT: Western Electric crystal set, c. 1922. Polished mahogany case, plug-in coils, BBC/PMG badge. ***

ABOVE: **GECoPhone BC2001 two valve (HF, Detector), 1923.** With BBC/PMG stamp, GPO reg. no. 2000. Beneath is its matching GEC BC2580 two-valve amplifier, BBC/PMG stamp, GPO reg. no. 3360. The combination was sold as a BC3400 receiver. Also pictured is a selection of accessories, left to right: headphone distributor (enables more than one listener), aerial and earth cables, three reactance coils, two loading coils and a lead-acid accumulator. Headphones are hung on the cabinet door. Each of these items is hard to find today, making this elegant period ensemble an extremely rare sight. ***

ABOVE RIGHT: **BTH (British Thompson-Houston) horn loudspeaker, c. 1923.** Type C2, using an aluminium 'swan's neck' with a painted aluminium flare, mounted on a Bakelite base. ***

RIGHT: **AJS (A.J. Stevens) two-valve battery receiver, 1925.** Slow-motion tuning, using plug-in tuning and reaction coils. Mahogany case. ***

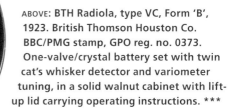

ABOVE: **BTH Radiola, type VC, Form 'B', 1923.** British Thomson Houston Co. BBC/PMG stamp, GPO reg. no. 0373. One-valve/crystal battery set with twin cat's whisker detector and variometer tuning, in a solid walnut cabinet with lift-up lid carrying operating instructions. ***

BELOW: AJS receiver with lid open to show access to valves and for coil changing.

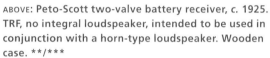

ABOVE: Peto-Scott two-valve battery receiver, c. 1925. TRF, no integral loudspeaker, intended to be used in conjunction with a horn-type loudspeaker. Wooden case. **/***

ABOVE: GECophone No. 2 crystal set, mid-1920s. A typical offering from GEC, complete with the requisite BBC/PMG stamp. ***

LEFT: Varley AP12 receiver with loudspeaker. This attractively contained receiver has proved hard to date conclusively, but it is likely to be from the end of the 1920s. ***

ABOVE: Graves two-valve receiver, c.1929. Two valves together with an efficient aerial and earth system provided just about enough power for modest volume horn loudspeaker reception of local transmitting stations, with the option of headphone use for longer-range reception. ***

ABOVE: Revophone Crystal receiver, 1920s. Cat's-whisker detector and tuned by coil tappings selectable by rotary slide switches, this simple receiver came supplied with full instructions pasted into the lid, including the erection of a suitable aerial. **

ABOVE: K-B 'Masterpiece' two-valve receiver manufactured for Godfrey Phillips. This battery receiver was given away by Godfrey Phillips, the cigarette manufacturers, in return for 500 cigarette coupons, one of which was to be found in each 6d packet of ten cigarettes. A three-valve K-B 'Masterpiece' upright radio was also offered by the cigarette company in 1931. **

RIGHT: Metropolitan-Vickers crystal receiver plus valve amplifier and horn, c.1923. Early valves were inefficient at radio frequencies, so crystal 'front ends' were sometimes used as tuners, with a valve amplifier to provide loudspeaker power. ***

How the Crystal Set Works

Is a radio with no apparent power source possible? Of course not. The crystal receiver derives its power directly from the transmitted radio signal, the main reason for its limited reception range. The necessarily long, high outdoor aerial, coupled with a good earth, forms a tuned circuit that receives the very small current induced in it by the transmitter. This radio-frequency current is made to flow through a wire-wound coil designed to select given frequencies within its range, the range being determined by its physical size and the number of turns of wire. The most common methods of selection – tuning, in other words – for these primitive receivers were either by some form of adjustable tapping, perhaps a slider running along the coil windings, or by variable capacitor wired in parallel with the coil. Whichever method, the result is that the tuned signal current can then be fed through a recti-fying contact created by a metal probe (nicknamed the 'cat's whisker') touching the surface of a mineral crys-tal. This converts the radio-frequency (RF) alternating signal current into a varying direct current, the varia-tions being an analogue of the transmitted speech or music. Sound can then be heard when headphones are connected in series with the crystal 'diode'. A small-value capacitor removes remnants of the RF signal. There were many practical variations of design but always the circuits used were straightforward, cost free in operation and reliable, whereas the early valve radios were definitely not, nor easy to operate.

Home-Built Radio

Numerous magazines devoted to radio construction appeared, offering plans and articles on the home building of crystal and simple valve receivers. People from all walks of life, some technically minded but most not, had their first experience of radio by building one, using magazines as a guide or by assembling a kit, which was said to be an economical alternative to the purchase of a ready-made receiver. This home-build phenomenon continued for many years, becoming the province of the keen amateur constructor who was supported by the ever-growing army of dedicated magazines, books, and component and kit suppliers. It can be difficult to tell the difference between home-built and commercial radios of the 1920s period, as radio 'factories' were far from automated. Assembly in what were often quite rudimentary workshops mir-rored the methods used at home; every wire placed by hand, every cabinet showing at least some signs of hand construction and finish. To blur the distinction even more, professionally built cabinets were available to house the home-built receiver.

One clue to a radio receiver's origin, though by no means reliable, is the presence or absence of a maker's label, transfer or plate and the official BBC mark or stamp of approval. Manufacturers proliferated, the great majority of them being very small 'back street' concerns, perhaps small shops with a workshop for radio con-struction, cycle works and garages, all with one aim in common: to make financial gain from radio.

Radio for All

After the haphazard, piecemeal start of radio manu-facture in the years following the end of World War I, when set-making concerns might have consisted of little more than a man and his apprentice working over a cycle repair shop or in a garden shed, things gradually became more orderly and the fledgling industry began to gain momentum. A great many makers, large and small, both well funded and under-capitalized, dipped their toes experimentally in the ever-deepening waters of radio manufacturing during the rapid expansion of radio in the late 1920s and early 1930s.

It really was a case of sink or swim! Many went under, either through sheer bad luck, poor judgement or lack of the ability to develop a sustainable range of marketable products, but others succeeded, expand-ing and developing into highly profitable concerns during the latter half of the decade of the 1930s – at least until war brought a temporary halt to radio empire-building.

RIGHT: **Burndept 'Ethodyne V', Mk. IV, mid-1920s.**

BELOW LEFT: **Pye 25C, 1927. Five-valve battery portable, L/M. Cone loudspeaker, internal frame aerial.**

BELOW RIGHT AND BOTTOM: **Pye 555, c.1925. This five-valve battery portable was designed to receive only the long-wave Daventry transmitter. It featured an** integral frame aerial, fine-tuning control and unusually, an Amplion horn loudspeaker unit. A later version was fitted with a moving-iron cone unit.

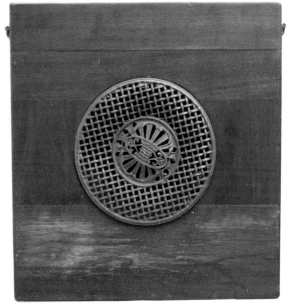

Post-War Activities

At the end of World War II hostilities, the bulk of these makers remained, and many, with an eye to restarting the expansion that had been curtailed, widened their remit to cover the growing television audience. Brave though their efforts were, and regardless of the fact that many makers had started production in the post-war radio and television industry of the UK, most of these were still relatively small business concerns; as the 1950s progressed, these smaller firms lost ground,

under-funded and unable to compete in an ever-growing and ever-costlier fight for market share. Slowly but inevitably, one by one they disappeared, sometimes lost into liquidation but more often being merged with the heavyweights in the industry, to produce an ever-reducing number of relatively large – and rapidly enlarging – concerns. Today, few of even the most successful of these once famous names remain under original control – though one notable exception is the Dutch electrical giant, Philips.

What Price Quality?

It is easy to forget, in these days of the inexpensive 'luxury' goods that electronic products have become, that in the early part of the last century, radio receivers were extremely expensive – and consequently highly prized status symbols. They were very costly to produce, too, but with retail price maintenance holding off competition, the UK market, at least, was certainly a lucrative one. The wooden cabinets that housed so many receivers were practically hand built, and could never be produced to sell in quantity or at a profit today. Even the Bakelite mouldings of those early days, denigrated by some at the time as a cheap and inferior alternative to the quality wooden cabinets, would today be too expensive to consider producing unless product demand and profit margins could be guaranteed.

It is also the case that the amount of hand production and assembly work that went into the assembly of even the most basic radio receiver chassis would today render it completely uneconomic to produce, at least to anything approaching the standards of

HMV were never producers of low cost receivers, and this advertisement is typical for its time. In 1936, '17½ guineas' represented a very considerable outlay, beyond the means of many – even with 'easy payment' options, known at the time as the 'never-never' because of the length of time it took to pay such debts off – and, of course, the added financial burden of interest they attracted.

physical construction commonly found in vintage sets. In truth, financial considerations caused the demise of almost all the UK radio and TV manufacturing base during the latter half of the twentieth century, and it is little wonder that makers went to the wall when faced with the economics of mass production from Far Eastern sources, where labour and resources were at that time extremely low in cost.

Production Values

Take apart any British radio built in the first half of the twentieth century and you will see evidence of surprisingly complex engineering. Once the chassis is free from the finely crafted wooden cabinet with its quality veneer

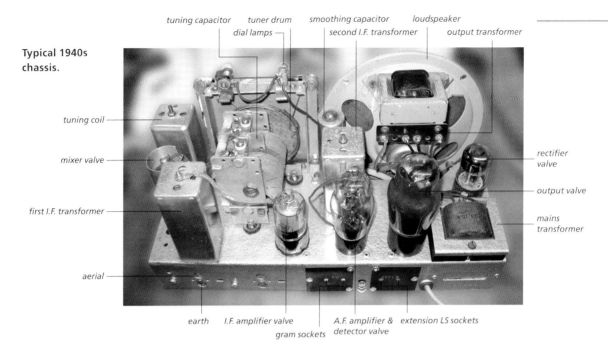

Typical 1940s chassis.

tuning capacitor · tuner drum · smoothing capacitor · loudspeaker

dial lamps · second I.F. transformer · output transformer

tuning coil

mixer valve

first I.F. transformer

aerial

rectifier valve

output valve

mains transformer

earth · I.F. amplifier valve · A.F. amplifier & · extension LS sockets

gram sockets · detector valve

or the smart, Art Deco overtones of the Bakelite moulding, you may find yourself amazed at just how very skilled and clever the designers and engineers employed by these makers were. In today's world, where the computer and the microchip simplify computation and design tasks, where flimsy cases consist entirely of thermoplastic injection mouldings, and where the once ubiquitous metal chassis has given way to the mass-produced circuit board, it is easy to forget that the radio engineers of yesteryear had no such facilities at their disposal – not even a pocket calculator. They seemed neither to value nor indeed even to understand the term 'simplification' either in circuitry terms or construction techniques. There was a very structural and mechanistic approach to the radio. Radios were built rather than assembled. The metalwork used in the average chassis is formidable in size, complexity, multiplicity, processing and accuracy. Evidence of the milling machine, the lathe and metal punch abounds alongside metal forming, casting, electroplating and screen-printing. The glass dials alone often show artwork of a high quality, and this is all before the components are even mentioned – the multiple ganged variable capacitors, the complicated switches, the power transformers, the variable resistors and, of course, the delicately hand-assembled engineering marvels of the valves themselves.

Radio Becomes User-Friendly

By the end of the 1920s, the presentation of wireless receiving sets had mostly changed from being typically a cluttered and perhaps untidy assembly of separate units, linked together by wires, to a less scientific instrument-like and much more easily understood and operated single box containing an integrated chassis, inbuilt loudspeaker and space within for batteries or transformers. Home or kit-built equipment, so similar to its manufactured equivalent in the 1920s, gradually began to lag behind the commercial developments and often a home-constructed radio of the early 1930s can be seen to have retained both the appearance and the technical features of late 1920s models.

By this time the range of controls needed had also been reduced – at least on the manufactured product, though less so on the home-built receiver – making the radio receiver less tricky to operate and therefore more inviting to the non-technically minded person; usually, in the chauvinistic 1920s and 1930s, this meant the lady of the house. By the end of the 1920s, attractive styling began to be employed as a selling point, rapidly bringing to a close the years of functionality.

RADIO COMES OF AGE

Philips 2531, 1930. Three valves plus rectifier TRF, M/L. Twin non-ganged drum-drive tuning, no internal loudspeaker. 'Philite' (Bakelite) cabinet. Medium/large table model. **/***

There can be little doubt that the decade leading up to World War II witnessed the golden days for radio both in the UK and the USA. An unprecedented rise in demand for, and ownership of, domestic radio receivers created an enormous impetus for manufacturing growth. The development from the small 'back-of-the-shop' makers of the early 1920s to the explosion of major companies of the early 1930s was indeed a phenomenon. By 1930, the uncompromising and complex presentation of the scientific instrument had virtually disappeared, with the effect that despite great advances in assembly and component technology, radios often had come to present a certain plainness of appearance – fewer knobs, dials and switches. True, fewer sets had separate loudspeakers, but functional rather than decorative styling had become the standard for most sets – but not for long.

ABOVE: Symphony battery portable, c. 1930. Four-valve long- and short-wave coverage (NOTE: the term 'short wave' in an early set such as this usually refers to what later became known as 'medium wave'). Internal cone loudspeaker. Some conductors were stamped from copper sheet and riveted to components, rather like a primitive precursor of the printed circuit. With the rear cover opened, the valves, battery compartment and cone loudspeaker can be seen. This appears to be elliptical, following the front grille shape. ***

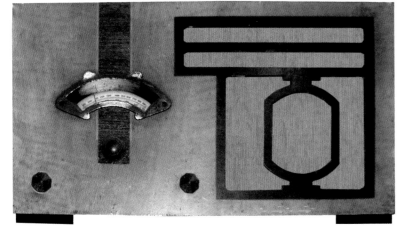

LEFT: Aerodyne Finch, c. 1933. Contained in a similar cabinet to the mains-powered 'Swan', the Finch is a battery TRF receiver. **

Gecophone-Osram 'Music Magnet' 4, *c.* 1930. Four-valve battery receiver, supplied as a kit. TRF, L/M. Oak cabinet with painted aluminium front control panel and lid for access to valves. No internal loudspeaker. Ganged tuning. **

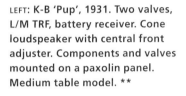

LEFT: K-B 'Pup', 1931. Two valves, L/M TRF, battery receiver. Cone loudspeaker with central front adjuster. Components and valves mounted on a paxolin panel. Medium table model. **

ABOVE RIGHT: Amplion Transportable, *c.* 1931. No details of chassis. Cabinet is walnut, both solid and veneer, with receiver controls beneath top lid. The grille design harks back to Art Nouveau with its organic styling. **

LEFT: Lissen 'Skyscraper 3', *c.* 1931. Three-valve battery TRF, M/L. Console style, one of a number of variations in presentation. **

RIGHT: Pye model 'Q', 1931. Four-valve battery portable. M/L, TRF, frame aerial. Walnut cabinet with carrying handle. **

ABOVE: McMichael Duplex Four, type 'S', 1932. Four-valve battery suitcase-style portable with the loudspeaker and the frame internal aerial in the lid. The wooden case is covered in black leatherette material, and the loudspeaker grille is brown Bakelite. Portable in name only! **

ABOVE: Pye 'MM', 1931. Three valves plus metal rectifier transportable AC TRF. Two separate chassis, one the receiver, the other the power supply. Chassis underwent several quite major technical adaptations over the production run. **

LEFT: Telsen 474, 1932. Three-valve plus rectifier TRF, L/M. **

ABOVE: Aerodyne 'Wren', c. 1933. Three-valve battery TRF, L/M, with PM speaker, Aerodyne patent 'clock face' tuning and walnut-veneered ply cabinet. Large table model. **

ABOVE RIGHT: Cossor 342, 1933. This is a mains version of the kit receiver, using a power supply on a separate chassis within the cabinet. A basic three-valve TRF design with L/M coverage. Same cabinet for battery version, for model 341, a battery TRF with a cone loudspeaker, and for model 344, another battery TRF, this time with class 'B' output valve and PM loudspeaker. **

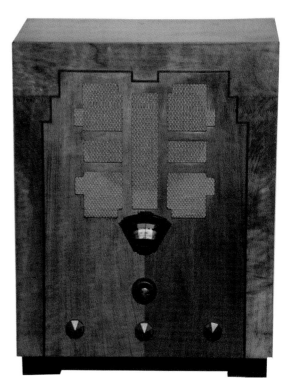

ABOVE: Psychon P500, *c.* early 1930s. Nothing is known about this receiver.

ABOVE RIGHT: Aerodyne SG 3, *c.* 1933. Three-valve battery TRF, M/L. Veneered ply cabinet. Large table model. **

RIGHT: Philips 634A 'Ovaltiney', 1933. Four valves plus rectifier AC TRF receiver, L/M. Housed in a mahogany cabinet with Bakelite escutcheon. The 'Ovaltiney' name stuck after a series of retro-styled (1930s) Ovaltine adverts during the 1980s. ***

LEFT: Aerodyne 'Raven', *c.* 1934. Three-valve battery TRF receiver with M/L coverage, balanced armature loudspeaker and, unusually, a small clock. The black cabinet provided the 'Raven' name, but the set was also available in a walnut-veneered cabinet. **

GEC 3445, 1934. Four valves plus barretter TRF, DC mains, M/L. Barretter-regulated valve heater current. **

ABOVE: Murphy B24, 1934. Five-valve battery-powered S/H, M/L. Large table model. **

LEFT: Pye PR-AC, *c.* 1934. Console with matching stand. No information available.

RIGHT: Ultra 22, 1934. Three valves plus rectifier valve AC S/H, M/L. Also 1935 four-valve battery version in identical cabinet. Large (upright) table model, veneered and inlaid ply cabinet, chromium knobs and escutcheon, mother-of-pearl scale plate. **

ABOVE LEFT: Aerodyne 'Bluebird' model 'A', 1935. Three valves, L/M, AC TRF. Reaction control. Model 'B', housed identically, was for use with AC/DC power supplies. **

ABOVE: Aerodyne Drake, c.1934. Three-valve plus valve rectifier AC TRF, M/L. PM loudspeaker. **

LEFT: GEC BC 3754, mid-1930s. Five valves plus rectifier valve S/H AC transportable, M/L. Veneered ply cabinet, very solidly built – and heavy. Internal frame aerial, chromium embellishment to grille and scale surround. Large table model with 'lazy Susan' rotating base for optimum reception on the frame aerial. **

Ekco AC85, 1935. Five valves plus rectifier valve AC S/H, L/M/S. 'Walnut' or black Bakelite cabinet (black version with chrome fittings). Large table model. ***

RIGHT: **Ekco AD36, 1935.** Three valves plus valve rectifier AC/DC TRF, M/L. Cabinet choice of walnut-effect Bakelite or black Bakelite with chromium fittings. One of the famous series of 'round' Ekcos designed for them by Wells Coates. Large table model. ****

ABOVE: **Marconiphone 235, 1935.** Three valves plus rectifier AC TRF, M/L. Black rexine- (leatherette-) covered plywood cabinet, chromium knobs, escutcheon and grille. Also model 238, in a wooden cabinet. Large table model. **

ABOVE: **Aerodyne Swan, c. 1933.** Three-valve plus valve rectifier AC TRF, L/M. Large horizontal table model with illuminated dial (metres only, no station names), PM loudspeaker and reaction control. Veneered ply cabinet. Quite rare today, perhaps partly due to the rather thin panels of plywood used for the cabinet. ***

Cossor 373, mid-1930s. Three-valve battery TRF, M/L, reaction. Open dial with station names, replaceable celluloid scale. One of Cossor's 'Super Ferrodyne' series. Large table model. **

ABOVE LEFT: Ekco AD65, 1934. Three-valve plus rectifier AC/DC, S/H. Marketed in a black cabinet with chromium trim, but also available in brown Bakelite. Large table model. Highly prized and sought-after. ****

ABOVE: K-B 321, 1932. Three valves plus rectifier AC TRF, M/L, illuminated drum-type scale. Large table model. **

BELOW: Philips 940A, 1935. Two-valve plus rectifier AC, medium wave only. A local station receiver. Brown Bakelite cabinet. Medium table model. **

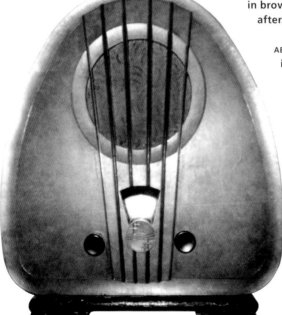

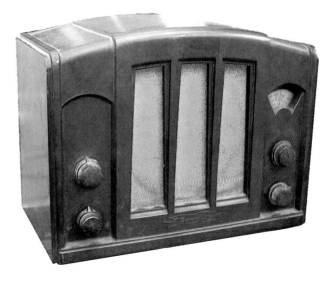

ABOVE: Philips 834A Superinductance, 1933. Four valves plus rectifier AC TRF, M/L, unusual cabinet construction using 'Philite' (Bakelite) front panel in mottled brown, and 'arbolite' (laminated plastic sheet) for the one-piece sides and top. Large table model. ***

RIGHT: **Portadyne S-AC, 1933. Four valves plus rectifier AC S/H, M/L. Walnut-veneered ply cabinet. Large table model. ** **

LEFT: **Ultra 'Tiger', 1932. Three-valve plus valve rectifier AC TRF, M/L. No reaction, but the well designed chassis works effectively without it. Note that this chassis and series were subject to considerable changes over two or three years, both in cabinet styling and in circuitry. AC/DC and DC versions were offered, along with at least three different cabinet designs and circuitry modifications (four valves plus metal rectifier). Large upright table model. ** * **

**Marconiphone 296, 1934. Four valves plus valve rectifier AC S/H, L/M. Fluid light TI. Veneered ply cabinet. The HMV 442 and 443 use similar chassis with minor cabinet differences. ** * **

LEFT: **Murphy A4, 1933. Four valves plus rectifier AC S/H, M/L.** Murphy often went about things in interesting ways, and this set is no exception, as it uses an AC/PEN output pentode valve as a self-oscillating frequency changer. Extension loudspeaker and pick-up input provision. Tone control. Veneered ply cabinet. Large table model. ******

Radio Cabinet Design Untrammelled

Within the first couple of years of the 1930s, tremendous changes took place in respect of visual design. The old boxes with their 'instrument' appearance and varnished oak construction were replaced by Art Deco-inspired creations – with some backward glances to Art Nouveau – housed within increasingly beautifully veneered and patterned wooden cabinets and, novel at the time, in Bakelite, the versatile thermosetting plastic that freed the designers from the 'developable surface' constraints of timber (bends cannot easily be created in more than one direction in sheet material such as plywood). A glance at the typical range of receivers from that era shows a wide variety of visual ideas.

Ekco Radio was at the forefront of Bakelite cabinet design and production in Britain. They opened a large factory at Southend-on-Sea, Essex, employing the services of highly regarded designers to create their Bakelite marvels, the most famous of which are arguably the 'round' series by Wells Coates, a brilliant and innovative Art Deco-influenced architect who had been involved in some of the design work for Broadcasting House.

TOP: **Bush SAC5, 1934. Four valves plus metal rectifier AC TRF, L/M.** Neon tuning indicator. The similar SAC4 features a small windowed scale and no tuning indicator. *******

ABOVE: **Bush SAC5 tuning scale detail.**

This 1930s Philips advertisement for their model 634 'Superinductance' boasts of excellent design. The performance certainly was impressive, though it was an expensive and ultimately futile exercise to bring a TRF design up to such a high standard at a time when the more advanced superhet circuit had proved its superiority.

Others included J.K. White (his cathedral-shaped cabinets of 1931/2, typified by the M23, though 'quaint', still stand the test of time) and the mainly self-taught but internationally recognized Russian immigrant and proponent of the 'modern' movement in design, Mischa Black.

Competition

The first stirrings of what was to become radio's greatest competitor and eventually, in terms of breadth of programme content, its nemesis, television first came about in 1925 in Britain by the experiments – and the dogged, against-all-odds persistence – of the Scots inventor John Logie Baird. By the early 1930s he had developed his system sufficiently to broadcast pioneering thirty-line television transmissions from Alexandra Palace, London.

At first, few if any manufacturers heeded Baird's invention, considering it to be little more than a curiosity, a toy with no chance of development, and it is true that his mechanical television was a blind alley; however, Baird himself came to recognize that the only viable way ahead was via electronics, even before his system was defeated by Marconi-EMI in the 1936 trials, after which he worked tirelessly towards non-mechanical television. Meanwhile, radio development and improvement forged ahead. By 1930, moving-iron cone loudspeakers, previously available mostly as stand-alone units housed in ornate cabinets, were offered as built-in to combined units to create single-cabinet radio sets. These low-cost cone units were sensitive, a useful advantage for the modest power output of the radio sets of the time, but they were hardly high fidelity. Despite their large cone size (typically 12in), bass notes in particular were poorly reproduced, an innate feature of the moving-iron cone drive system, and the general quality was such that, at the higher frequencies, it was said that distinguishing between a flute and a fiddle was almost impossible.

The Moving Coil Loudspeaker

A great improvement occurred when energized moving-coil loudspeakers began to appear at the start of the decade. These worked by electromagnetism, drawing their energy either from the rectified mains in mains-powered receivers, or from the batteries in the battery models. Although the quality and frequency range of these devices was much in advance of the older units, there was a price to pay in terms of lower sensitivity, and higher power output valves had to be devised to make the most of them. The alternative to energized units was the permanent magnet speaker, but the magnets for these were costly and difficult to manufacture in the early days, although they began to appear in quality receivers during the early 1930s.

Standardization

Slowly, standardization of components, component identification codes and circuitry began to take hold, with fewer makers building parts 'in house'. This fuelled the growth of the component supply industry. Some firms went so far as to supply complete standard chassis for 'makers' to build into their own designs of cabinets, whilst others supplied the cabinets for chassis makers, a similar situation to today's 'badge

engineering' of much home electronic equipment, where the same internal product is packaged slightly differently and labelled to suit a range of so-called 'manufacturers'.

Blue Spot extol the virtues of their PM loudspeakers in this 1933 advertisement.

RIGHT: **Ekco AC86, 1935. Five valves plus rectifier AC S/H, L/M. Black Bakelite with chromium trim, also in mottled brown Bakelite. Large table model. *****

LEFT: **Belmont 368, c. 1935. S/H, eight valves including 'magic eye' and rectifier. **/*****

Ferguson 378U, c. 1935. Seven-valve S/H plus twin separate valve rectifiers. Push-pull output, L/M and two short-wave bands, tone control. AC/DC. Ferguson model 378AC is kept in a similar cabinet. **

Cossor 364, 1935. Four-valve plus rectifier AC S/H, LMS, replaceable tuning scale for programme frequency allocation changes. The set features an unusual thermometer-style tuning system. Chromium-plated fittings and Bakelite knobs on a walnut-veneered cabinet. **

LEFT: Cossor 348, 1936. Three valves plus rectifier valve, AC. Unusual, in that for long- and medium-wave reception, the receiver works as a TRF, but on short wave it becomes a superhet: the triode-hexode frequency changer valve works as an HF amplifier on L/M. **

RIGHT: Ekco AC97, 1936. Four valves plus rectifier plus TI. S/H, AC. An unusual 'robotic' appearance marks this receiver as different. The tuning indicator was known by Ekco as a 'mystic eye'. The circuit features a 'fidelity' control which adjusts the I.F. bandwidth. Also available in black Bakelite with white trim. ***

LEFT: Wayfarer portable, 1930s. Made by London Electrical Appliances Ltd (Londonelec). Four-valve battery TRF, M/L. Wet cell for 2V filament supply plus separate HT and GB batteries. **

RIGHT: Philco 444, 1936. Three valves plus rectifier valve AC, S/H, M/L. Bakelite cabinet, seemingly styled after the rear view of a Volkswagen of the 1930s, hence the title 'People's Set'. Large table model (but high, rather than wide). Similar chassis used in Philco model 269 (wood cabinet).

LEFT: Pye battery table receiver, c. 1936. No information on this model.

ABOVE: Invicta AC47, 1936. Four valves plus rectifier valve, AC, L/M. *

LEFT: Decca 77, 1937. Four valves plus rectifier valve AC, S/H, L/M/S, veneered ply cabinet. **

LEFT: Ferguson 503, 1937. Two short-wave bands plus M/L, S/H. AC, eight valves plus rectifier valve, featuring push-pull audio output. **/***

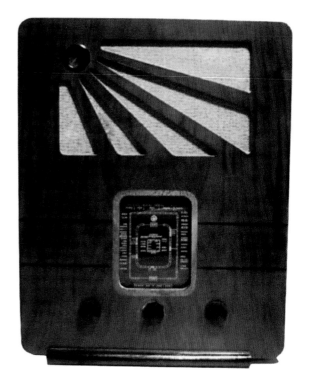

ABOVE: McMichael 374, 1937. Five valves plus rectifier valve plus TI AC S/H, L/M/S. Described as transportable by McMichael. Medium (upright) table model. Sunray grille design with the tuning indicator as the 'sun'. **

ABOVE: HMV 651, c. 1937. Five valves plus rectifier AC S/H, L/M/S, walnut-veneered plywood cabinet with contrasting inlay, metal grille mesh and Bakelite escutcheon. Large table model. **

RIGHT: Philips 785AX, 1937. Four valves plus rectifier and TI. Monoknob control, AC L/M/S S/H. **

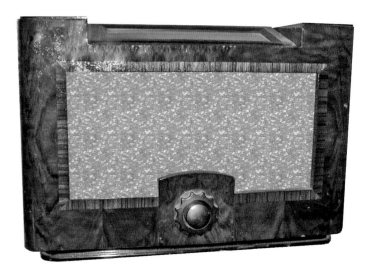

RIGHT: **Philips 747, 1937.** Four valves plus rectifier, AC S/H, L/M/S. **

LEFT: **Ferguson 771, 1938.** Four valves plus valve rectifier AC S/H, L/M/S, push-button and manual tuning and band selection. Veneered ply cabinet. Tone control, gram and external LS provision. Typical for HMV of the period, a mains-energized loudspeaker is fitted. Large upright table model. **

RIGHT: **Invicta 500, 1938.** Four valves plus valve rectifier plus TI, AC S/H, two short-wave bands plus medium and long, and featuring five preset stations by rotary switch, which is also combined with gram and wave-band selection. A choice of seven different pre-set station groups were offered, identified by suffixes from A to F after the identification number; also sets with the suffix 'S' were supplied to individual station requirements. Large upright table model. **

LEFT: **Lissen 8453 'Kenilworth', 1938.** Four valves plus rectifier valve AC S/H, L/M/S, seven press buttons for pre-set stations and one for on-off, plus manual tuning. Veneered plywood cabinet, large table model. **

RIGHT: **Cossor 77B, 1939.** Three-valve receiver with two-valve power unit on a separate internal chassis. AC S/H, L/M/S. In a brown Bakelite cabinet. **

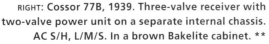

LEFT: Ekco PB505, late 1930s. Three valves plus rectifier plus tuning indicator AC S/H, press-button and manual coverage of L/M/S. Brown mottled Bakelite. Variations of presentation but identical chassis: PB506 and C509. Very similar is the AC/DC model range PBU505, PBU506 and CU509. Short superhet, using a EBL1 (CBL1 in the AC/DC versions) combined detector/output valve. All valves Mullard side-contact types, but the same Bakelite cabinet was used for an updated chassis in 1946. Large upright table model. **

BELOW: Defiant (Co-Op), model unknown, late 1930s.

ABOVE: Ekco AW70, 1939. Three valves plus rectifier AC S/H, L/M/S, brown Bakelite cabinet. Large upright table model. ***

MIDDLE RIGHT: GEC BC4040, 1939. Four valves plus rectifier AC S/H, M/L. Six pre-set station press-buttons plus manual tuning. Tone control. Medium table receiver, Bakelite cabinet. **

RIGHT: Pilot 'Little Maestro', 1939. Walnut-veneered wood cabinet, four valves plus rectifier valve, AC/DC S/H, L/M. Precursor to the first Bakelite Little Maestro, released in 1940. Other wooden cabinet finishes were also available. **

Pye MP, 1939. Three valves plus valve rectifier AC S/H, L/M/S. Pye marketed this receiver as being great value for money, but this goal had been achieved by cutting quality where it didn't show – the chassis. A 'short' superhet circuit was employed, which effectively saved a stage of amplification; not an especially unusual move, but the circuit itself is cleverly arranged so as to use as few components as practicable. Also the construction of the IF transformers was somewhat novel – instead of adjustable trimmers or coil cores, fixed capacitors tuned the windings which, Pye advised in their service data, could be fine-tuned by releasing the adhesive holding one of the coil windings in place on its former and sliding it to change its position relative to the other winding. Despite this limitation, the set works well. Veneered ply cabinet – no corners cut here. Large upright table model. **

LEFT: Blue Spot 'Aristocrat', late 1930s. Five valves plus rectifier, AC S/H, L/M/S. Veneered ply cabinet. Large table model. **

Ferranti Una, c.1936. Three versions were marketed: AC, AC/DC and battery. All were TRF. The mains receivers used a valve rectifier. L/M. Large table model. Battery version was consolette. **

From the tiny little windowed tuning dials of 1930, full-vision illuminated dials became fairly standard by the middle of the decade, even, sometimes, on battery radios where the dial bulb consumed costly battery power. All but the most luxurious British sets tended to have no more than three or four receiving valves plus rectifiers, perhaps due to the protective cartel of valve manufacturers entitled BVA (British Valve Association). This alliance deliberately kept the cost of valves high, whereas in the USA, valves were in a 'free' market where all but small economy receivers commonly had a larger valve complement. By contrast, the high cost of valves in Britain led to limits being placed on the number of them fitted in each set.

Deco Extravagance

By the mid-1930s much of the technical invention and development of radio had been completed, and after that time radio design remained – in technical respects, at least – fairly static. Inevitably, improvements and refinements continued to valves, components and

Radio came into its own at a time when the design movement now known in the UK as Art Deco was in vogue, although the term itself is relatively modern. Exactly what it is that constitutes Art Deco is arguable; but from the start point of a Paris exhibition in the mid-1920s, the movement gathered pace. Always eclectic, Art Deco exhibits visual evidence of influences from many sources, including the ancient or primitive art forms of Egypt, the Aztecs and Africa: sun rays, stepped 'architectural' forms, zigzags, lightning bolts, stylized fountains, fans and sunbursts. Although its beginnings were in handcrafted high applied-art form, often small-scale objects such as items of jewellery, by 1930 it had been adopted – and adapted – almost universally, especially in the high-rise architecture of the skyscraper, a prime, gloriously excessive example being New York's Chrysler building.

Its use for radio design became widespread, but as the 1930s progressed, modernist tendencies such as 'streamlining' were evident in some radio cabinet designs, in particular Bakelite ones, where the sharp corners dictated by the earlier Art Deco motifs and relatively complex detail styling became more material-friendly rounded and simplified, a fair example of this trend being the Philips 727A.

The trend in the 1930s was for the wooden cabinets of economy receivers to be planar – that is, flat-sided and often simple box constructions – with their Deco motifs taking the form of inlaid veneering, with added decoration in the form of shaped grilles and escutcheons. Even the control knobs came under the Deco influence, often faceted and octagonal in design. Conversely with Bakelite cabinets, textured surfaces, angles and decorative motifs abound, sometimes taken to excess and running the gamut of design ideas. Inevitably, too, some show a not entirely successful mix of the ancient and modern, perhaps with an anachronistic grille design that belongs in the earlier Art Nouveau period but mounted into the clean lines of a modernistic cabinet. In visual terms at least, those that do work, succeed astoundingly.

The cover of an early 1930s Aerodyne advertising leaflet. The receiver pictured shows the hallmarks of Deco influence.

This Philips 727A must have looked very 'modern' in 1936.

A good example of a remarkable stylistic range in cabinet design can be seen in the work done by Richard Russell for Murphy Radio. He produced some uncompromisingly modernistic and very individual wooden Deco cabinet designs, either loved or hated, it seems. Richard was the brother of the somewhat better known designer Gordon. Another designer to produce outstanding work for the Murphy company was Eden Minns, who designed the ultra-modernistic, machine-like Bakelite cabinet to house the AD94 chassis.

Betty Joel, a famous woman designer of bespoke furniture in the 1930s, was recruited to design the K-B 'Rejectostat' table model (1933), an eye-catching design by any standard. In fact, many anonymous designers contributed to the broad mix of style that Art Deco evolved into. Whether in Bakelite or wood, the lightning flashes, sun rays, bevelled surfaces and intricate geometric grille forms abounded throughout the 1930s. As the decade progressed, design simplification evolved from the sometimes overstated work of the earlier years.

Ekco were well to the fore with their design trends, especially in Bakelite mouldings, yet 'streamlining' had a rather more limited take-up, at least in Britain. An early and impressive example of this approach is the Ritz 'Airflo', which used a cabinet formed from veneered bent plywood to create a smooth, sleek and eye-catching design that still looks fresh today, belying the fact that it first appeared in 1934. Only the small dial aperture offers a hint of the receiver's true age.

In fact, a radio hardly needs to be actually aerodynamic, and although other British makers nodded in the direction of streamlining, they were cautiously moderate in its application, with the result that the trend made only a token appearance in British sets as rounded cabinet edges and simplified grille designs.

An enormous variety of interpretation of the term 'Art Deco' ensured its popularity, with seemingly endless variations appearing up to the onset of World War II. Post-war, simpler Deco-influenced styling continued in the UK right up to the start of the 1950s, with such sets as Bush's DAC10 and DAC90 series and Pilot's Little Maestro Bakelite earlier models. America, too, was well to the fore with Art Deco design, though they knew it at the time as 'moderne'. Streamline styling remained in vogue there in the post-war years, creatively evident in many small American Bakelite and Catalin radios. The term 'Modernism' is often applied to this period.

The Ritz 'Airflo' of 1934 shows to good 'streamlining' effect how plywood could be formed into planar curves.

Summer 1936, and Burndept have brought out a portable radio that, they claim, really lives up to its name.

especially to user convenience; some offered a genuine advance, but others were little more than gimmicks – selling points – and offered no great technical innovation. During the middle years of the decade, cabinet design seemed to know no bounds, as if it was intended to provide some measure of an antidote to those depressed times. Art Deco, the phenomenon of which began in the 1920s as a sharp 'modern' alternative to the organic softness of Art Nouveau, found expression in the large and impressive wooden cabinets of the time, a few of which have truly become design classics. Whilst Murphy and others went with cabinets shaped and decorated in geometric forms constructed from veneered plywood, Bakelite, first pioneered in Germany for radio cabinets, was used with great success by the Ekco Radio Company.

Radio Takes Pride of Place

Despite the invention and gradual perfection of television, in the years prior to World War II it was never given the chance to compete due to financial and practical limitations, plus seemingly obstructive tactics from the BBC's John Reith – a story in its own right – so radio remained in pride of place in almost all households, where each receiver represented a considerable investment for working people who quite naturally wanted the best they could obtain for their hard-earned money.

Families gathered around the radio much as we do with today's television. Historically, purchasers had tended to equate size with quality, even with portable receivers, seeing no reason to think 'small', such was the importance of radio in households across the nation and beyond. In any case, even so-called 'portables' were still powered by large and heavy HT batteries and LT accumulators; in other words, most were portable in name only. Mains receivers were mostly massive, heavy and often ornate in styling.

Meanwhile, the scramble to become top in what had rapidly evolved into a very lucrative market gave impetus to what might today be seen as outrageous or simply downright falsity in advertising. GEC's claim that their batteries offered an improved purity of tone seems to be stretching the truth to breaking point, and Burndept's somewhat dubious *Hindenburg* disaster advert distastefully uses a tragedy as a selling point.

Hyperbole that today's Hi-Fi accessory manufacturers would be proud of! In 1935, GEC clearly thought they could convince *Practical Wireless* readers that their batteries offered greater purity of tone.

BELOW: Radio manufacturers were always looking for an advertising opportunity, even one as tasteless as this, the *Hindenburg* airship disaster of 1937.

War Looms

Still, by the close of the 1930s, smaller 'second' sets had been gradually introduced. Sets such as the 1939 Pilot Little Maestro (the first of which were wooden-cased) started to find a market. Suddenly in 1939, things changed when war was declared, and the people of Great Britain held their breath as the second appalling conflict of the twentieth century plunged the free world into darkness – though British recovery from the depression was at least partly due to the perceived threat from Nazi Germany, which created a boost in work as massive rearmament took place. At the onset of war, domestic radio production stopped as factories switched to providing for the war effort. It was imperative, in terms of public information, to keep the old sets in working order often far beyond their expected life, but this was no easy task due to an acute shortage of valves and components, not to mention a shortage of people with the expertise to fit them and repair the faulty sets. The skilled radio engineer was needed urgently elsewhere.

As the German Nazi movement gathered momentum, the great proselytizer Goebbels, the minister for National Enlightenment and Propaganda, used the media to full effect and lost no time in declaring the radio to have a revolutionary impact upon the spoken word, giving it a hitherto unparalleled value in mass communication. However, in the Germany of the early 1930s, fewer and fewer people could afford to buy a radio receiver. The production of an affordable 'people's set' was made a priority, and to that end, the **Volksempfänger VE301** made its first appearance at the tenth German Radio Fair of 1933. From the outset, the VE range was designed to be affordable but not so low in cost that it adversely affected the sales of radio manufacturers' normal output.

Deutscher Kleinempfänger (People's Set) 1938.

Volksempfänger VE301GW, 1935, brown Bakelite.

The model number is significant, as it represents the day on which Hitler came to power: 30 January 1933. The production values of the radio – intended for the masses, a 'people's radio' in much the same way as the Volkswagen was a people's car – were designed above all to keep costs down, and it was, at 76 Reichsmarks, lower in cost than even the cheapest of other radios on the German market at the time. Despite that, Germany, in common with most of the rest of the Western world, was in the midst of a depression, and such a sum of money remained beyond the pocket of many. To alleviate the problem, a finance scheme was available, as was a form of means test that allowed successful participants to obtain a radio free of charge. After several models with similar production aims, the target was finally achieved when the **Deutscher Kleinempfänger** was introduced, selling in 1938 for 35 Reichsmarks (about 35 shillings at the time in the UK).

SOME OF THE GERMAN RECEIVERS

VE301 'Volksempfänger' This was the first of a series of 'people's sets', each proudly bearing the 'Calling Eagle' emblem of the Third Reich. From 1933 onwards, the set featured a very basic two-valve TRF circuit with reaction, one valve acting as the detector and the other providing the AF output. Long- and medium-wave coverage was provided, and the receiver was fitted with a directly driven moving-iron loudspeaker. There were variants for use with AC, DC and AC/DC mains, and also a battery-powered version (VE301B) using three receiving valves.

RIGHT:
Volksempfänger
VE301GW, 1933–35,
black Bakelite.

FAR RIGHT:
VE301G, c. 1934.

BELOW:
Volksempfänger,
VE301Dyn, 1938.

VE301G It seems that the German wood industry, based around the vast forests of Thüringen, was in the doldrums in the early 1930s, another victim of the widespread depression. To provide at least some relief, wooden cabinets were ordered; in effect, this was a small-scale and relatively early National Socialist attempt at economy management. The cabinet was also used on the VE301B and VE301B2 receivers.

VE301Dyn 'Volksempfänger' Appearing in 1938, this was the final development of the VE301; it cost 65 Reichsmarks, and featured a twin-pentode mains-powered receiver circuit, a moving-coil loud-speaker and an illuminated glass scale. Two variants were marketed. The presence of the swastika emblems at each end of the dial has led to the erroneous belief that the set was available only to Nazi party members; it was in fact advertised in contemporary wholesale catalogues.

continued overleaf

F121, close-up of DKE emblem

DKE: Deutscher Kleinempfänger *c.* 1938* This receiver, like the other 'people's sets', was produced by the German radio manufacturers with one aim in mind: it was to be affordable by the masses, a true 'people's set'. The receiving section consisted of one double valve (that is, two valves within one glass envelope), with a small rectifier valve supplying the power. Tuning and wave-change were combined. The dial, marked only in degrees, moved continuously around, and as it passed the 180-degree setting, a switch changed the waveband. The loudspeaker again was an anachronistic moving-iron type, obviating the need for a relatively expensive output transformer. The absolute minimum of components and metalwork ensured low production costs. The receiver was designed to run from AC or DC mains, but an alternative three-valve battery version was also produced for use in areas without mains supplies. Modified versions of the DKE became available in 1940 and again in 1944, all with only relatively minor changes to the basic nature of the circuitry.

In the 1930s Germany was in the thrall of National Socialism. Goebbels was Hitler's minister for propaganda, hence the irreverent title the radio attracted. Although ideal to receive Hitler's stirring speeches, the receiver was limited in power, being similar to the British 'local stations' type of low-cost receiver. However, a *Wireless World* review of the time contradicts the idea that the sets were extremely lacking in sensitivity, saying that during the hours of darkness, Droitwich could be received on a typical aerial. This may not have been precisely what the National Socialist state wanted because it seems that when war started, labels were attached to the radios warning that listening to foreign broadcasts was a crime against German national security, with the risk of severe punishment, by order of the Fuehrer.

It is worth noting that some manufacturers continued production of the DKE after World War II – without the swastika emblems, naturally – and survived long enough to employ B9A-based valves.

Quelle (a catalogue company) made a repro of the DKE in the 1970s/1980s, presented in either a cream or orange cabinet with a glass scale and a transistorized AM/FM chassis.

Once war was at an end, many of the German Volksempfänger and DKE sets and associated items such as the VL34 extension loudspeakers were brought back to Britain by servicemen as souvenirs. All Bakelite models have plain black or brown finishes. These sets are collectable, in part because of the Nazi emblems moulded into the Bakelite cabinets, although these may be found to have been defaced by owners wishing to distance themselves from the meaning behind the symbols. Where such damage has occurred the sets are – perhaps paradoxically – less collectable.

ABOVE: **A neatly designed extension loudspeaker, this VL34 model was moulded in Bakelite to match the receivers in the range.**

LEFT: **A low-cost option offered to the German populace, this extension loudspeaker has a case made from thick cardboard.**

---

* *People's set – the term 'Klein' is the Dutch and German term for 'small', but these receivers were colloquially known as 'Goebbelschnauze', Goebbel's Gob.*

A TIME OF AUSTERITY

Propaganda and the Wartime Civilian Receiver

By 1944 the British government had come to realize what the German authorities had known for many years, namely, that radio was invaluable as a propaganda tool, and could be used to great effect in keeping up the nation's spirits. The wartime economy receiver was brought out, manufactured by a range of British makers in both battery- and mains-powered forms. The sets had single waveband coverage (medium wave), but there were a few marketed towards the end of production that provided both medium and long wavebands. All models were built to a common design by a consortium of major British radio manufacturers. The sets employed standardized parts, valves and cabinets.

The presentation of these sets was basic indeed and deliberately so: softwood ply cabinet panels and painted metal tuning dials, no pretence of art, almost a return to the purely functional object of the late 1920s in terms of the crude presentation – but the chassis, designed by Murphy staff, was well made and sensitive, and satisfied the pressing need for war news – mostly with a positive spin – to be fed to the British population. Good, clean examples of these receivers are quite popular with collectors.

At the cessation of hostilities, radio production began again, though haltingly at first, still hampered by general shortages of valves and components. Essential exports accounted for a fair proportion of output, necessary to bring in much needed revenue to the war-ravaged British economy. Even so, by 1948, over 11 million

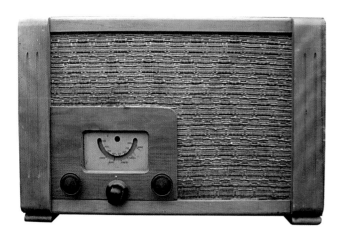

ABOVE: **Wartime civilian economy receiver, battery version. Despite the basic crudeness of the cabinet, the chassis within is capable of a very fair performance on its single wave band. ****

ABOVE RIGHT: **Wartime civilian economy receiver, mains version. Mains power removes the battery problem and makes this the more desirable of the two war-time receivers. *****

licences were taken out – and this figure includes 45,000 combined radio and TV licences.

Radio still reigned supreme in almost all households, but by this time television was waiting in the wings, limited transmission having been resumed in June 1946 in the London area. In 1949 the first regional TV transmitter was opened at Sutton Coldfield.

Recycling in Post-War Times

Much of the radio production in the immediate postwar years was based upon pre-war designs, one example among many being Ekco, who issued a receiver (model A21) using the Bakelite cabinet from the late

ABOVE: **1947 and the austerity of post-war Britain,** *Wireless World* **carry an advert for the first radio show of the decade.**

LEFT: **The post-war years often meant the modification and re-marketing of older designs.**

1930s PB505 model fitted with a chassis using octal-based valves (the original receiver used side-contact types). The Philips 371U of 1948 comes in a Bakelite cabinet that bears a more-than-passing resemblance to the 1938 model 470A. Even as late as February 1949, Philips marketed two versions of the radio: model 371 was for AC mains operation, and model 371U was an AC/DC version. In fact, most of the range on offer from Philips at that time had strong echoes of pre-war design, as an advert from 1948 shows clearly. Significantly, all but one of the models shown in the advert were in Bakelite cabinets.

This kind of measure would have been taken at the cessation of hostilities to use up existing stocks held 'in limbo' and to get around the immediate problem of component and material shortages.

LEFT: Bush AC71, 1940. Four valves plus rectifier valve AC S/H, L/M/S. 'Teleflic' dial, styled like a circular telephone dial. Veneered ply cabinet. Large table model. ★★★

RIGHT: Cameo U54A, 1947. Four valves plus valve rectifier AC/DC S/H, L/M/S. Wooden cabinet with Bakelite grille. Model EL80 has identical presentation but uses a modified chassis. Small table model. ★★

Philips 414A, *c.*1949. Another receiver using the Philips post-war chassis, this time fitted with the later miniature 'lockfit' valves instead of octal types. Four valves plus valve rectifier AC S/H, L/M/S, switchable settings for tone control. The set shown has been fitted with incorrect control knobs. Brown Bakelite cabinet. Large table model. ★★

Portadyne A43, 1940s. Nothing known about this receiver. Large table model. ★

LEFT: **Portadyne U1, 1940s. Nothing known about this receiver. Bakelite cabinet. Large table model. ***

ABOVE: **Cossor 71B, 1940. Four valves plus rectifier valve AC S/H, L/M/S. Medium table model. ****

BELOW: **Ferguson Mains Minor, 1940. Four valves plus rectifier valve, AC/DC, M/S. Small table model. ***

ABOVE: **Ekco AD75, 1940. Three valves plus rectifier AC/DC S/H, M/L. Bakelite cabinet. Designer: Wells Coates. Intended to meet wartime economy specifications. The receiver was re-marketed in 1946 with only minor chassis variations but with the addition of an on-off switch mounted on the cabinet side. *****

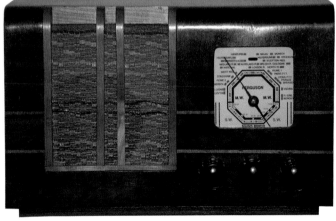

ABOVE: **Murphy A92, 1940.** L/M and six
short-wave bands. Five valves plus
rectifier, manual and push-button tuning,
AC S/H. The A92 is believed to have been
one of the official receivers used at the
World War II BBC listening station,
Caversham, Berkshire (the present BBC
world monitoring station). **/***

ABOVE RIGHT: **Philips 206A, 1940.** Three valves
plus valve rectifier 'short' superhet, L/M/S, AC.
Brown Bakelite cabinet. Medium table model. **

RIGHT: **Aerodyne 301,** c. 1945. Four valves plus valve rectifier
AC S/H, L/M/S. Gram and extension loudspeaker sockets. Simple
top-cut tone control. Veneered ply cabinet. Large table model. *

Alba 472, c. 1945. Four
valves plus rectifier valve
AC/DC S/H, L/M/S. Large
table model. *

RIGHT: **Ferranti 145, 1945. Four valves plus rectifier AC S/H, L/M/S, metal mesh grille, Bakelite. Large (upright) table model. *****

TOP: **Philco A535B, 1945. Four valves plus rectifier valve AC S/H, L/M/S.** Also three export versions with some technical differences, in particular the addition of a 100V tapping on the mains transformer primary. Also two of the export types are built to tropical standards. All versions come in both Bakelite or wooden cabinets. The 'B' suffix is for Bakelite cabinet versions, the 'W' for wood cabinets. **

ABOVE: **Ultra U405, 1945. Four valves plus rectifier valve AC/DC S/H, L/M. Bakelite cabinet. Small table model. ****

RIGHT: **K-B 870, c.1945. Four valves plus rectifier valve AC S/H, L/M/S. Medium table model, veneered ply cabinet. ****

Bush DAC90, 1946. Four valves plus rectifier valve AC/DC S/H, M/L. Very successful receiver in terms of sales, the DAC90 continued in production for at least three years before being replaced with the arguably even more successful DAC90A, which, although housed in a superficially similar cabinet, uses a very different chassis. Bakelite in cream (urea) or plain black or mottled brown Bakelite. Small table model. ***

ABOVE LEFT: Decca 'Double Decca', 1946. Four valves plus metal rectifier AC/DC/battery powered, M/L/S, S/H. Small table model. **

ABOVE: Ekco A23, 1946. Four valves plus rectifier valve AC S/H, L/M/S plus TV sound channel, press-button selectors and four-position tone control. Mottled 'walnut' Bakelite cabinet. Large table model. **

LEFT: Ever Ready table-model battery receiver, 1946. M/L, brown Bakelite cabinet. S/H. Manufactured using various valve ranges, the earliest being side-contact types but later production used octal-based valves and still later, miniature B7G valves. ***

RIGHT: Ever Ready model 'C', 1946. Four-valve all-dry battery portable. M/L, S/H. Curved acrylic cabinet with painted plywood side panels. Similar in appearance to the slightly later models C/A and C/E. **

BELOW: Ferranti 146, 1946. Four valves plus rectifier AC S/H, L/M/S, black Bakelite cabinet with white grille/dial surround. Medium table model. **

RIGHT: Philips 170A, 1946. Four valves plus rectifier valve plus TI, AC S/H, Bakelite cabinet. Mullard models MAS292 and MAS281 have identical chassis in wood cabinets. Large table model. **

Philips 186A, 1946. Bakelite cabinet, identical chassis to Philips 170A and Mullard MAS281, differing only in presentation (the Mullard has a wooden cabinet). Four valves plus full-wave rectifier valve plus TI. AC S/H, L/M/S, gram sockets. **

Philips 209U, 1946. Three valves plus rectifier valve AC/DC S/H, L/M/S, Bakelite medium table model. Exposed scale glass and slender Bakelite grille bars are vulnerable to damage. Medium table model. ***

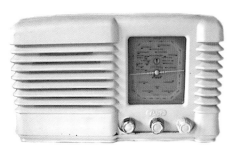

ABOVE AND RIGHT: **Pilot 'Little Maestro', 1946.** Post-war version of the series, which began immediately prior to World War II. Available in a choice of wood or Bakelite cabinets, but also offered post-war were sprayed Bakelite versions in several colours; one example is shown here – before treatment, with its worn cream paint, and after stripping and polishing, the same receiver with its mottled brown Bakelite exposed. Five valves, AC and AC/DC versions – but all with live chassis technology. L/M, S/H. Small table model. **/***

RIGHT: Regentone U22, 1946. Four valves plus rectifier AC/DC S/H, L/M/S. Top cut tone control, gram sockets. Large table model. *

RIGHT: Roberts P4D, 1946. Four-valve all-dry battery portable S/H, L/M/S. ***

BELOW: Romac 106, 1946. Four-valve battery-powered S/H portable styled like a 35mm camera, with shoulder strap containing the aerial wire. M/W only, but other variants in similar cases are models 126 (slight modifications to circuitry and case fittings), 136L and 236L (both with long- and medium-wave coverage) and 136S and 236S (medium- and short-wave coverage). Models 236L and 236S also have a mains adapter unit fitted as standard. The adapter unit was available separately for the other models in the range. **/***

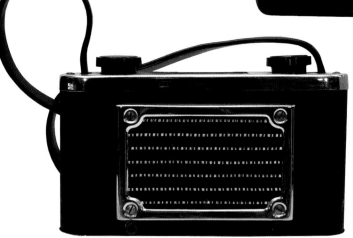

BELOW LEFT AND RIGHT: Ultra T401, 1946. Three valves plus rectifier valve AC S/H, L/M/S. Supplied in brown Bakelite or in a range of sprayed colours, one of which is shown here. Small table model. **

RIGHT: Amplion HU610 'Delegate', 1947. Four valves plus rectifier plus barretter (constant current voltage source). AC/DC, L/M/S, S/H. **

BELOW: Ekco 'Radiotime' A33, 1947. Three valves plus rectifier, S/H, M/L, AC. No manual tuning, stations selected by rotary switch. Electric clock can be used to set switch-on time. **

RIGHT: GEC 4850, 1947. Four valves plus rectifier AC S/H, L/M/S. Model 4855, in an identical cabinet, is AC/DC. Medium table model. **

Goblin 'Time Spot', 1947. Four valves plus rectifier valve AC S/H, L/M/S, synchronous clock for controlling on-off times automatically. Large table model, veneered ply cabinet. **. If clock is functioning, ***.

K-B BR20, 1947. Four valves plus valve rectifier AC S/H, L/M plus two short-wave bands, each with bandspread. Tone control, gram and extension loudspeaker sockets. Veneered ply cabinet. Large table model. ***

Marconiphone P17B, 1947. Four-valve medium-wave-only portable radio with frame aerial in lid. Lid spring-loaded, switches set on when opened. **

ABOVE: Philips 381A, c. 1947. Four valves plus rectifier, S/H, L/M/S, AC. Gram and extension LS sockets, tone control. **

LEFT: Philco A547B, 1947. Four valves plus rectifier valve AC S/H. Two short-wave bands plus M/L. Tone control, pick-up (gram) sockets. Brown Bakelite cabinet, medium table model. **

Philips 462A, 1947. Three valves plus valve rectifier AC S/H, L/M/S; comments made for Philips model 209U apply equally to this receiver. Check especially for repairs to grille moulding bars. Medium table model. **/***

BELOW LEFT: Mullard MAS 305, 1947. L/M/S, S/H, AC 230V with tapping for 100V. **

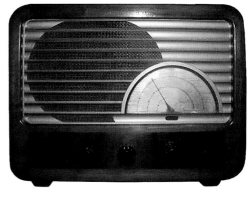

ABOVE: Sobell 516, 1947. Four valves plus valve rectifier AC (model 516AC) and AC/DC (model 516U), S/H, L/M/S. AC model employs parallel valve heater supply and 6.3V heater octals, AC/DC model uses series supply and higher heater voltage octals. Medium table model. **

LEFT: Ekco 'Consort' U76, 1948. Four valves plus rectifier valve, L/M/S, AC/DC, internal aerial. The somewhat unusual cabinet design is actually quite practical, but the large Bakelite control knobs have smooth, unmilled edges and can be rather difficult to turn. They also have a tendency to distort with age. **

Etronic RA640, 1948. AC S/H, six valves including rectifier plus TI. L/M/S, gram sockets and tone control. Veneered ply cabinet. Large table model. **

BELOW: Ferranti 248, 1948. Four valves plus valve rectifier AC S/H, L/M/S. Sockets for gram and extension loudspeaker. Tone control. Veneered ply cabinet. *

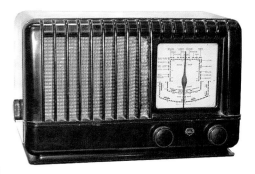

ABOVE RIGHT: Mullard MAS221, 1948. Four valves plus valve rectifier S/H, AC, L/M/S. Brown Bakelite cabinet. **/***

RIGHT: HMV 1117, 1948. Four valves plus valve rectifier AC S/H, L/M/S. Eight press-button select bands, pre-set stations and manual tuning. Twin loudspeakers (one ME, the other PM), and separate bass and treble tone controls. Provision for gram and extension loudspeaker. Veneered ply cabinet with Bakelite escutcheon and press-button assembly (check the latter for cracks). Large well-made table model; its appearance seems to hold its value down. **/***

Mullard MAS281, 1946. Four valves plus rectifier valve plus TI AC S/H, L/M/S. Using the 'new' Philips post-war chassis fitted with Mullard octal valves, this receiver has an RF amplifying stage allied to a short superhet circuit, making it very sensitive. Sockets for gram and extension loudspeaker. Tone control. Veneered ply cabinet. ***

Pilot Major Maestro, 1946. Four valves plus valve rectifier AC/DC S/H, L/M/S. Provision for pick-up (gram) input – not to be recommended with live chassis technology – and extension loudspeaker. Mottled Bakelite cabinet with spring-loaded carrying handle. Medium/large table model. ***

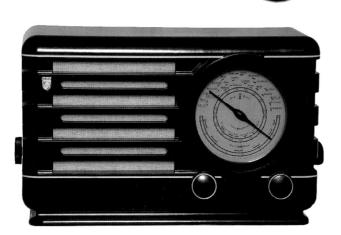

Philips 371A, 1948. Four valves plus rectifier valve AC S/H, L/M/S. Plate aerial. The same Bakelite cabinet was used on other Philips models, and the chassis is identical to the Mullard MAS221. Medium table model. **/***

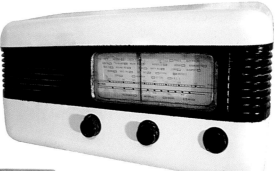

LEFT AND BELOW: **Pye 47X, 1948.** Three valves plus rectifier S/H, AC/DC, L/M. Brown Bakelite cabinet. Also as two-tone (part sprayed) finish. Identical to Invicta 200. ***

Pye 19D, 1948. Four valves plus rectifier valve AC S/H. Five bandspread short-wave ranges in addition to M/L. Model T19D is in similar container, but with variations of the ranges covered and some circuit divergencies. Large table model. **

Bush AC11, 1949. L/M/S, S/H. Four valves plus rectifier valve. A large table model housed in a wooden cabinet. Unusual in that the chassis was designed to be converted, if required, from AC operation to AC/DC; valve heaters are in series configuration, and the conversion involved removal of the mains transformer and the fitting of a series dropper resistor, making the receiver into a DAC11. **

Cossor 494AC, 1949. Four valves plus valve rectifier AC S/H, L/M/S. Tone control. Walnut-effect Bakelite cabinet, provision for gram and extension loudspeaker sockets. Not to be confused with later models using a very similar presentation, the 494 can be recognized externally by the escutcheon around the grille and dial, which is moulded as part of the cabinet. Later receivers used a separate thermoplastics moulding, which invariably distorts or cracks. Also, 494U, 1950 AC/DC version. Large table model. ★★★

ABOVE: Bush BP10, 1949. Four-valve all-dry-battery portable S/H, L/M. The set switches on when the scale shutter is opened. Bakelite cabinet is two tone. ★★

ABOVE RIGHT: Bush BP10, scale shutter closed.

RIGHT: Marconiphone T18DA, 1949. Four valves plus valve rectifier AC/DC S/H, M/L. Cream-sprayed Bakelite cabinet, designed to slip over the chassis from above. Small table model. ★★★

ABOVE LEFT: **McMichael 463, 1949.** Four-valve all-dry portable S/H, M/L. Ply cabinet in crackle paint finish. **

ABOVE: **Murphy A146C, 1949.** Six valves plus valve rectifier S/H, M/L, AC, switched tone control. Note: receiver uses an auto transformer, and so is not isolated (chassis could be live). One of several 'baffle' models, so named because of the large front panel, said to give improved loudspeaker response. Console. *

ABOVE: **Pye 39J/H, 1949.** Eight valves including rectifier valve, eleven wave bands, S/H. Push-pull audio output. AC. Veneered ply cabinet. Large table model. ***

ABOVE: **Ekco A144, 1949.** Four valves plus rectifier valve, L/M/S, S/H, tone control. Similar chassis to model A104 and export model A129, also AC/DC versions U109 and U143. Although AC only, the A144 has heaters wired in series to allow for easy conversion to AC/DC operation by removal of the mains transformer and the substitution of resistive elements. Large table model. **

Ekco A104, c. 1949. A slightly earlier and differently presented version of the A144. **

LEFT: **K-B ER30, 1949.** Four valves plus rectifier valve plus TI AC S/H, L/M/S, tone control. Two-tone walnut-veneered ply cabinet. Large table model. **

BELOW LEFT: **HMV 1120, 1949.** Four valves plus rectifier valve AC S/H, with three short wavebands plus M/L. Large table model. **

BELOW: **Pilot 'Blue Peter', 1949.** Four valves plus valve rectifier AC (110–250V) S/H, L/M plus two short-wave bands, one being the trawler band of 60–180m. Large table model. **

Sobell 439 'Sobellette', 1949. Three valves plus rectifier valve AC/DC S/H transportable, M/L. Bakelite cabinet in a variety of paint finishes and mottled brown. A 'short' superhet with a single IF transformer and a throw-out aerial wire. Miniature table model. Highly collectable. ***

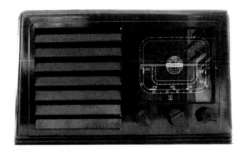

Derwent, model unknown. Bakelite. No identification, but probably dates from late 1940s. Live chassis (AC/DC), but little else known. Medium table model. *

ABOVE: Derwent, unknown. Another of the reclusive Derwent series, this time in a wooden cabinet. Again, nothing is known about the receiver, but these may have been made exclusively for a rental company of the same name. *

LEFT: Ultra R586, 1949. Three valves plus valve rectifier AC/DC/dry battery S/H, L/M. Bakelite cabinet. The 1950 Ultra 'Twin-50' is very similar but has a few technical changes. Small table model. **

Bush PB73, 1940. Four valves plus rectifier AC S/H, L/M plus four bandspread short-wave bands. Wave change via push buttons. Gram and extension LS sockets, tone control. Large table model. **

Murphy U124, 1948. Four valve, AC/DC S/H, L/M/S. Medium table model. */**

BELOW: **Sobell annoyed other radio manufacturers with this 1949 offering, made in an attempt to maximize sales.**

Whitewashing the Black sheep...

After-sales service is the black sheep of the radio retailer's flock—an expensive beast that feeds exclusively on profits. Fortunately Sobell are wielding a very effective whitewash brush. The Sobell 2 year guarantee provides 2 years' free maintenance in the home with every Sobell Receiver—a service that's provided *and paid for* by the manufacturer. Sell Sobell—free yourself from servicing worries—and take *all* the profit.

SOBELL RADIO

★ **2 YEARS' FREE ALL-IN SERVICE IN THE HOME**

SOBELL INDUSTRIES LTD., LANGLEY PARK, NEAR SLOUGH, BUCKS.

The First Signs of Recovery

By 1949, Philips were hinting at a more modern approach to cabinet design with their model 681A, a Bakelite cabinet in which was a chassis that offered, so it was claimed, an incredible twelve waveband coverage (Philips classed switch-selected band-spread frequency groupings as wavebands in their own right, when in reality they were small spread-out sections of the usual waveband coverage). Various other attempts at maximizing sales potential were tried. Sobell were quite radical in offering a full all-inclusive two-year guarantee for their range, an offer that angered their competitors.

There was still a demand for table model battery-powered radios, typified by the GEC's model BC4956. This receiver required a combined high-tension and grid-bias battery, plus a 2-volt accumulator for the valve filaments, very much a throwback to the late 1930s – yet it went on sale in August 1948. There was a strong drive for export to bring in much needed revenue to the country, and trade press adverts appeared extolling the fine performance and looks of sets whilst at the same time warning that stocks were extremely limited – 'but look to the future'. Export performance had been mediocre for the British radio industry as a whole before the war, but the figures for 1946 reveal a performance

five times greater than the best that had been achieved pre-war. Some enterprising makers, always on the look-out for a fresh selling angle, claimed that the experience of war had helped to prove the quality of their products.

The Boom in War-Surplus Stocks

At the same time vast stocks of war-surplus components, transmitters and receivers came on to the market, some stocks of components being procured by set

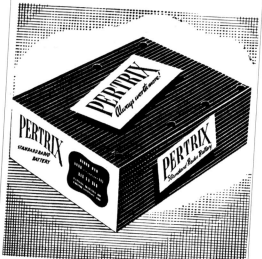

PERTRIX REDRESSED FOR PEACE

PERTRIX BATTERIES have emerged from the testing ground of war as more reliable, more efficient than ever before. You will soon see them in the smart new post-war pack shown above. It denotes the finest battery for radio use yet made.

★

HOLSUN BATTERIES LIMITED

137 Victoria Street, London, S.W.I.

ABOVE: Batteries were in short supply immediately post war, but this 1947 advert confidently predicts the imminent availability of batteries 'demobbed for peacetime'.

manufacturers to help their production. The availability of war surplus also had the effect of reviving interest in home construction, including for the first time television receivers, often using small green-faced cathode ray tubes of ex-forces origin. Many were the articles in radio magazines devoted to the adaptation and modification of military radio equipment. Octal valves and others of similar physical size continued to be used in many mains receivers, though miniature all-glass valves began to appear in portable receivers, especially in the more compact ones where space was at a premium.

1949, and the Ultra 'Twin' makes its appearance in the trade magazines.

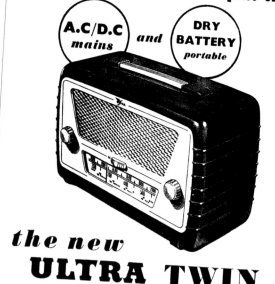

August 20, 1949   THE WIRELESS AND ELECTRICAL TRADER   (Advt.) 307

Offer your customers 2 sets for the price of one

A.C/D.C mains *and* DRY BATTERY portable

the new ULTRA TWIN

As soon as people read the advertising in all the papers about the new "Ultra Twin" they will be coming to you to tell them more about it — and to see this wonderful set for themselves.

The "Ultra Twin" is two sets in one, and you can show them that they can plug it in anywhere on AC or DC mains *or* use it as a battery portable wherever they go, indoors or out of doors.

Everyone will be amazed at the fine performance of the four valves plus rectifier, and delighted beyond words that the

"Ultra Twin" is so light (11 lbs.) that you can take it anywhere without the slightest effort — in fact a child can carry it.

Another point that will please you as much as your customers—the change over switch from mains to batteries is *automatic* and trouble-free, which means that there is much less servicing for you to do.

So give the "Ultra Twin" the place of honour it deserves in your window and be ready to demonstrate it.

£15 . 16 . 6 TAX PAID

let your customers

see it...hear it...walk about with it

ULTRA ELECTRIC LTD., WESTERN AVENUE, ACTON, LONDON, W.3
SCOTTISH BRANCH: 40 WELLINGTON STREET, GLASGOW

Early 1950s. Batteries were expensive, and portable sets were reserved for the odd day out and annual holidays, under-used until makers came up with ideas such as this one, where mains power could reduce running costs.

IT'S *SENSATIONAL*
IT'S *NEW*

THE RAYMOND

Threeway

★ Operates AC-DC Mains or Batteries.
★ To operate on AC-DC Mains, simply insert Mains plug, which automatically isolates Batteries.
★ Loud Speaker of new design giving large sound and deep tonal output.
★ Valves—4 all glass miniature.
★ 2 wave bands.
★ Case of strong durability with light alloy fittings and unobtrusive carrying handle, weight less Batteries 8½lbs.

The set millions have waited for!

BATTERY AC/DC PORTABLE
PRICE **£15.15.0**
(excluding Batteries)
Plus Tax £3.7.9.

RAYMOND ELECTRIC LIMITED, 26 WADSWORTH ROAD, PERIVALE, MIDDLESEX.

Receivers needing accumulators to power valve filaments gradually became a thing of the past, and so-called 'all-dry' battery radios contained within a neat briefcase format and employing valves with very low current drain filaments powered by a dry cell supply finally enabled receivers truly to merit the name 'portable'. Even so, batteries were still a recurrent expense and did have a finite life; to get around the problem and maximize their sales potential, by the end of the decade most makers began to produce, within their portable ranges, receivers capable of operating from either battery or mains, fitting a mains power supply unit, which in effect echoed the eliminator of old.

This led to sets that spanned the range from obviously portable and designed for occasional mains use, to others that were equally obviously intended for the mains with occasional portable use, such as the 1950 Ultra 'Twin' mains/battery receivers that had the appearance of a small table radio but with an added carrying handle. London-based company Raymond Electric also attempted to please all by producing a receiver that looked like a cross between a table receiver and a portable, powered by AC mains, DC mains or self-contained batteries, complete with carrying handle. They named it the 'Threeway'. Many other makers also offered a similar degree of versatility in their designs.

Market Changes

As the decade of the 1940s progressed, some makers continued to introduce visually innovative and more expensive designs – the product ranges of Murphy, Bush and Pye come to mind in this respect – but for many prospective purchasers in the austerity-stricken country the large, rather grand and therefore expensive receivers of the 1930s were neither affordable nor, it seems, as desirable as they once were, though combined radio-gramophone units, a cumbersome name quickly shortened to 'radiogram', were popular. Television was waiting impatiently in the wings to take pride of place in the home, and the mass radio market evolved towards the smaller radio and second set sales, especially those with Bakelite cabinets. Despite the fact that the quality of sound reproduction resulting from the paring down in size never equalled the resonant warmth of the big cabinets and loudspeakers, there is no doubting that some at least of these smaller, less pretentious receivers were design gems in their own right; the Bush DAC90 and 90A and the first Bakelite 'Little Maestro', still in production post-war (though less so the subsequent Little Maestro versions), remain as prized examples of this pared-down, cost-conscious but attractive style of set.

Radio Normandie (Fecamp) was the first continental daytime English-language commercial station, broadcasting on medium wave in the 1930s. Programming varied, but much was musical in content, as might be expected. Among the voices heard was that of Roy Plomley, better known for his later *Desert Island Discs* for the BBC. Radio Luxembourg also began in the 1930s, broadcasting its commercial fare on the long wave. Hilversum, the Dutch station, was also a popular alternative choice for British listeners seeking popular music. Along with all continental stations, Normandie and Luxembourg went off the air at the start of World War II. The Nazis used Reichsender Hamburg to broadcast propaganda and 'entertainment' programmes to British listeners. The most famous – or, more accurately, infamous – voice of this station was undoubtedly that of Lord Haw-Haw (William Joyce). Another station was AFN, the American Forces Network. Listeners who owned sets capable of short-wave reception could listen to *The Voice of America*, which, at the beginning of the 1950s, regularly broadcast a 'jazz hour' and a 'pop hour', on records.

After the war, only Luxembourg resumed broadcasting in the English language. In 1950 they moved from the long waveband to 208 metres, medium wave. Many famous and soon-to-be famous voices were heard from this ground-breaking commercial station; listeners found it a refreshing alternative to the somewhat stuffy BBC fare, especially on Sundays, which, as far as the BBC was concerned in the immediate post-war years, were a time for sober reflection, not light-hearted entertainment. David Jacobs, Hughie Green, Jimmy Saville and Pete (later Peter) Murray were all heard at times. Pete Murray was for a long time the station announcer, on permanent staff, rotating his hours with Peter Madren.

To support the obligatory music on disc, Radio Luxembourg in the early 1950s offered stories, serials and audience participation shows such as *People are Funny*, *Opportunity Knocks*, *Dan Dare* and others, along with reruns of American radio programmes such as *The Bogart and Bacall Playhouse* and *Perry Mason, Lawyer Detective*.

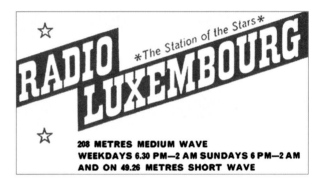

Gradually these succumbed to the pressures of scheduling costs and the rise in popularity of record sales, and by the early 1960s programming basically consisted of recorded popular music. Jack Jackson hosted the Decca Record programme, and other record companies such as Capitol had their share of the airwaves. The BBC, meanwhile, placed the accent on live music as the Light programme, the main BBC source for light music, was restricted to a few hours per week of recorded material. The Light still had quiz shows, soap operas and comedy series redolent of the 1930s in format, if not in style. The space between these was mostly filled with live or recorded material, a fair proportion of which was by BBC staff musicians and orchestras, although one perennially popular record request show was Forces' Favourites, later to become Family Favourites.

If there was a problem at all with Luxembourg, it was the quality of reception. Broadcasting its English output during the evenings, the medium-wave transmission was subject to severe fading effects caused by the phenomenon of ground-wave/sky-wave propagation cancellation, plus the crowded band and evening conditions ensured that the moment Luxembourg faded, other stations in French or German would fade in to take its place for a few moments whilst the frustrated listener had little choice but to await the return of 'the station of the stars'.

BRITAIN RECOVERS

The involvement of Britain in the Korean War caused rearmament to slow domestic radio production as companies were engaged in servicing government contracts and pushing much-needed exports. Despite this setback, by 1953 other transmitters were adding to the spread of TV availability, among them being Holme Moss, Wenvoe and Pontop Pike. Domestic receiving licences neared the 13 million mark, but of these and for the first time, over 2 million were combined sound and vision. The radio industry was about to enter a period of unprecedented growth. More than ever, sets were sold on their appearance, and cabinet design needed to reflect the times. More setmakers offered television receivers alongside their range of predominantly multi-powered receivers in a variety of guises.

TOP: Baird 204, c. 1950 (Radio Rentals). L/M/S S/H, tone control. *

ABOVE: Bush DAC10, 1950. Four valves plus rectifier valve, L/M, S/H, AC/DC. Features push-buttons for preset stations, wave change and manual tuning. Bakelite cabinet designed in two halves – back and front – so no fibreboard back. White plastic knobs, push-buttons and escutcheon. **

RIGHT: Bush DAC90A, c. 1950. Four valves plus rectifier valve, L/M, S/H, AC/DC, gold-anodized aluminium grille. In production for several years with only cosmetic changes (later knobs have flanges, dial colour schemes varied). Appearance similar to the DAC90. The 90A has a metal grille (the 90 uses cloth), and the 90 wave-change switch is placed higher. Especially popular in the cream urea cabinet. **/***

Bush DAC90A showing switch. This view shows the right side of the receiver. Note the position of the wave-change switch: on the earlier DAC90 series, this switch is higher on the side panel.

LEFT: DAC90A, cream. This example of the popular receiver is in a urea formaldehyde cabinet. Not as tough as phenol formaldehyde, these cabinets often exhibit stress cracks, especially on top above the mains dropper. The relatively rare ones with no evident cracks generally attract a lot of interest and a higher price.

BELOW LEFT: HMV 1121, 1950. Four valves plus rectifier valve, two short-wave bands plus M/L, AC, S/H. **

BELOW: Etronic 'Triplet' EPZ4213, 1950. Four valves plus rectifier AC/DC/internal batteries portable S/H, L/M. Two-tone Bakelite case. **

LEFT: **HMV 1122, 1950.** Four valves plus valve rectifier AC S/H, L/M/S. Tone control, provision for pick-up and extension loudspeaker. Veneered ply cabinet, full-length twin tuning scales and side controls. Large table model. ******

BELOW LEFT: **Home-built kit receiver using Little Maestro styling,** *c.* **1950.** One of many such offerings in the early 1950s, this strange little set bears the hallmarks of economy. Probably built from a kit, the circuit is a primitive form of superhet in that it has the necessary mixer-oscillator valve, but no IF amplification stages. A regenerative detector stage helps increase signal strength – there is an adjustable preset trimming capacitor, accessible through a hole in the rear chassis runner. No form of maker or kit supplier identification is evident. The tuning arrangements have been simplified by fitting the tuning control knob centrally on the dial, leaving a hole where the centre knob would normally be. This appears to have been covered from the inside of the case. Curiosity value only. *****

BELOW: **Olympic receiver using 'Little Maestro' styling,** *c.* **1950.** Another radio employing this ubiquitous cabinet mouldings. Probably a kit offering. Maker or supplier unknown. *****

RIGHT: **Electradix crystal set,** *c.* **1950.** Built into a meter case (believed to have utilized ex-government parts). *****

LEFT: Ivalek crystal set, early 1950s. A simple, tiny, extremely basic receiver in a plastic case. As with any crystal set, headphones and a good aerial and earth system are essential for reception to work (medium wave) – but no batteries required! A very small case, but still lots of room inside. Oddly, quite a popular collectors item. */**

RIGHT: K-B FB10, 1950. Four-valve plus rectifier superhet in a painted Bakelite case. M/L, AC only, but because an autotransformer is used, the chassis may be 'live'. **

LEFT: Marconiphone T26A, 1950. Four valves plus rectifier AC S/H, L/M/S plus three switchable pre-set stations. Tone control, veneered ply cabinet. Well built, typical of the marque. Large table model. **

RIGHT: Philips 581A, c. 1950. Four valves plus rectifier valve, S/H, four short-wave bands plus M/L. Tone control. Side-mounted controls, Bakelite cabinet. **

LEFT: **Pye 445U, early 1950s. Five valves plus valve rectifier, AC, S/H. L/M plus two short-wave bands and bandspread coverage of short wave in five sections, making nine bands in all. Large table model. ****

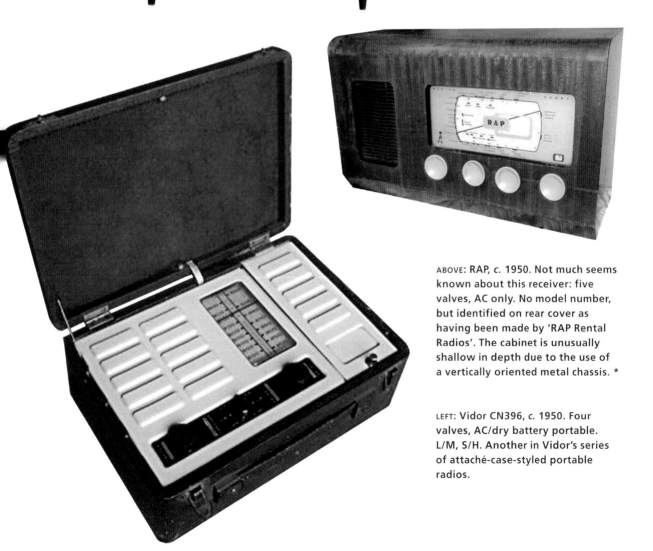

ABOVE: **RAP, c. 1950. Not much seems known about this receiver: five valves, AC only. No model number, but identified on rear cover as having been made by 'RAP Rental Radios'. The cabinet is unusually shallow in depth due to the use of a vertically oriented metal chassis. ***

LEFT: **Vidor CN396, c. 1950. Four valves, AC/dry battery portable. L/M, S/H. Another in Vidor's series of attaché-case-styled portable radios.**

ABOVE: Ekco 'Festival', 1951. Produced to mark the Festival of Britain. The receiver appears to be an adaptation of the earlier A110 Connoisseur. No manual tuning, stations pre-set. */**

ABOVE RIGHT: Ekco U159, 1951. Four valves plus rectifier valve, AC/DC, M/L, S/H, urea formaldehyde cabinet. This example shows the stress crack that often appears under the centre of the moulded carrying handle. */**

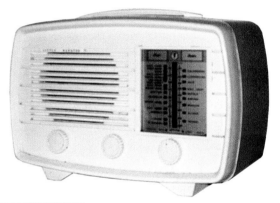

RIGHT: Pilot Little Maestro T66, 1951. Four valves plus valve rectifier AC S/H, L/M. Bakelite cabinet. Model T65, identical in appearance, is an AC/DC version using a different series of valves, a half-wave valve rectifier and a resistive dropper as a replacement for the heater transformer of the AC-only model. Small table model. **

Mullard MAS243, c. 1952. Four valves plus rectifier valve, M/L/S, TI, S/H, AC, Bakelite cabinet. Chassis probably based upon the Philips 411A. *

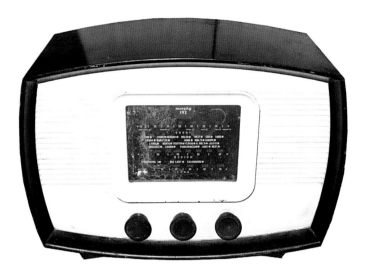

LEFT: Murphy A192, early 1950s. Four valves plus rectifier valve, L/M/S, AC S/H. Bakelite cabinet. *

BELOW: Philips 200U, 1951. Four valves plus valve rectifier AC/DC S/H, L/M. A no-frills Bakelite receiver with a stylish grille design. Small table model. **

BELOW: Champion 784, 1952. Three valves plus rectifier TRF. Broadcast band only (medium wave). Fitted with line-cord resistive mains lead. The urea formaldehyde cabinet is rather thin-walled and prone to stress cracks. Designed and built entirely with economy in mind. One of the last low-cost TRF receivers to be marketed. *

RIGHT: Ekco U199, 1953. Four valves plus rectifier AC/DC S/H, M/L. The rotary wave band selector switch also offers a choice of three pre-tuned medium-wave stations. Bakelite cabinet. **

Ever Ready Sky Queen MkI, 1953. Four-valve all-dry portable, M/L. Leatherette-covered wooden cabinet, frame aerial, clear acrylic handle: from the name onwards, a radio unashamedly aimed at 'lady listeners'! However, the physical size of the set, the weight of the combined HT/LT battery, plus the uncomfortable handle design, would surely have limited portability to short distances. *

Philips 141U, *c.* 1953. Four valves plus rectifier valve, M/L S/H, AC/DC. **

Portadyne 'Minx', 1953. Three valves plus rectifier AC S/H, M/L. Identical in appearance to the Portadyne 'Princess', available in brown or in blue-, cream- or green-sprayed Bakelite cabinets. Small table model. Also marketed under the 'Noble' brand. The 'Minx' name was also used by Portadyne on a 1962 transistor model. *

LEFT: **Pye P75A, 1953. Four-valve plus valve rectifier AC S/H, L/M/S, internal frame aerial, veneered ply cabinet. Provision for gram and extension loudspeaker. These Pye chassis have a reputation for being solidly built. Medium table model. ****

BELOW LEFT: **Pye P76, 1953. Four valves plus valve rectifier AC S/H, L/M plus two full short-wave bands, one offering coverage from 65.5–200m. Veneered ply cabinet, negative feedback tone control. Provision for gram and extension loudspeaker. ****

ABOVE: **Ultra R786 'Coronation Twin', 1953. Four valves plus metal rectifiers S/H, AC/DC/ battery-powered, M/L. Bakelite case. ****

LEFT: **Ever Ready 'Sky Prince', 1954. Four-valve all-dry (combined HT/LT battery) M/L S/H transportable table receiver. Medium table model. ****

Ferguson 353A, 1954. Three valves plus rectifier valve AC S/H, L/M/S. Features an unusual reflex circuit. Veneered ply cabinet. Medium table model. *

Murphy U198H, 1954. Four valves plus rectifier valve S/H, M/L, AC/DC. Bakelite cabinet. Medium table model. *

LEFT: Ekco U245, 1955. Four valves plus rectifier AC/DC S/H, L/M. Bakelite cabinet. Small table model. *

The Battery Problem and Some Solutions

A revealing trade advert by Ever Ready in 1951 shows a picture of their model 'K' receiver and promises radio dealers that if they sell just one Ever Ready battery radio they will be certain of the future sales of a multitude of batteries. That, of course, was the problem: batteries were very expensive, and when operating

Ever Ready are seen here turning heavy battery consumption, a major drawback of valve portable radios, into a selling point in this trade magazine advert in the summer of 1951.

An old idea revived, the Amplion Company advertise their mains units designed to convert battery receivers.

power-hungry valved radio receivers, they offered a limited life. As the battery failed, the voltage dropped, and with it went both the sensitivity and volume that the fully powered valve set was capable of providing. At a certain point the receiver would simply refuse to work at all. The answer, as Ever Ready knew (and as many listeners found, to their cost), was to purchase a replacement battery.

However, the rival Vidor Radio Co. had produced an optional mains power supply unit for their battery-only 'Riviera' model in 1949, followed by an AC/battery version of the set, despite the fact that Vidor, along with a number of other makers including GEC, were also in the business of battery manufacture. In 1951 the Amplion company revived an old idea when

they advertised their 'Convette' battery eliminator designed to power most all-dry battery radios from the mains supply. This saved on the purchase of batteries, but it meant that any radio using the device could no longer be classed as truly portable – not that purchasers seemed to mind, as in those years of long working weeks and pitifully brief holiday breaks, most radios stayed within reach of the home power socket.

Amplion also offered a complete receiver when they produced their 'alternative', a valved universal (that is, AC/DC mains or battery-operated) receiver marketed by them in 1956. Ultra brought out a very successful new version of their popular mains/battery 'Twin', including one christened the 'Coronation Twin', a very collectable receiver today.

Home Construction

From the start in the 1920s, amateur radio con-struction had continued apace, both from kits and from scratch, with most home constructors helped along by guidance from one or more of several pop-ular radio construction magazines. This remained a creative hobby interest for many people until well into the 1950s and beyond, by which time the complexities of radio had evolved to a point where it became mainly the preserve of the technically minded. For some of these enthusiasts the hobby developed into a career. Although it is the case that the zenith for home construction was probably the 1930s, its popularity was boosted, as mentioned previously, in the years following World War II by the availability of masses of war-surplus equipment and components, thus creating a market of its own.

During the latter half of the 1950s, very gradually but inevitably, home construction began to lose ground until, by the early 1960s and perhaps because of the development of television and the transistor, conven-tional radio construction was limited to a relatively few true enthusiasts as opposed to the occasional experi-menter, although the best stereophonic amplifiers and Hi-Fi systems of the time were valved – and usually, very good they were, too, either built as kits or purchased complete. The hobby construction magazines that had

ABOVE: Ultra's neat little mains-portable range was topped off nicely with this so-called 'Coronation Twin' of 1952, one version of which had the royal coat of arms mounted in the grille centre.

RIGHT: F.J. Camm specified exact components for his *Practical Wireless* plans, and many component manufacturers advertised in the magazine's pages; an example of co-operation for mutual benefit, presumably. *Practical Wireless* magazine, 1935.

F.J. Camm created and edited *Practical Wireless* for many years, starting in the early 1930s right up to his rather untimely death. Under his guidance, a magazine was developed to suit the needs of everyone interested in the practical side of radio construction. Not for him the theoretical musings of other more laudable tomes; his approach was essentially practical and easily readable. By these means he encouraged many thousands of people to self-build and enjoy a fine hobby activity that, had they not seen the content and presentation of *Practical Wireless*, might well have felt that the subject was just too technical and complex for them.

In order to cater for as large a potential readership as possible, FJ made a point of offering a range of constructional articles suitable for everyone, from the beginner to the experienced and knowledgeable radio amateur and radio service engineer; these were always accompanied – though sometimes to the annoyance of more advanced readers – by clear wiring diagrams designed to assist

ABOVE: *Practical Wireless*, January 1935.

LEFT: Features and series across the range of ability were an important part of *Practical Wireless* over the years.

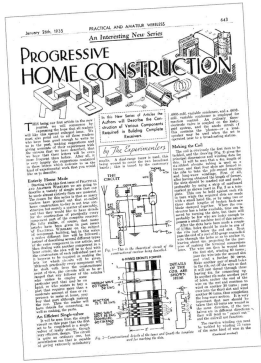

those not too sure of theoretical circuitry, plus well drafted theoretical schematics. The magazine was for many years 'required reading' for radio enthusiasts of all ability levels, and especially for the hobby constructor. The advertisements were almost as useful as the articles, because for many readers, especially those in remote areas, purchasing spares by post was an essential facility.

Practical Wireless remained successful throughout the 1930s, and as FJ forged ahead, one by one the competitor magazines fell by the wayside. At least one was taken over by *Practical Wireless*: *Amateur Wireless* can be seen as part of the banner on the cover shot of the 1935 issue.

continued overleaf

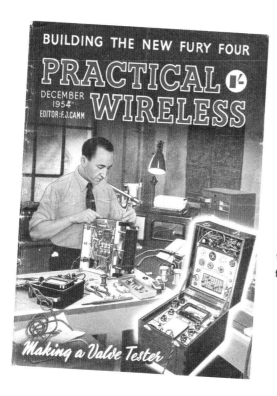

To make sure of a broad appeal, the magazine was aimed at every potential radio enthusiast, regardless of ability. Anyone requiring more rigour could always find it in other magazines, for example within the pages of *Wireless World*, a journal of technical distinction. Many chose to read both – and other journals vying for a market share. The secret of Camm's success was the mix of clearly explained theory, sound practical advice, constructional articles of a good standard, and guidance to the newcomer with clear, straightforward explanatory text and especially good graphic work. *Practical Wireless* outlived all similar contemporary publications, and continued in more or less the successful form that F.J. Camm originally intended for it, many years after his demise.

**Practical Wireless,
December 1954.**

Cossor were early on the home-construction scene with their kits, and with this 1935 valve advert they aim to catch the eye of the more experienced experimenter.

once seen a very high sales turnover were by this time facing ever-increasing staffing and production costs, coupled with falling sales year-on-year. The fight for market share was becoming a fight for survival.

Britain Finally Gets FM Transmissions

Invented by the American Edwin Armstrong, America had FM transmissions in 1939, at first admittedly on a small scale. In Britain, it wasn't until 1955 when the popularity of British radio, steadily losing in audience terms to TV, saw a slight reprieve as the first VHF/FM transmitter opened at Wrotham, frequency modulation being chosen over amplitude modulation as the best compromise for quality after many years of testing and experimentation. That year, the number of receiving licences issued approached the 14 million mark, although fully 4.5 million were combined radio and television. The following year, PAM, at that time an unheralded subsidiary of Pye, brought out the first all-transistor receiver to be manufactured in the UK (though not the world's first, as this was the 'Regency' of 1954, made in the USA), pointing the way to the demise of the widespread use of the thermionic (vacuum tube) valve, and bringing to a lingering end the great days of valve radio. Although the set itself was not entirely successful, mainly due to the great variations in performance of the then primitive

transistors, the trade was greatly impressed; the way ahead was signposted.

Valves are, by their very nature, power-hungry devices, even the low-consumption types developed in the twilight years of the technology. Batteries were required to supply high voltage at relatively low current – which meant a large and heavy battery assembly – and also a low voltage at a relatively high current which meant, self-evidently, a further large and heavy battery assembly. Some receivers, in the name of 'user convenience', were powered by a combined High and Low Tension battery (HT/LT) but these suffered when one section wore down before the other, rendering both useless and necessitating the purchase of yet another battery. Other makers exchanged convenience for efficiency and stuck with two separate batteries. Some small radios, especially of the attaché-case style, used very compact and lighter weight batteries. Sacrificing battery longevity for ease of portability, these suffered inevitably from an even shorter lifespan than their larger cousins. The fact remains that, even when in possession of the facts regarding battery expense and weight, such was the conservatism of the British buying public that valved battery-operated portable radios continued to be manufactured for several years before reaching an end in 1961, when the transistor finally replaced the valve for portable radio use.

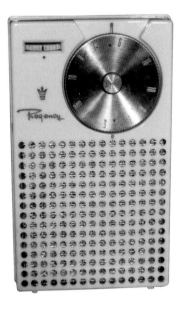

Regency TR1, 1954. The world's first transistor radio, manufactured in Indianapolis, USA, by the Regency division of IDEA (Industrial Development Engineering Associates).

RIGHT: **Ever Ready 'Sky Monarch',** **1955. Six valves including TI,** **L/M/S all-dry battery-powered** **S/H table radio with push-pull** **output. In similar cabinet, and** **released the same year, was the** **'Sky Monarch AM/FM', which** **used nine valves and covered** **M/FM. Again, dry-battery** **operated. Large table model. ★★**

RIGHT: **Cossor 524 'Melody Maker',
1955.** Five valves plus rectifier
valve AC S/H, L/M/FM medium
table receiver. One of a long line of
Cossor receivers to use the
'Melody Maker' name. Mottled
'walnut'-effect Bakelite cabinet. *

BELOW: **Ekco U243/1, 1955.** Five
valve plus rectifier valve plus
TI, AC/DC S/H, L/M/FM.
Medium table model. *

ABOVE: **Murphy A362, 1955.**
Five valves plus rectifier AC S/H,
L/M/FM. Autotransformer, so the
chassis is 'live'. Valve heaters are
series connected. Half-wave rectifier.
A very cost-conscious chassis.
External appearance is pleasing for
the period, but the knobs are flimsy
and can cause problems. Bakelite
cabinet. Medium table model. *

LEFT: **Pye 'Fenman II', 1955.**
Nine valves plus valve rectifier
AC S/H, L/M/FM. Four loudspeaker
units, bass and treble tone controls,
compensated volume control
(loudness control). Wood cabinet.
Large table model. ***

ABOVE: **Pye 'Jewel Case' portable, 1955.** All-dry four-valve portable, M/L, S/H, frame aerial. *

ABOVE: **Ultra R906, 1955.** Four valves plus metal rectifier AC/DC/dry battery transportable, M/L. Shown here are two differing presentations: top example is covered in a simulated crocodile skin, bottom example is covered in a simulated snakeskin. Small table model. **

ABOVE: **Ekco BP257, 1956.** Four-valve all-dry portable S/H, M/L. Printed circuit. *

RIGHT: **Philips 353A,** c. **1956.** Six valves plus rectifier valve, L/M/FM, S/H, AC. Brown Bakelite cabinet. *

Bush VHF61, 1956. Six valves plus
rectifier valve plus TI, L/M/FM S/H, AC.
Bakelite cabinet, piano-key band
selection. **

Bush VHF64, 1957. Six valves plus
rectifier valve, plus TI, L/M/S/FM,
S/H, AC. Walnut-veneered cabinet,
piano-key band selection. **

ABOVE: K-B OB10 'Minuet', 1957. Four valves plus rectifier
A/C S/H, M/L. *

RIGHT: Pye P123BQ, 1957. Perhaps the first transistor
receiver issued under the Pye brand name, this is a six
transistor plus one diode S/H M/L battery portable. **

LEFT: Bush VHF90, 1956. Six valves plus metal rectifier AC/DC S/H, M/FM. Also VHF90C, as VHF90 but with the addition of aerial and earth sockets for improved medium-wave reception. Do not confuse with VHF90A, which is a totally different receiver. Small table model. *

BELOW: Bush VHF90A, 1958. Six valves plus metal rectifier AC/DC S/H, FM only. Bakelite cabinet. A poor successor to the DAC90A, assuming that is what Bush had in mind when this receiver was named. Small table model. *

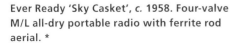

Ever Ready 'Sky Casket', *c.* 1958. Four-valve M/L all-dry portable radio with ferrite rod aerial. *

Bush DAC70, *c.* 1958. Four valves plus valve rectifier, L/M, S/H, AC/DC. Bakelite cabinet. Often found with the gold plastic trim shrunk back from the front inner edges of the cabinet, also the translucent plastic backing for the dial tends to melt due to the heat of the dial lamp. *

Murphy U598, c. 1958. Four valves plus valve rectifier AC/DC S/H, L/M. Wooden cabinet. Medium table model. *

LEFT: Pam TR30, c. 1958. Six valves plus rectifier valve plus TI, L/M/S/FM, S/H, AC. This is a large table model with many features including three loudspeakers, treble and bass tone controls, internal aerials for both AM and FM reception. Rather let down by cost-cutting with the chassis design and construction. Identical chassis to the Invicta model 40. **

BELOW: Roberts RT1, 1958. Roberts' first commercial transistor radio. Battery-portable S/H with M/L. ***

MIDDLE LEFT AND BELOW LEFT: Roberts RT1, 1958. Six transistor M/L battery portable. Subsequent versions shown here are 'Starry Night Black' and 'Starry Night Yellow', both from 1959. ***

Stella ST239U, *c.* 1958. Six valves plus rectifier valve, L/M/FM, S/H, AC/DC. Maroon Bakelite cabinet. *

ABOVE: **Decca TP22, 1959. Six transistor battery-powered portable, M/L, metal chassis. Model TT22 is a table model variant using an identical chassis. ***

ABOVE: **GEC BC402, 1959. Five valves plus valve rectifier, AC/DC, L/M/FM, S/H. Ferrite internal aerial for AM reception and separate internal aerial for FM. Sockets for external aerials and for extension LS. ****

RIGHT: **HMV 1376, *c.* 1959. Five valves plus valve rectifier AC/DC S/H, L/M/FM. Large table model. ***

LEFT: **Philips B2G81U, *c.* 1959. Three valves plus rectifier valve, AC/DC S/H, L/M. Employs printed circuit board. Small table model. ***

RIGHT: **Pye 444 'Cruiser', 1959.** Six transistor M/L plus trawler band S/H battery portable. An early example of a transistor receiver offering trawler-band coverage. **

BELOW: **Philips 310A, 1952.** Four valves plus valve rectifier AC S/H, L/M/S, combined loudspeaker grille and scale plate in acrylic. Brown Bakelite cabinet. Medium table model. Grille bars are easily damaged: look for cracks or repairs. **

ABOVE: **Stella ST240U, 1959.** Six valves plus rectifier valve, L/M/FM, S/H, AC/DC. Wood cabinet. *

LEFT: **Decca 66, 1955.** Five valves plus TI plus rectifier AC S/H, L/M/S/FM. Fitted with high frequency loudspeaker (tweeter) in addition to large elliptical unit. Separate treble and bass tone controls, veneered ply cabinet. Large table model. **

Valves and Stereo Sound

For practical and financial investment reasons, rather than consideration of public reluctance to embrace new technology, mains-powered valve radios continued to be produced well into the 1960s. From around 1954, mains radios and radiograms featuring the new VHF/FM band became increasingly available. The availability of long-playing stereo gramophone records in 1958 created a fresh market for radiograms as well as more trans-

portable (but usually still valve-powered) record players, some of which were fitted with radio tuners. The invention of a stereophonic disc-recording method by the brilliant EMI scientist A.D. Blumlein in the 1930s had waited for the quality of recording techniques to improve until the point was reached when stereo sound could be successfully sold to the public, though stereo tape recording, the province of audio enthusiasts, was no longer novel by that time. Radio broadcasting in stereo remained as an enticing future prospect.

INTO THE TRANSISTOR YEARS

Bush MB60, 1957. Five valves, M/L A/D battery-portable/AC mains-powered. Metal rectifiers. Easily confused with later Bush transistor receivers using similar case. **

Although valves remained in use for many years in mains radios and then in televisions – even first-generation colour TVs – where they continued to outclass the early and primitive transistors for sheer power handling, the great valve radio days were all too soon consigned to history. As far as the popularity of radio itself is concerned, a further respite in the slide of radio broadcasting from its once-dominant position with the public was offered by the rapidly developing solid state electronics of the transistor radio. Radio programming itself continued to contract into a mainly music-based offering.

Crossing Over

Some makers put their early transistor receivers in cases that were similar in all respects to the ones they had previously used for valve chassis. In fact, other than the fact that transistor radios invariably were more expensive than their valve-driven counterparts, and remained so for some time, the cross-over from valve to transistor portable became somewhat blurred. A good example of this is the KB Rhapsody, produced in 1955 as a four-valve mains/battery receiver in the typical upright

styling for portable radios of the period. By 1958 the Rhapsody had become a transistor receiver, but maintained the external appearance of the earlier valve model. It therefore pays to check inside radios of the era to see exactly what it is you are buying, although most of the first generation of transistor radios were proudly and sometimes flamboyantly badged as 'transistor' to distinguish them. The case used for the Bush MB60, a portable mains/battery valve receiver of 1957, reappeared in 1959 as the popular TR82 transistor portable, and was also used with other Bush models.

A few unusual combined transistor/valve receivers were marketed towards the end of the 1950s. The reasoning behind these was that the early transistors were poor at handling high frequencies, and were relatively low power: they were still in no way equal to the valve for performance in these two important areas. Examples of this type of hybrid receiver are the HMV 1410B (B for blue case), 1410G (G for grey case) and Marconiphone P60B. All used the same chassis, which featured three valves working at RF and IF, feeding a matched pair of Mullard OC72 transistors working as a push-pull output stage, the output of which approached the power that would have been offered by a single-ended output valve, but at a lesser current drain. The differing power requirements of the valves and transistors were catered for by connecting the filaments of the valves in series and using three single cells to provide 4.5V as LT, which doubled as a power source for the transistors, with a conventional HT battery for the valve HT. It sounds rather clumsy and it was, but this stopgap measure didn't last long once transistor development had advanced sufficiently.

The relatively short-lived British Perdio Company (*Personal Radio*) produced several interesting receivers, all of which were transistor designs. Tentative production started in late 1956 but was beset with many difficulties and technical problems, and it wasn't until 1959 that

their products began to attract mass sales. Competition from Hong Kong and Japan gradually eroded their profit margins until, by 1965, the struggling company was wound up. Their 'Continental' PR73 of 1959 had quirky styling with the three controls set diagonally 'sun-and-planet'-wise across a control panel, the small volume and wave-change knobs set one to each side of the main tuning knob/dial. Their PR167 featured a rather unusual bandspread tuning facility over a section of the medium wave. Their PR25, released in March 1961, was electrically identical to both the PR36 released in January 1962 and the PR37 released in July 1962, although externally they were each in very different cases and gave the appearance of three distinct receivers.

Some classic designs came about during this period as Roberts, in common with all other makers, made the transition from valve to transistor when they produced the RT1 in 1958. Although not in an exactly identical case to any Roberts valve receiver, this all-transistor portable has styling values in common with the maker's previous valved receivers. As mentioned above, the popular Bush TR82 transistor radio of 1959 used the same thermoplastic moulded case as the earlier MB60. These receivers have recently been remarketed as a classic design, featuring updated circuitry and components whilst keeping their appearance. Being non-original and having a rather flimsier feel, they cannot be considered as truly vintage.

ABOVE: **Perdio PR73 'Continental', 1959. This relatively large (280 × 230 × 100mm) seven-transistor battery portable was unusual in offering trawler band coverage in addition to the usual medium- and long-wave reception. Leatherette-covered wooden case with blue plastic control panel and gold colour grille cloth. ✶✶**

RIGHT: **Dynatron 'Linnet' TP12, 1960. Seven transistor M/L table model, battery powered. Chassis also used in the Dynatron 'Nomad' of 1959. ✶✶**

ABOVE: **Ekco PT352 transistor portable, 1960. Six transistor battery-powered receiver, M/L – preset on long wave for Light programme reception. Optional carrying case. ****

ABOVE RIGHT: **Ekco U332, 1960. Four valve plus rectifier AC/DC S/H, L/M. Ferrite internal aerial, extension loudspeaker provision. Black plastic cabinet. Medium table model. ***

RIGHT: **Ekco U332, red casing. Possibly later production, the different and updated presentation conceals an identical chassis to the model above.**

Ferguson 'Flight', c.1960. Five valves plus rectifier valve AC/DC S/H, L/M/FM. Tone control. Printed circuit board, internal aerial. Sprayed Bakelite cabinet. Medium table model. The 'Flight' name was used for at least one transistor model. *

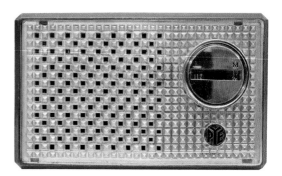

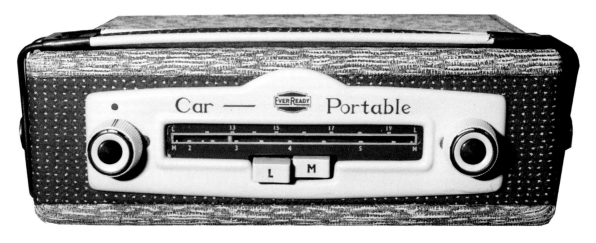

TOP LEFT: **Perdio c. 1960, model unknown. ***

TOP RIGHT: **Pye pocket portable, 1960. A basic M/L receiver. ***

ABOVE: **Ever Ready car portable, 1960. Six transistor M/L with metal mounting box and additional external loudspeaker for in-car use. ***

LEFT: **Perdio PR24 'Mini-6', 1960. Six transistor pocket portable. ***

ABOVE: Regentone seven transistor, early 1960s. *

ABOVE RIGHT: Bush VTR103, 1961. Nine-transistor S/H M/L/FM portable. Identical cabinet to several other Bush receivers. **

RIGHT: Ekco PT378 'Vanity', 1961. Six transistor battery portable, M/L. *

BELOW: Marconiphone T96B, 1961. Six transistor battery portable, M/L, S/H. *

Ekco A455, c. 1960. Transistor table model, mains-powered. Seven transistors plus one diode and a bridge rectifier. M/L, S/H. Similar to Ferranti A1149. **

RIGHT: K-B WP21 'Lyric 9', 1963. Nine transistors (one working as a diode), M/L battery portable. Microphone pre-amp for baby alarm or for use with telephone attachment.

BELOW: Roberts R500, 1963. Transistor battery S/H portable, L/M/S. **/***

BELOW RIGHT: Philips B4G17U, 1963. Six valves including rectifier, AC/DC, L/M/FM. Stella model ST154U uses identical chassis. **

RIGHT: Perdio PR110 'Grosvenor', 1964. Seven transistors, L/M/S battery portable. **

BELOW: Ever Ready 'Sky Queen' Mk III, 1964. Seven transistors and two diodes, battery portable S/H. Car aerial socket. Uses AF, AC and OC-type transistors. *

BELOW RIGHT: Standard 'Micronic Ruby', 1962–65. Various models, some with FM band. Seven to nine transistors, battery-powered. Silk-lined presentation box with carrying pouch, strap, ear piece and mercury batteries. Gold-plated loudspeaker grille. **

BELOW: Standard 'Micronic Ruby' presentation box.

LEFT: Sanyo 8U604E, 1965. Eight transistor L/M/S, S/H portable. **

RIGHT: Sanyo 6C64B transistor portable, 1965. Six transistors, medium-wave (broadcast band) reception only. *

LEFT: Bush TR130, c. 1966. Seven transistor battery portable, M/L, featuring a preset Luxembourg setting, push-button wave change, manual tone control, car aerial socket and earpiece or extension loudspeaker socket. **

BELOW: Ferranti A1149, 1967. AC mains-powered table radio, S/H, L/M. One diode, seven transistors (three in the Mullard LP1156 IF module) and a full-wave bridge rectifier. *

BELOW: Ferguson 3R05, late 1960s. L/M/VHF. Battery/AC mains transistor receiver. *

Hacker 'Helmsman' RP36, late 1960s. Eleven transistor battery portable, M/L and three short-wave bands, including the marine/trawler band of 63–190m. Telescopic and ferrite aerials. **/***

ABOVE: Sinclair 'Micromatic' Mk II kit, 1969. Two transistors. **

National Panasonic R70 'Panapet', 1970. Six transistor medium-wave portable, globe-shaped case, battery operated. Optional neck chain. *

Roberts RIC2, 1971. Three transistors plus TAD100 integrated receiver microchip. M/L, S/H. Battery portable, housed in a mustard colour case. **

Bush VHF81, 1964. Six valves plus rectifier valve AC/DC S/H, L/M/FM. Internal aerials. Push-button wave-change. Slim design with vertical chassis. Veneered ply cabinet. Chassis similar to the Bakelite-housed VHF80 from 1960. Quite a 'pared down' design with rather flimsy cabinet, but performance is good. Small/medium table model. *

Styling and Technology Changes in the 1960s

Cabinets moulded from thermoplastics began to replace the more expensive to produce thermoset types, sometimes treated by a rather unpleasantly cheap wood-grain printed finish to disguise the material's true nature – a sop to the conservatism of the buying public, in much the same way that the Bakelite cabinets of the 1930s were said to be 'walnut effect', though the latter colour usually permeated through the Bakelite, providing a finish that was both permanent and of high quality, whereas the printed wood grain, being a surface effect, was prone to wear – especially on the sharp corners favoured by designers at the time – and was also fatally easy to scratch.

One marked styling trend during the early 1960s was the appearance of long, low cabinets. This form appeared both in wood, often teak or teak-veneered ply/chipboard, and in plastic 'wood-grain', and can be found housing mains-powered valve table radios and transistor table models. On a larger scale the same styling was used for radiograms, where the console cabinets of earlier years were ousted in favour of slimmed-down sleekness, usually supported on splayed legs, whether long or stubby. Sometimes the additional loud-speaker required for two-channel stereo was fitted in an additional matching cabinet.

Despite the success of test transmissions for stereo radio by the BBC in 1962 using the Third Programme's Wrotham transmitter, it was to be some years before such transmissions became standard. Stereo long-playing records were by that time well established, and

Although wood and Bakelite were by far the most common materials used in the construction of cabinets, they were not the only ones. Examples can be found using pressed steel, such as the Vidor CN411 'Lido' portable mains/battery receiver. The metal origin of the casing is neatly hidden beneath a rexine (leatherette fabric) covering. The top surface of the lid is the only part of the case to be made from plywood – metal here would prevent the action of the lid-mounted directional frame aerial. Whilst most valve portables were finished with a covering of 'rexine' or similar leathercloth in one form or another, Ever Ready used thermoplastics to make their Model 'C', which featured plywood sides with a curved acrylic front/top panel. Acrylic was also used by Pye for their ill-fated and now highly collectable M78F.

This Vidor all-dry suitcase-style portable is large and heavy, much of the weight being due to the leatherette-covered steel case.

Especially interesting was the development of 'Catalin' cabinets in America. These were made using a form of thermosetting resin that was cold pourable, and put into carefully prepared moulds. The person casting the resin was able to mix colours during the process in such a way as to produce unique and often quite beautiful translucent colour effects. These Catalin radios are naturally highly collectable, and command very high sale prices when in fine condition.

McMurdo Silver built sets where the chassis and coil cans were chromium plated: these were often not intended to be hidden within a cabinet. They were American designs, but in the late 1930s, Silver established a British factory. The British RAP company produced their 'table model' in 1946, which had a chromium-plated chassis, and a plate-glass back to the cabinet to allow the chassis to be seen and admired.

Although not completely unique, the McMichael model 463 portable had a highly unusual craquelure-effect paint finish to its otherwise conventional plywood case.

Ever Ready built a radio into a saucepan – well, just about, as the cabinet was made from aluminium by a saucepan manufacturer. The receiver was intended for Central African regions, and the cabinet was tropical insect-resistant. There was little space available in the 9in- (23cm-) diameter 'pan', so the battery was connected externally.

There are other oddities: radios built into world globes, statuettes, papier-mâché figures, beer cans… the list is constantly growing, even today.

Another trend of the early post-war years, odd in hindsight, was to paint the Bakelite cabinets used to contain smaller 'second set' receivers. Makers such as Pilot and Ultra offered lower-cost sets in a range of pastel colours; knobs, too, would be sprayed to match. Inevitably the colour on these sets, being a very thin surface effect, wears through or becomes scratched, showing the dark Bakelite beneath. This is especially the case on the knobs and any sharp corner on the moulding, with the result that finding such a receiver with a perfect original paint finish is almost impossible.

From a collector's standpoint it might seem sacrilegious to cover perfectly good Bakelite with paint, but we need to remember that sales above everything else were what counted to the survival of any manufacturer. The demand must have been there or they would never have produced such cabinets, and it was also a way of extending the market life of a given design. It can work to the collector's advantage, oddly, as it often happens that the Bakelite surface beneath is in perfect condition, having been protected by the paint. This gives rise to a dilemma: should the paint be stripped away to make an untidy set look beautiful, or should the set be left 'as is' in order to maintain authenticity? It is a personal choice, but remember that most models were available both painted and unpainted.

accordingly, makers brought out radiograms that were stereophonic for record reproduction but monophonic for radio. A couple of Ferguson designs serve to illustrate these tendencies. With their Model 602RG, twin audio channels carried either the twin-channel stereo information from records, or single-channel mono radio. Loudspeakers were built in, but a separate loudspeaker cabinet was available as an extra should a wider sound spread be preferred. With their follow-up model 604RG, Ferguson chose to use a twin channel of a single-ended form as an amplifier for records. When switched to radio, the twin output valves were combined to provide monophonic push-pull output.

Monophonic record players were still marketed at the budget end of the spectrum, and these were fitted with monophonic but 'stereo compatible' cartridges, designed to track stereo records without damaging them by having a stylus with the compliance to move both vertically and horizontally. Reproduction was, of course, mono. It is a matter of conjecture as to just how many stereo recordings were ruined by playing on the vertically non-compliant stylus of a mono cartridge.

As the 1960s progressed, transistors began to encroach on the valve's dominance of mains-powered receivers, and transistor portables took on the look that is still in vogue today: a case of rectangular form with wooden end panels and spun silver knobs of a simplified form mounted along a full-length slide-rule type dial on the narrow case top. The carrying handle was usually full length and rigid in structure. Many makers used, and continue to use this presentation, or variations of it. Identifying the make of a receiver by its looks alone became difficult as Fidelity, Ferguson, Philips, Ultra, Hacker and others all began to market somewhat similar-in-appearance products.

The last valve portables appeared in 1961, a late contender being the Ever Ready 'Sky Captain'. Vidor, always in competition with Ever Ready, produced transistor portables from 1958. Valve mains-powered radios had effectively become a thing of the past by the late 1960s. Some radiograms were still being produced either fully valved or more commonly in 'hybrid' form, where perhaps a single output valve was used in each channel of the stereo amplifier. Valves in television, and especially in the first colour television receivers, hung on until the

early 1970s before the transistor replaced them. HT battery production for valve portables came to an end in 1973, effectively rendering useless many thousands of battery-only receivers.

Finale

By the early 1970s it was obvious that the transistor was the successor to the valve, and in what appears – in retrospect – to be a surprisingly short time period, gone was the individual flair and elegance of design that characterized the best of the period from 1930 to 1960. The emphasis was on miniaturization. No longer was there interest in, or demand for, the occasionally startling, occasionally even banal, but sometimes brilliant creative flair of those pioneering designers with their big cabinets and sonorous loudspeakers, high gloss in Bakelite or beauty in natural wood; perhaps too soon replaced by the anonymous uniformity of style, form and colour that we know today. The Art Deco motifs and special sound quality that only vacuum-tube electronics seem to create were outmoded and unfashionable as home entertainment sources. The great convenience, compactness, novelty and immediacy of the transistor radio left the lumbering valve radios of old unfashionable, unloved and unwanted. Many thousands were scrapped, simply thrown out along with the rubbish or doomed to the attic, cellar or, worst of all, the rickety damp shed complete with mildew and voracious woodworm.

In their place came lightweight – and sometimes downright flimsy – transistor portable radios, and despite the characteristically thin, reedy sound and lack of volume of many of the early models, they were very low in running costs and needed no big and expensive batteries, which in turn contributed to their lack of bulk and weight. Some of these radios, for the first time, truly earned the accolade 'pocket portable', and they became extremely popular. Despite the general trend towards miniaturization and cheapness of appearance, not all were cheaply constructed or inelegant in design, by any means. Roberts and Hacker, among others, produced some stylish and well made products, despite the limitations on innovation imposed by the small size.

BASIC PRINCIPLES

First it is important to distinguish between two very different forms of electricity: DC and AC. DC is *direct current*, the sort of current that flows when you switch on a battery-powered torch: this is electrical current that flows steadily in only one direction. All radios are powered by direct current. AC is *alternating current*, an electrical current that constantly changes polarity; the speed at which this happens is called its *frequency*.

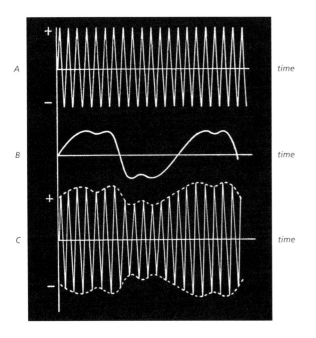

A: unmodulated carrier wave
B: audio signal
C: carrier wave modulated by audio signal

The high-frequency radio wave is modulated in strength by the audio signal. The receiving radio demodulates and discards the carrier, keeping the audio signal for amplification.

One complete reversal of polarity is called a cycle, or rather, it was. Nowadays it is denoted by the symbol Hz, for Heinrich Hertz, the German physicist who pioneered practical work with alternating current. AC is versatile: it can be fed through a transformer or coil, where the process of induction can be put to good use (*see* later). The household mains power supply in Great Britain is AC, 50Hz, which means that in any one second the current cycles through fifty direction reversals. In order to operate a radio from AC mains, a method of converting AC to DC is needed, and this is the function of the power-supply components built in to all mains radios.

In very simple terms, a radio transmitter consists of a high power AC generator producing continuous waves (oscillations) at the pre-determined transmission frequency. All radio frequencies are far above the range of frequencies encompassed by human hearing and are, of course, electrical in nature, unlike sound waves which are impressions carried in air, water or some other sound-conducting medium. An aerial circuit connected to the output of a high frequency generator causes the emission – radiation – of radio waves. Superimposed upon these so-called 'carrier' waves are the actual low-frequency AC audio signals of the broadcast programme.

The TRF (Tuned Radio Frequency) Receiver

A receiver must first be able to select the frequency of the carrier of the wanted station, and yet reject all other unwanted ones. Without this capability, a mass of transmitting stations would be heard at once, perhaps an interesting but not a particularly useful result. The property of this sharp *tuning* is called *selectivity*. In the most basic form, this is typically achieved by using a *tuned circuit* consisting of a coil and a variable capacitor to select the required transmission frequency. Once tuned in to a given carrier frequency, the second task for the receiver is to separate the wanted audio signal from the carrier, a process known as *detection* or *demodulation*, for which a diode is used. Then the carrier wave, having done its work, must be discarded.

The principle described above of the tuned circuit and detector could as easily be applied to a crystal set as to a valve or transistor radio, the crucial difference being in the way the effects are achieved and the essential amplification that valves and transistors provide. No crystal receiver can amplify, so in their case at this point in the proceedings, headphones are needed to hear the detected radio signals. A single tuned circuit is needed for crystal receivers. It should be noted that the above simplified description applies to AM (amplitude modulated) transmissions, such as can be received on vintage equipment and are at the time of writing still transmitted on short, medium and long wavebands. FM (frequency modulated) transmissions use a different method of carrying the audio information. Digital transmissions do not transmit audio in the same way, but use a coding system.

In practice, two or more tuned circuits are necessary to obtain sufficient sensitivity and selectivity. Even after amplification by valves or transistors, radio signals cannot be heard because they are still in AC form. Demodulation, known as *detection* in vintage radio terms, converts the alternating signal into a unidirectional form, leaving a direct current of varying potential, which is an analogue of the original audio. Filtering is used to remove remnants of the carrier wave, then further amplification is needed before sufficient power is available to drive a loudspeaker. With no valves to amplify signals before detection, crystal sets relied entirely upon the power of the tiny signals received by the aerial, and so needed very efficient aerial and earth systems before headphone reception could be made to work.

In many sets of the TRF type, so-called 'reaction' or 'regeneration' – invented by the American Edwin H. Armstrong (1890–1954) – was employed to increase sensitivity, and these would tap off the signal at the anode of the detector valve and feed it back to the grid to be re-amplified, effectively using the same valve to amplify the signal instantly, many times over. The use of reaction definitely enhanced the performance, but at a cost: very careful design and physical layout of components was needed to prevent instability, a tendency for a radio to burst into uncontrollable screeching, howling or 'motorboating', the latter being a term used to describe a sound similar to that of the engine of a motorboat as it chugs along a canal. A variable capacitor was generally used to set the critical level of feedback, which for greatest sensitivity was just before the circuit went unstable and burst into the howls of oscillation that were a feature of the old TRF receivers of the 1920s and early 1930s.

The TRF was the earliest valve radio type and generally, in terms of the electronics employed, the simplest. It works by picking up the radio transmission and amplifying it before detection, as described above. With any TRF there is the difficult problem of making two or three tuned circuits work in unison, a process known as tracking, over the wide range of received frequencies – and all the tuned circuits must be fully and simultaneously variable over the reception bands. Another problem that often beset the TRF was poor selectivity, where two or more stations may be heard at once, though well designed and well made coils, such as those used in the Philip's 'superinductance' range or in TRF receivers, eliminated this.

Then there is a tendency for circuits to become unstable and burst into oscillation when high signal gain is aimed for, yet high gain is essential for good reception. Reaction, as described above, improves performance, but this can require a certain knack on the part of the operator, especially when striving to receive some distant or weak station that is at the very edge of the set's sensitivity. Some makers fitted additional trimming tuners, perhaps as a control knob concentric with the main tuning knob, to allow the user some manual adjustment to the tracking.

The name 'F.J. Camm' appeared for many years on the covers of essentially practical magazines covering DIY, motoring and television, and on the first and most important as far as vintage radio is concerned, *Practical Wireless*. Other than his initials being a virtual guarantee of quality, most readers knew little about the man behind the name.

Frederick James Camm was born in Windsor, UK, in 1895, the second of two boys and the younger brother, by two years, of Sydney Camm. Their father, George, was an accomplished craftsman, and there can be little doubt that both the brothers gained much from the skills and attitude of their father. Both Sydney and 'FJ' were very keen on aeronautics and flying machines, and were founding members of the Windsor Model Aeroplane Club, during which time they planned to build a full-size man-carrying glider, before World War I brought their venture to a halt. Sydney went on to design the famous World War II 'Hurricane' fighter aircraft.

In 1910, FJ began his long and varied career when he gained an apprenticeship with Brown Brothers Coachbuilders. His gift for lucid technical writing became apparent early in life: a 1915 edition of *Flight* magazine carries his notes to do with the loading, balance and thrust of flying model aircraft. FJ married Dorothy May Field in 1919; their only son, Frederick William Sydney, was born in 1920.

FJ then worked for Pitmans in London, where his excellent draughtsmanship and technical writing abilities were put to good use. He contributed to a number of publications including *Hobbies* (offering articles on wireless telegraphy and modelling) and *Everyday Science*, all the while building a store of material and ideas for the soon-to-be Newnes publications *Practical Mechanics* and *Practical Wireless*. In 1919 his first book – the first of many, over several decades – was published, entitled *The Design of Model Aircraft*. By the time the second edition hit the streets he could claim to be model editor of *Flight* and technical editor of *Everyday Science*. He continued to develop a growing interest and ability in all branches of engineering, and freelanced his journalistic work. Always versatile, he designed a five-cylinder compressed-air model aeroplane engine, and developed numerous designs for flying model machines of all kinds. He introduced the 'Reader's Queries' sections in his journals, a free 'help' service, which continued throughout his long career.

F.J. Camm.

With the help of his brother and father, George, he built a three-wheeler car that he christened 'The Cambro'. These cars were manufactured by The Central Aircraft Co. of Kilburn, and were offered for sale at 79 guineas. Later, as editor of *Practical Mechanics*, he designed a home-build car which had three and four-wheel versions. Editing *Hobbies Weekly* for Newnes, he began a 'Practical Wireless' section in that magazine, and by 1932 this title had become a fully fledged magazine of its own. By 1935, *Practical Wireless* had incorporated its competitor *Amateur Wireless*, and the combined magazine was edited – of course – by FJ. A product endorsement by him was seen as a valuable sales aid.

Always outspoken, when using the pseudonym 'Thermion' in the *Practical Wireless* column 'On Your Wavelength', FJ could give vent to the things that irked him in life. Reading these pages gives an insight into the man behind the pseudonym. A stickler for accuracy, he suffered fools not at all, and disliked Americanisms and the BBC penchant for affectation in pronunciation. Typical of his mistrust of 'novelty', he denigrated the long-playing record upon its arrival, when 'Thermion' expressed considerable reservations. He preferred 78 rpm discs at the time, though doubtless he would have been persuaded otherwise in later years.

continued overleaf

A restless workaholic, throughout his career he wrote and edited constantly, and many were the books published (most, but not all, concerned with radio) bearing his name as author or editor. As well as writing he continued to edit the range of Newnes' *Practical* magazines. An insight into the character of FJ can be gained by reading his own editorial comments made on the occasion of the passing of twenty-one years as an editor of *Practical Wireless*, in which, for once, he talks about himself:

The years slip past unnoticed, and it scarcely seems possible that twenty-one years have elapsed since I passed the proofs of the first issue… I have had little time for reflection or retrospection… I can look back with justifiable pride on twenty-one years of successful achievement… a glance at the bookshelves in my office provides reminders of my output during that time… did I really produce all that?… In those years I have written over 21,000,000 words, and probably far more, in the form of articles and books… I have shunned delight and lived laborious days, but they have been pleasant days. I have made a hobby of work… I do not like holidays… the best way to lengthen your days is to steal a few hours from the night… work does not kill!

WB loudspeaker advert featuring F.J. Camm, 1935.

He goes on to state that his work is all his own, no ghost writers for him. Most of his work was, he said, dictated or taken in shorthand as he talked.

As well as being fluent as a writer, FJ was also a highly skilled draughtsman, designer and model maker. It seems that many who worked with this multi-talented man found him to be a hard taskmaster, and he could be opinionated and abrasive at times, but without doubt he was a gifted teacher, the ample evidence of which can be found in any of his technical books, all of which ran to multiple reprints. Purists, sticklers for complexity in technological texts, would sometimes complain that his work was too 'accessible', but his concise and jargon-free explanations were welcomed by the great majority of readers. Much of his output reflected the nature of its time and he tended to stay in the present, rarely venturing very far into speculation about the future, and staying with tried and trusted technology.

It is self-evident to anyone reading his books that much of the material has a dated feel, even by the original publication date, because he recycled material constantly. This fact was obvious even in the early 1950s. Even so, everything he wrote reads easily, and there can be little doubt that his voluminous contribution to the development of radio as a national hobby – not to mention car mechanics, cycling, model engineering and early do-it-yourself material – was far-reaching, and a very great debt is owed by all of us to this remarkable and truly inspiring man. Unfortunately for him – and for us – it seems that work, despite his 'Victorian ethic' claim to the contrary, did kill: FJ died in February 1959, still working hard at the time of his passing at the relatively early age of sixty-four.

FREDERICK JAMES CAMM, 1895–1959

The Superhet

Problems inherent in the TRF are largely overcome by the use of the *Superheterodyne* principle, usually shortened to *superhet*. This is another of Armstrong's brilliant inventions, though it has to be said that the German physicist Walter Schottky (1886–1976), working independently of Armstrong, can also be credited with the discovery of the technique, remarkably in the same year (1918). Superhet receivers are inherently rather more complex than their TRF counterparts. They employ a process known as 'beat reception', where the received radio-frequency signals as selected by an aerial-tuned circuit are combined with the signal generated by an oscillator in the receiver. This *local oscillator* is often part of a combined valve that does the two tasks, namely generating the local frequency and mixing it with the incoming signal. Not surprisingly, the valve is often called the 'mixer-oscillator'. The result of this mixing process is a *beat* frequency, well away from the radio-frequency signals and so not subject to interference by them. We call this the *intermediate frequency*, or IF, and it is this frequency that is amplified, along with the received signals carried on it, before being demodulated for AF amplification.

Because the IF is fixed, it does not require variable tuning no matter what actual radio transmission frequency is being received, so the IF circuits are less of a problem to design and can offer greater and more stable gain, resulting in a more sensitive and powerful receiver. The price paid is complexity of circuitry, and the need for a higher number of components compared with the simple TRF, two factors which made the typical superhet a more expensive receiver to manufacture – and therefore to purchase. Nevertheless, because of its clear benefits, the superhet became the virtual standard for receivers from the mid 1930s onwards, although the TRF lingered in use for some battery receivers throughout the decade. It is notable that Edwin Armstrong's 1912 experiments in regeneration form the basis of the continuous wave-radio transmitter, which forms the key to radio and television transmissions. Armstrong went on to invent, among other things, Frequency Modulation (FM).

Radio Components

Resistors used in valve radio receivers are commonly made from carbon. These types are low-wattage ones, which means they can only handle modest amounts of electrical power. They limit current – and therefore drop voltage – by converting the electricity into heat, which is dispersed by radiating it into the surrounding air. In many elderly radios they are in the form of a carbon stick with wire loops bonded to the ends as contacts. Physically they are quite large. Modern equivalents may be much smaller in size and capable of dissipating higher power levels. Higher wattage resistors are made as ceramic tubes with resistive wire wrapped around them. They act almost like electric fire elements, though hopefully nowhere near as hot, of course. These are used as *ballast* resistors in AC/DC sets, dropping the mains voltage to a suitable supply level for a chain of valve heaters.

The excess power is always dissipated as heat, which is one of the reasons why the case tops of small AC/DC valve radios become hot in use. They are also used for HT smoothing in conjunction with *electrolytic capacitors*. Ballast resistors fail when breaks occur in their wire. Care must be taken to fit correct values and wattages when replacing these, and they also need to be placed with care to allow the safe dissipation of the heat they generate.

Inductors/Transformers

Wind a length of wire around something to create a coil, making each turn of the wire lie adjacent to the turns alongside it, then pass an electric current through the wire. There will be little effect upon a direct current (DC) from, for example, a battery, but if the current is alternating (AC), the coil will limit the current flow. This is because having each turn alongside each other creates a complex electromagnetic system that acts as a 'brake' to the current, impeding its progress. This is roughly where the term impedance comes from. With a loudspeaker, the coil is wrapped around a thin former, which slides freely over the pole of a permanent magnet. The fluctuating, alternating signal through the speech coil is translated into movement of the coil due to magnetic attraction/repulsion (remember from your schooldays: like poles repel, opposites attract). The movement of the coil former is linked to the loudspeaker cone to create sound.

With the *transformer*, inductive coupling occurs from one winding (the primary) and is linked closely to another (the secondary), either by physical proximity or more generally by the sharing of a common core, but not electrically connected. Induction transfers the AC current. The versatility of the transformer comes from the fact that altering the primary-secondary turns ratio allows the secondary voltage to be increased or decreased. This is known as 'step up' or 'step down'. 1-1 transformers are often called 'isolation' transformers as they give a measure of protection due to the finite limit of current available from the secondary. AC-only valve radio sets were mostly, but not entirely, fitted with transformers both to step up the voltage and to isolate from the mains. Radios with such transformers are considered to be, electrically speaking, somewhat safer in operation than sets – AC/DC, usually – that use the mains power directly, dropping the supply for the valve heaters by resistive means as described above.

Capacitors

Capacitors – or to give them their vintage name, condensers – are made in many different sizes and shapes, and from a variety of materials, but they all have certain things in common. There is a metallic conducting material used for the 'plates' (something of a misnomer, but a hangover from the days when capacitors were built like a sandwich from layers of metal plate and insulating material), and there is a non-conducting material that is used to keep the two plates electrically separate. This insulator is known as the *dielectric*. For the greater part of the valve era, this was made from paper, mica, rigid plastic or air.

Capacitors function by storing an electrical charge, but only for short or extremely short periods, not like batteries. They are used in a number of ways, for example in radio power supplies, where electrolytic capacitors are used to store power and give it back as needed, thus acting as a reservoir for power. When used in conjunction with a second 'smoothing' capacitor and an inductance (choke) or resistor, they form the standard system used to filter out the slight AC ripples left after the AC mains has been converted to DC by rectification, something that must occur in all mains sets. Electrolytic capacitors are used in these circuits and in other applications whenever large values of capacitance are required, because the capacitance within them is large, even though their physical size may be quite small. They use 'damp' paste electrolytes and are usually polarized, which means they must be connected correctly or they will 'leak' (pass DC): this could lead to rapid, even catastrophic breakdown at the high voltages used in radio power supply circuits. Non-electrolytic capacitors cannot be made to the same capacity values without becoming unwieldy in size.

At audio frequencies (in vintage terminology, LF), capacitors can effectively pass alternating signals such as analogues of speech or music, at the same time blocking any direct current that the alternating signal may be carried upon. At radio frequencies (vintage: HF), variable capacitors are used in tuning and to bypass unwanted RF signals after detection. In tuned circuits they work together with an inductance in the form of a coil or transformer to select wanted signals and reject unwanted ones. This is the way the tuning works – large adjustable air-spaced ganged capacitors wired in parallel across the inductance of a tuning coil allow the frequency selected to be varied across a given band. In conjunction with resistors, capacitors form so-called 'time-constant' circuits, allowing timing functions, integration and differentiation of waveforms. This type of circuitry can be found in television equipment.

Capacitors are measured for their amount of capacity by a unit called the farad, named after the electrical pioneer Michael Faraday. The farad is a very large unit, and in electronics the values most encountered are the microfarad (μF), the nanofarad (nF) and the picofarad (pF), of which the largest measurement is the microfarad. Note that in the valve era, the nanofarad was not in common use.

The Transistor, a Landmark in Electronics

John Bardeen and Walter Brattain were scientists working in the American Bell Laboratories as members of William Shockley's investigative team. Between them, Bardeen and Brattain effectively invented the first transistor in December 1947, although Bell kept its discovery a secret until June the following year. Exactly what part was played by Shockley remains unclear, and there are conflicting reports about the level of his involvement; even so it is his name, above the other two, that is generally mentioned in connection with the invention of the transistor. To state, as many authorities do, that the transistor was invented in 1948 by William Shockley does seem therefore too simplistic, and credit must also be given to his team.

Shockley (seated), Bardeen (left) and Brattain. The men who created the transistor.

Experimenters had been working for years in an attempt to make a crystal that would provide gain – to amplify. There are stories, probably mostly apocryphal, that a few experiments along the same lines actually succeeded in the earlier years of radio. Whatever the case, the first known successful transistor appeared in the late 1940s, and started the process of development towards today's microchips, a process still continuing. As far as vintage transistor receivers are concerned, the germanium P-N-P transistor is the one that matters, although it should be pointed out that more robust and efficient silicon-based transistors soon replaced them.

How Transistors and Valves Work

What follows is simplified, and readers wishing to know more about the technicalities should consult the reading list in the appendix.

Transistors

Between the absolutes of conduction and insulation lie a group of materials called *semiconductors*. As you might expect, and the name suggests, these are neither perfect insulators nor very good conductors, although that is incidental to the other important properties that semiconductors have. For one thing, the resistance of a semiconductor falls as it gets hotter, unlike metals which increase in electrical resistance as they heat up. For another, current flowing through semiconductors can be either a flow of electrons, or a flow of 'holes' – gaps where electrons once were.

The atoms that make up solid materials such as metals and minerals tend to align themselves into *crystalline* structures to form *lattices*, a regular arrangement of atoms. *Germanium* and *silicon*, the two important semiconductors used in the manufacture of transistors, both possess four electrons in their outer – or *valence* – rings. These form *co-valent bonds* with adjacent atoms in the crystal lattice. When heat is applied, a valence electron may take up sufficient energy to escape from its parent atom, and if a voltage is applied to the crystal, this 'free' electron, and others like it, can move through the lattice to create a current flow. Each time an electron escapes its parent atom, a positive 'hole' is created. Hole conduction is therefore in the opposite direction to electron conduction.

Precisely calculated amounts of an element with a differing valence electron number are added as crystals are grown to create impurity conduction: an impurity with only three valence electrons is said to be 'P' type (for positive), and an impurity with five valence electrons is said to be 'N' type (for negative). Crystals are grown with both types of impurity within the same crystal structure, the junction formed at the change point being named the P-N junction.

The crystal diode is a P-N junction. The old 'cat's whisker' crystal detectors were crude contact forms of a P-N junction. Grow a crystal with impurities added to create two P-N junctions back to back, and you have the basis of a transistor.

There are numerous configurations for transistor amplifiers, but one used very often is the *common emitter* circuit. A small varying signal current applied via the base causes a matching but much greater variation in the current flow from emitter to collector – and across the load resistance, causing a corresponding voltage change. This current gain, converted into voltage, is how the transistor amplifies. (Remember this is a simplified explanation.)

Valves

The radio valve, alternatively known as the vacuum tube or thermionic valve, was the key that opened the door to successful radio broadcasting. The valve remained as the only amplifying device available until the introduction of the first transistor radios in the 1950s. Lee DeForest patented his triode valve in 1906. The amplifying valve was born, and with it, radio for the masses. All the early valves had directly heated filaments and were designed to run from DC supplies, which meant in practice batteries or accumulators. The development of the separate heater allowed sets to be designed for AC mains.

What a valve is: There are many variations, but a typical radio valve consists of a glass bulb not unlike a light bulb in some respects, although the shapes of the valve vary greatly. With earlier valves there is usually a plastic base with connecting pins that can be plugged into suitable valve sockets located on a radio chassis, commonly with four or five pins from the early 1930s and eight pins – octal-based – at the end of that decade. Later, miniature 'all-glass' valves have no base as such; the connecting pins pass directly through the flat glass bottom of the tube-shaped bulb. There is a filament within all battery valves, but unlike an electric lamp this does not glow brightly. With mains valves the filament becomes a heater and is enclosed within a narrow tube called the 'cathode'. The simplest amplifying valve has two further electrodes within the bulb. A metal tube known as the anode or 'plate' surrounds the cathode. Situated in the gap between the anode and the cathode, but closer to the latter, is a finely wound frame of wire known as the 'grid'.

Valve amplification in simple terms: The cathode is coated with a metallic element that, once heated, is able to emit electrons. The process by which this occurs is called *thermionic emission* and also the *Edison effect*, as Thomas Alva Edison, the American inventor, first noticed it when experimenting to improve his invention of the light bulb. Although he patented the process he did not understand its importance, and never exploited it. Even he wasn't the first to notice it, however: in 1873, British professor Frederick Guthrie noticed ionic discharge into a vacuum – and there were several other contributors to have seen and recorded the effect around the same time.

The principle is as follows: electrons, being negative in electrical polarity, are released through the oxide coating on the hot cathode, attracted by and flowing through the vacuum in the valve to the anode, which is supplied with a high positive charge. The grid, situated very close to the cathode, is a controlling element; small negative voltage changes on it can impede or stop the electron flow because like-for-like polarities repel (the negative electrons are repelled by the negative grid voltage). If a resistor is placed in series with the anode supply, the available voltage will drop across it – and the greater the current flow through the valve, the greater is the voltage drop due to the resistance. It follows that if a high-voltage source of power is supplied to the anode, *and* a suitable value of resistance is present in series, *and* a varying negative-going signal is applied to the grid, the voltage changes at the anode will be an inverted copy of those at the grid, with the important difference that grid voltage changes are very small, often little more than a single volt or so, but the anode voltage changes created at the anode can be as much as several hundred volts. The fact that the amplified signal is electrically inverted is matterless as far as audio is concerned, but if needed, a further stage of amplification can be used to correct this.

THE INVENTION AND DEVELOPMENT OF THE VALVE

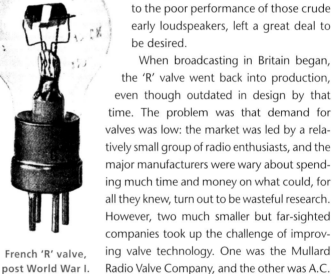

Continuous development of ever-better forms of radio valve followed the early work of DeForest. Arguably the greatest obstacle to overcome was the difficulty of creating a high vacuum; early valves suffered serious reliability problems from contamination due to residual gases, which made them both uncertain in operation and short-lived. The much-needed breakthrough occurred in 1913 when the brilliant American scientist Irving Langmuir (1881–1957) perfected techniques for high vacuum production. The earliest successful high vacuum valve became known as the 'R' type, and the use of this valve led to true radio telephony (transmitted speech) by the latter years of World War I. The 'R' valve was actually developed by French military scientists. To look at, and to some extent in its construction, it had the appearance of a light bulb, understandable because the valve was mass-produced in French electric lamp factories.

French 'R' valve, post World War I.

As the war ended, considerable stocks of 'R' valves were disposed of on the surplus market and were snapped up by amateur radio experimenters for use in their receivers. Despite the advances that had been made, the 'R' valve still suffered from a relatively short life, typically 100 hours, necessitating frequent and expensive replacement, one compelling reason why in those early years the crystal receiver outnumbered the valve receiver. However, horn loudspeakers could be operated because of the amplification the valve provided, and valve sets were much more sensitive,

although the audio quality, in part due to the poor performance of those crude early loudspeakers, left a great deal to be desired.

When broadcasting in Britain began, the 'R' valve went back into production, even though outdated in design by that time. The problem was that demand for valves was low: the market was led by a relatively small group of radio enthusiasts, and the major manufacturers were wary about spending much time and money on what could, for all they knew, turn out to be wasteful research. However, two much smaller but far-sighted companies took up the challenge of improving valve technology. One was the Mullard Radio Valve Company, and the other was A.C. Cossor Ltd. The former were first off in 1921 when they marketed their 'successor' to the 'R' valve. S.R. Mullard had been involved with the manufacture of the 'R' valve for some time and was able to claim that his new valve, the 'ORA', though based directly on the old valve, offered a significant improvement. In fact, the ORA was no better than a good 'R' valve, but the refined production process led to far fewer rejects and the new-found reliability boosted sales enormously.

Following on in 1922, Cossor produced their own successor to the 'R' valve. It was nothing like the old valve in appearance; all the electrodes were of a different shape, and great claims were made for its efficiency – claims which were, by and large, substantiated. Its success placed the company in the forefront of valve manufacture.

The next advance came with the change from 'bright emitter' to 'dull emitter' filaments. Bright emitters such as the 'R' valve and its immediate successors gave out an amount of light quite similar to that of a light bulb. This was very wasteful of power, and as the filaments were heated by accumulators, the frequent recharging of these was both expensive and an often inconvenient nuisance to listeners. This led to the development of dull emitter types where the filament was coated with various metallic elements that were capable of freeing copious quantities of current-carrying electrons when heated only to a dull red. This important development saved a great deal of accumulator power, but the valves themselves needed even higher (harder) vacuums to limit the 'poisoning' of the filament's emitting surface.

As the years progressed, improvements came by degree: 'gettering' was developed, first by high frequency firing of magnesium: in this process a small quantity of magnesium was placed inside the envelope of the valve and then, after evacuation, the valve was exposed to a high frequency wave that instantly heated and evaporated the magnesium, in the process trapping any residual gases and leaving a characteristic silver flare inside the valve glass. This was a 'one shot' process, but in later years, getters were produced that were activated by heat, mopping up residual gas molecules each time the valve was powered.

In 1926 the British Valve Manufacturer's Association was formed. Despite its altruistic and lofty-sounding objective of promoting, encouraging, fostering, developing and protecting the interests of the trade, the public and valve manufacturers, it was self-interest alone that was behind this price-fixing cartel of major valve producers.

Building radios at home was a popular alternative to purchasing one that was factory made, because at the time it was apparently thought extravagant and, oddly, slightly effete to do the latter. Unfortunately, radio building from scratch was not an easy option, despite the claims of hobby magazines to the contrary; it was far too easy to invest a lot of money in parts and valves, only to end up with a tabletop full of unworkable junk, even allowing for the relative simplicity of the typical radio of the time. The answer to this concern came in the form of the kit receiver. Kits were marketed by a number of suppliers including some who also manufactured complete receivers, a good example of one such supplier being Cossor. Their 'Melody Maker' kits, marketed as they were by a respected radio maker – a fact which itself engendered buying confidence – cut out much of the

British valves, early 1930s. British five- and seven-pin valves like these were in use from the late 1920s through to the early 1930s, fitted with the four-pin base of earlier valves. Where needed, a central pin was added, making the base into five pins, plus, for certain output pentodes, a side connection cap. Seven-pin bases belong to the early 1930s.

Cossor 'Melody Maker' TRF, 1928. This three-valve battery radio from Cossor was supplied in kit form. It has seen better days. Its painted steel cabinet has corroded and the lid is missing altogether, but it is still restorable. **

possibility of error. They certainly proved successful: from their first kit, marketed by them in 1927, they went on producing new kit designs yearly until 1936. To return to the 1920s, even as late as 1928, radios, complete or as kits, were still sold as 'sets' – in discrete boxes or units containing the receiver proper, the batteries and the loudspeaker – but by this time the trend-setting fully integrated (that is, all units in a single box) radio receiver had begun to make its appearance.

Another milestone was the development of true mains-powered valves. Filament valves could not be run efficiently from the mains supply (even DC supplies were noisily subject to unstable fluctuations), which meant, at first, that all radios were battery powered. Listeners wishing to economize by running their receivers from the mains could use an eliminator for the HT supply, but the sets still needed a rechargeable accumulator for the filaments of the power-hungry valves. Some makes of HT eliminator even had built-in charging facilities. Then, in 1926, a patent valve heater design was produced in the form of a combined heater and cathode. In essence, this consisted of a metal sleeve (the cathode) that slid over and lay in close proximity to the filament, and it was the sleeve that gave off the requisite supply of electrons as the filament within it heated its surface. The filament in these valves was renamed more accurately the heater. This heater arrangement allowed the valve to be operated fully from the mains, when, in the case of AC-only receivers, the heater supply would be commonly provided by a step-down transformer.

The heater also gave rise to the characteristic slow warm-up of mains-powered valves, typically 30 seconds or so before the valve reaches operating temperature. Due to the construction of the heater/cathode assembly, the heater itself could run relatively cool in all but output valves, and the valves themselves had both improved performance and longer life compared with the old-style directly heated types.

Manufacturing Problems

Before successful valve production could be achieved, many practical problems had to be overcome. One considerable problem was how to prevent the connections to the internal electrodes from breaking loose at the points where they passed through the glass envelope. A solution was found by using a plastic base to the valve, bonded to the glass and acting as a support for the lead-out wires that terminated in strong metal pins. The British four-, five- and seven-pin series are examples. To eliminate perceived problems with pins, a series of side-contact valves – rigid plate contacts spaced around the plastic base – were

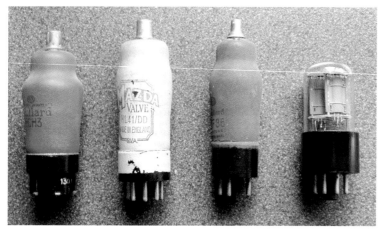

Late 1930–1940s valves. By the mid-1930s, side-contact valves were in use, but before the decade was out they had been largely supplanted by the so-called 'international octal'-based valves. This base was American in origin and used a central locating pin with a spigot to ensure alignment of the valve in its socket. On the left of the picture is a typical side-contact valve. Immediately right of this is a Mazda octal valve, which used a British octal base with pin spacing such that it is incompatible with the American octal holders. The red Mullard valve, centre right, dates from the end of the 1930s and uses the American 'international octal' base. At the right of the picture is a typical glass-tube (GT) octal valve.

LEFT: **From side-contact to octal. Many of the later octal valves were electrically similar to the earlier side-contact range.**

tried for a while in the mid-1930s. These, and later types that were either all-glass or with a metal base with a 'pip' on one side, snapped into spring-tensioned valve holders (sockets) to prevent valves working loose.

Clearly this was a sensible idea for War Department communications equipment subject to tough working conditions, but for most domestic radios, especially those with standard horizontal chassis, the problem simply didn't exist. The later miniature valves – B7G and B9A – needed no such fixing, as the holders gripped the pins quite firmly, though whenever the chassis they were used in were disposed vertically, as in many television sets, there would be a wire clip – or alternatively they were held in place by a spring-

loaded bayonet fitting screening can where needed – for security. The side-contact valves quite quickly lost ground to the American 'octal' eight-pin range that came on the market at about the same time.

Another problem to be overcome was that of heat causing a failure of the seal between the pin and the glass due to expansion. As a solution, valve pin wires were designed with distinct parts: a stiff wire within the envelope for welded connection to the electrodes; a short intermediate section of wire with a similar co-efficient of expansion to the glass it passed through; and, with all-glass miniatures, a thicker, tough section of wire to form the actual external pin.

Another problem, briefly mentioned above, was adequate electrical screening to prevent feedback (instability, sometimes in the form of audible howling). Valves were often encased in metal tube screens, or separate metal plate screens were built around their holders. Lots of early valves designed for use at RF were 'metallized', either with a grey or a gold conductive coating. The grey in particular tended to flake off. As this screening was an essential part of the structure of the valve, carried by a fine wire to earth (chassis) through a convenient pin, failure of the screen-to-wire connection created problems, as described. Mullard's red coating, as used on their octal and some of their side-contact range, has generally proved durable. However, the later and physically smaller valves dispensed with screening and opted for a return to external metal cans and/or internal screen mesh tubes; a very well known example of a valve with an internal screen is the EF80.

Battery Valves

Battery valves were at first the only type of valve available for any radio, but by the 1930s they were intended for use in portable or transportable sets or for the dwindling number of homes without mains access. Their design gradually improved over the years. From the 2-volt types that required an accumulator for their high consumption filaments came the so-called 'all-dry' range that used 1.4-volt filaments. 'All-dry' meant that the filament current consumption was so reduced in comparison with the older valves that a dry cell was adequate as a power source, which was accordingly rated at 1.4 volts to suit the 1.5-volt output of a dry

cell. In case you wonder where the missing 0.1 volt has got to, the reason was, that had the filaments been rated for the full 1.5 volts, there would have been a rapid fall-off in valve performance as the power cell aged. The important point was that, for the first time, the radio user was freed from the inconvenience of regular accumulator recharging.

The first of these low consumption valves were octal in style, usually in a tubular form with a plastic base, although a short-lived range was made with side-contact bases. Both these types were used until they were supplanted by miniature B7G all-glass valves which retained the 1.4 volt filaments. The miniature valves themselves underwent further development until a range emerged close to the end of the valve era, which possessed the extremely low filament current consumption of 0.025A.

From their appearance in the early 1950s, the all-glass B9A-based valves had proved successful, and this became the dominant base type from the mid-1950s onwards. Valves using the base were fitted virtually as standard to radio and television receivers – both monochrome and early colour – until the valve era effectively came to a close; the exceptions were colour television line output stage valves that were physically larger, and consequently used a more substantial but still all-glass base arrangement.

Valves, late 1940s onwards. On the left of the picture is a typical B8A valve with the characteristic metal base with its locking spigot. Later B8A valves dispensed with the metal base but retained the spigot, formed in the glass. From the early 1950s, B9A (Noval-) based all-glass valves became increasingly the industry standard. This base configuration continued in use throughout the later valve years. Valves fitted to portable radios during this period used the B7G base, again all glass, but with seven pins.

LOUDSPEAKERS

The earliest loudspeakers were really little more than a telephone (that is, headphone) earpiece positioned horizontally, with an acoustic exponential horn attached. These horns amplified the sound in much the same way as the horn in an acoustic gramophone amplified the vibrations produced by the needle on a diaphragm, but hi-fi they certainly were not. The main limitation was the poor audio frequency coverage, which was especially lacking in bass response. Due to the lack of bass, 'tinny' was one of the words often used to describe this sound, a problem mostly due to the necessarily limited horn size, although the inefficiency of the driving unit at low frequencies was a contributory factor. Horn speakers were needed because of their ability to amplify (in the acoustic sense, not electronically) the very modest signals, all that was available before true power output valves had been developed. Despite their non-linearity (uneven response) across the audio frequency range, they were very sensitive in action. The very poor audio quality of these cumbersome devices was improved in the latter part of the 1920s by the cone loudspeaker, as described next.

Cone Loudspeakers

As radio development gathered pace, it became imperative that a better solution to the problem of loudspeaker reproduction was found. The first cone-type loudspeakers were of the moving iron form, where the peak of the paper cone was attached to a strip of iron by means of an adjustable bolt. Fixed at one end but free at the other, the iron strip 'armature' was placed closed to the core of a small electromagnet, the winding of which was often fed directly from the output valve anode. Current variations through the winding varied the magnetic pull on the armature, so vibrating the cone to produce sound.

Invariably fitted with large cones, these loudspeakers were sensitive, and suited the simple TRF designs of the late 1920s/early 1930s. Although a marked advance on the earlier horns, inherent design weaknesses in this simple form again limited the quality. Large cone size, typically 12in (30cm), was needed to partly offset the very limited bass response. Inbuilt distortion was unavoidable due to the mechanical design, in that the lack of damping created resonance due to the 'bounce back' of the cone after every pull on it, as well as the non-linear nature of the cone movement – the cone rod actually moves through a slight but significant arc, adding a false edge to the sound. As if that wasn't enough, the most powerful audio signals tended to cause the armature to contact the magnetic pole piece, giving rise to objectionable buzzing or rattles. Increasing the spacing between the armature and the pole piece prevented this, but at the expense of sensitivity to the weaker signals. Careful manual adjustment was required, and this was provided for by a knurled knob to set for best sensitivity whilst avoiding contact. The adjustment knob was mounted on a spindle central to the cone, and accessed either conveniently from the enclosing cabinet front, or less conveniently from the back.

Some further degree of improvement was gained with the balanced armature type, where the armature slots between a split magnetic winding. This arrangement gave better control over the movement of the cone and allowed for a wider spacing of the gap between pole pieces and armature, but being inevitably slightly less sensitive, the balanced armature loudspeaker was suitable only for sets with a relatively high output power.

The Development of the Dynamic Loudspeaker

This device was developed to minimize the design faults of its predecessors. A twin armature was fixed to a cone rod suspended by leaf springs between the pole pieces, resulting in a truly linear movement of the cone, with no likelihood of contact chatter. The springs were only required to be very light in action, resulting in a sensitive unit of quite good basic quality. Cone loudspeakers in general possessed the great advantage that they could be housed in a cabinet, either a stand-alone unit containing only the loudspeaker (sometimes with space for the radio's batteries), or as part of an integrated receiver where everything was in the one cabinet, once problems had been overcome regarding 'microphony' – where valves vibrated under the influence of sound waves from the loudspeaker, causing odd echoing, howling and 'pinging' effects.

Many of the early cone loudspeakers were fitted with a sensitivity adjuster in the form of a knurled wheel or knob, and as the more advanced moving coil loudspeaker units were never so fitted, you can be sure that if the cabinet you are examining has such a control, contained within is a cone loudspeaker of the vibrating reed type.

Moving Coil Loudspeakers

The invention of the moving coil loudspeaker immediately proved, at least in terms of dynamic range, far superior to the earlier efforts – so good, in fact, that it survives to this day in universal use. Tracing the invention of this device is difficult; certainly, Ernst Siemens of Germany patented a device in 1874 'for obtaining the mechanical movement of an electrical coil from electrical currents transmitted through it', and three years later patented a cone made from parchment to act as a sound radiator for a moving coil unit. This flared design of cone formed the basis of the exponential horns used on most acoustic gramophones.

In 1898, Oliver Lodge took out a patent for 'an improved loudspeaker with non-magnetic spacers to keep the air gap between the inner and outer poles of a moving coil transducer'. The 'Phonetron', patented in 1921 by C.L. Farrand, was the first coil-driven loudspeaker available in the USA. A research paper published in 1925 by Chester W. Rice and Edward W. Kellogg of the General Electric Co. showed a coil-driven free-edged paper cone, held by a rubber membrane around the edge to a circular support, the assembly mounted on a baffle board – in other words, the moving coil loudspeaker we all know today. By 1927 the moving coil loudspeaker had been virtually perfected, although at that time it still suffered from the twin drawbacks of being expensive to produce, and exhibiting a definite lack of sensitivity compared with the low cost and more sensitive cone loudspeaker. It did, however, produce a quality of sound never before heard. The earliest units were mains energized with a field coil creating the required magnetism; this was probably due to the initial difficulty of making sufficiently powerful permanent magnets.

Once power-output valves had been devised that were truly adequate to drive them, a typical early example being Mullard's PEN4VA, the moving coil speaker, both in mains-energized (ME) and, subsequently, permanent magnet (PM) form, became the preferred choice of domestic radio receiver manufacturers across the developed world, though units fitted with massive exponential horns continued to be used in cinemas. These were essential to increase acoustically the relatively modest valve amplification of the film soundtracks.

There were several other attempts to overcome the dominance of the moving coil design, but most have faded into obscurity. One notable exception is the electrostatic loudspeaker, forms of which may occasionally be found as tweeters in quality radio sets. These utilize two plates with an air gap, rather like a simple capacitor: variations in electric potential applied to the plates produce movement and therefore sound. Although the electrostatic principle has been used by certain hi-fi manufacturers for full-range transducers, the moving coil loudspeaker has remained as the mainstay of domestic electronic audio.

THE STORY BEHIND SOME FAMOUS NAMES

Bush AC3, 1932. Three valves plus rectifier AC TRF, L/M. Note that these receivers were produced with no cabinet back covers. ★★★

Bush

The Graham Amplion company were successful makers of horn loudspeakers during the 1920s, but like so many others they succumbed to the depression of the early 1930s. Their managing director, Gilbert Darnley Smith, persuaded the Gaumont British film organization that had acquired Baird Television Ltd that they would benefit from a foothold in the radio market. Accordingly a new company was created in 1932 with Darnley Smith at the helm. A factory was established in Shepherd's Bush, London (hence the 'Bush' brand name), and in that year, their first receiver, a mains TRF design featuring a cabinet in the American-influenced 'Gothic' or tombstone shape, was marketed with modest success.

They were hampered in their sales by the depression, which prevented them from joining the Radio Manufacturers Association, who were at the time concerned with the survival of existing members and had closed ranks, refusing to take on new members. This in turn prevented access to the Wholesaler's Federation, so Bush used the Gaumont name to help with advertising as they set up dealerships. Bush concentrated on neat, value-for-money table receivers and radiograms during the 1930s, and used Christopher Stone, a popular radio personality and a man credited by some to have been the first true 'disc jockey', to help in their advertising campaigns. They made a great play of the reliability of their sets, offering a year's guarantee when most makers limited their guarantees to ninety days, and Stone's genial image was used effectively in competition with the other well known pipe-smoking gent, Frank Murphy, in many

advertisements. To be fair, those adverts did have a ring of truth, as the chassis construction of the typical Bush receiver is generally strong and well thought out.

Their very first radio, model AC3, had a distinctive tombstone shape bearing a remarkable similarity to a well known American receiver; otherwise most of the 1930s sets were based upon the geometric forms of Art Deco, and as the 1930s progressed, cabinet forms, still exclusively wooden, became simpler and more 'streamlined', in common with many makers. In the latter half of the 1930s Bush produced a wide range of receivers from modest, relatively low-cost sets to imposing and highly specified radiograms.

In the immediate post-war years the Rank organization – who already controlled Murphy – took control of Gaumont British and with it, Bush. Wooden cabinet models continued, though limited at first due to supply conditions, but no-frills radios in Bakelite housings soon became a big seller for the Bush brand, starting with the DAC90 and the AC91, and followed by the DAC10 and the DAC90A, all success stories in their own right, especially the latter. The DAC90A, very popular today with collectors, looks at a glance to be much the same as the earlier DAC90, but the chassis inside is very different and miniature valves replaced the octal types of the latter. Externally the DAC90 can be recognized by the cloth loudspeaker grille that is usually fitted* (the 90A has a gold anodized expanded aluminium grille) and the higher positioning of the side-mounted wave-change switch.

The DAC10 has the hallmarks of late Deco styling, with extravagant horizontal louvres that run around the front and sides of the walnut-effect Bakelite cabinet. It also features top-mounted push-button station and waveband selection. To save space within the cabinet, the loudspeaker unit has its magnet mounted in front of the speech coil rather than in the usual rear position, a somewhat unusual arrangement that can be a problem when a replacement unit is needed. Performance aside, the DAC10 is quite popular with collectors for its distinctive appearance.

The BP10 is unusual in that it is a portable receiver contained in a Bakelite case at a time when most portables on the market were of wooden or metal case construction. The valved MB60 started life in the mid-1950s, and became a design classic, presaging the appearance of many transistor portable radios to come, including the Bush TR82 of 1959. The 'MB' in its title indicates mains or battery operation.

In 1958 a model was introduced that was designed to receive FM/VHF transmissions only. This was the VHF90A, which, other than its title, has little in common with the DAC90A. It is a mains-powered radio contained in a small and somewhat undistinguished Bakelite case. The DAC90A itself stayed in production for almost ten years until replaced by the inferior styling of the DAC70.

---

* It may be that some very late DAC90s
were fitted with a metal grille.

ABOVE: **Bush PB53, 1938. ****

BELOW: **Bush VHF80, 1960. Six valves plus rectifier valve L/M/FM, AC/DC S/H. ***

BOTTOM: **Bush VHF80C, 1961. Six valves plus rectifier valve L/M/FM, AC/DC S/H. An updated version of the VHF80, this model was presented in a black plastic case with grey trim and a red scale plate. ***

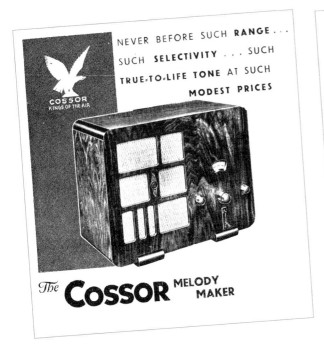

ABOVE: Detail from 1951 Cossor advertisement.

RIGHT: Cossor's Melody Maker kits, advertised in *Popular Wireless*, 1933.

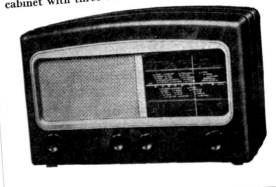

Late valve receivers from Bush include the VHF80 series, available in 1960 in a plastic cabinet in brown and gold trim; it was improved a year or so later with the introduction of the VHF80C, then in 1964 by the VHF81 with a wooden casing. Both sound quality and FM performance are pleasing with these economic models.

Cossor

A.C. Cossor Ltd was based in Highbury, London. The company had been in existence for many years in the early twentieth century as thermometer and barometer manufacturers, and had gradually built up a good reputation as specialist makers of electric glassware as used in the manufacture of Crookes tubes, cathode-ray tubes, X-ray tubes and the early low-vacuum radio valves. By 1922, Cossor were marketing a greatly improved successor to the old 'R' valve, the design of

which proved a sales success and placed them in the top rank of valve manufacturing. Cossor continued to develop their valve range and became strong competitors for Marconi-Osram and Mazda, though well behind the sales leader, Mullard. In the early years kits were an essential part of Cossor's product range, but by 1930 the company started the production of complete receivers.

Although they were still a small concern, much smaller than the major manufacturers, the years of 'Melody Maker' radio kit sales had provided them with the skills and capacity to manufacture components. They opened two new factories in Highbury, and rapidly expanded their range into ten models by 1932. Such was the rate of expansion that soon factory space was again at a premium, prompting the move of cabinet production to Leyton.

Post World War II, Cossor restarted radio and television set production, but also branched out into radar; in the 1950s, they merged into Philips.

Ekco

W.S. Verrells was only nine when his father died. He went to work, and at the age of twelve toiled in a Welsh coal mine, studying at night school. During World War I, Verrells fought for his country, at which time his lungs were badly affected (presumably by mustard gas) and his health was so poor it was feared that his life would be greatly shortened. His doctor advised him to go to Southend: 'The ozone will do you good.' So he did, and his lung condition improved. He became a freelance writer, and in 1924 sent in an article to a Southend newspaper concerning the possibility of using the mains supply to power the battery-only sets of the time. The letter caught the eye and the interest of Eric Kirkham Cole, who also had been considering the problem independently.

At the time, Cole was the proprietor of a small electrical business and was making Ekco radios as a minor sideline, producing six sets per week on average from a workforce of just two: Cole himself, aided by his future wife. After some discussion and development, Cole showed Verrells his design for a battery eliminator to replace both the high tension and low tension batteries. When it was advertised in the technical journals, the response was so encouraging that the two men went into partnership with a working capital of just £50. Verrells sold the eliminators that Cole built, by the simple expedient of calling at every house where he saw an aerial. The drawback to this first full eliminator was that it operated only on DC mains. A new eliminator capable of utilizing AC mains as a power source was needed, and Cole, feeling slightly out of his depth, sought technical help to develop a successful one.

Business Begins

In October 1926 E.K. Cole Ltd was formed. This limited company had a capital of £2,500; Verrells was chairman, Cole vice chairman, and the complement of directors was made up from three local men who had been astute enough to finance the operation. In 1927 a factory at Leigh-on-Sea was opened, with a staff of fifty or so, and soon went into profit, which for 1929

was in the region of £30,000. When indirectly heated valves were developed it became clear that future radio development would be based around mains-powered receivers, something that would close the market for the sales of their battery eliminators. It was a case of 'adapt or perish', and the decision was taken to enter into full-scale radio manufacturing without delay.

Further qualified staff recruitment followed, and by 1930 E.K. Cole Ltd went public. The first task was to build a factory big enough to allow for the expected unprecedented expansion; experience had already shown them the need for room to grow, as, due to the phenomenal growth in popularity of radio, they had already outgrown several other locations where they had set up their operations. They chose a greenfield site on the outskirts of Southend-on-Sea, and opened Britain's first purpose-built factory for radio manufacture.

A Lucky Break...

By chance, Michael Lipman, a representative of the German company AEG, visited them even as the factory was under construction, in response to an enquiry regarding insulating materials. Legend has it, though possibly apocryphally, that when asked as an aside if he knew of anything that might aid the mass production of radio receivers, he showed Ekco's buyer a Bakelite cabinet he just happened to have in the back of his car.

It was there, apparently, because he had shown it to other set manufacturers in the hope of gaining sales, but he had been disappointed, and no interest had been engendered. If we speculate why that might have been, one reason is obvious. The high initial cost of tooling meant that the AEG company needed a large minimum cabinet order to make it worthwhile, and cautious manufacturers would have good historical reason to doubt the popularity of the new and virtually untried material, besides which the rather conservative radio makers were apt at the time to be dismissive of the future value of Bakelite, sure that the sceptical buying public would find it hard to accept anything other than 'quality' wooden cabinets. However, the idea of ordering a considerable quantity of cabinets did not put off the confident Ekco team in the slightest. Neither, apparently, did they perceive any problems with selling, and orders for two types of cabinet were very soon placed.

The first Ekco receivers using the Bakelite AEG cabinets proved to be a hit at the 1930 radio show. Michael Lipman was offered, and accepted, the post of production engineer for the factory, and as it was still under

EKCO AND BAKELITE: A SUCCESS STORY

Set makers in Holland and Germany used Bakelite cabinets for some early models, and Philips in particular used a form of thermosetting resin laminated board (Arbolite) for some of their British receiver cabinets – but this material was planar, meaning that it could not be formed into compound curves, and therefore cabinets made with it had to be assembled – built up – from separate flat or single-curvature sheets. Ekco is credited for being one of the very first British radio manufacturers to introduce Bakelite in Britain as a radio cabinet material – at least in fully moulded form.

By the early 1930s Bakelite had become well established as a versatile material for the manufacture of various radio-related items such as knobs and dial escutcheons, but British makers had yet to employ the material in the mass production of entire one-piece cabinets. Ekco had seen, and been impressed by German Bakelite radio housings, and at first were content to import them from Germany, where Bakelite radio cabinets had been in production for some time. But changes in import duties soon put a stop to that process, and caused Ekco to push ahead with their own cabinet production plant. The great hydraulic presses – essential to the production of Bakelite mouldings – were installed at the Southend works, and mass production began. An early production run was set in operation for model RS3, a straightforward TRF in the current 'one-cabinet' self-contained form,

One of Ekco's giant hydraulic moulding presses.

its cone loudspeaker built into the mottled Bakelite case. Within a few years, the innovative ideas that Ekco commissioned from top-flight designers began to build a formidable reputation for the company.

Freed from the constraints of timber, designers created some of the most interesting and complex forms, previously difficult if not impossible to produce economically in 'conventional' wood construction. The finished cabinets were strong and elegant, often showing the influence of Art Deco. Perhaps the most famous of the many Ekco designs was, and still remains, the so-called 'round' series, commissioned by Ekco from the avant-garde architect and designer Wells Coates. Simpler in concept than earlier designs such as the M23, the 'round' series was based upon the geometric forms of arcs, circles and lines, which may be the reason for their continuing popularity: timeless, uncluttered elegance.

construction he had a free hand to equip it. He called upon a personal friend from Ford to help him plan an adaptable conveyor system for the rapid production of radio receivers. The factory was up and running by 1931, and even the government's 'anti-dumping' law that added a punitive 50 per cent import duty to many goods, including the AEG cabinets, only served to spur Ekco on to manufacture their own. A deal with AEG was negotiated and the plant installed.

The factory floor shown in a contemporary article in the *Southend Standard* is enormous, employing over 2,000 workers, the vast majority being women. They worked alongside the conveyor belt, soldering, riveting, drilling and assembling the completed chassis of radio receivers from tiny component parts, often produced in house by Ekco.

Although women were employed in great numbers throughout the factory, one bastion of male supremacy remained: the complex metal moulds needed for the Bakelite pressings were created by a skilled team of men. Three great hydraulic presses created the famous range of Bakelite cabinets, each operating at pressures up to 1,000 tons or more, unique at that time in Britain for their capacity.

... and Disaster

Then disaster struck. In early 1932, while production was under way of the RS2 TRF receiver with its cathedral-style Bakelite case designed by J.K. White, the Ekco design and research laboratories were destroyed by fire, and with them went the designs for the following year's models and also items of production equipment for the RS2 and similar models. In fact the hiatus allowed a rethink of the RS2, and the M23 was the result, identical in appearance to the earlier receiver but with circuit modifications, and employing a moving coil loudspeaker instead of the primitive vibrating-reed cone of the earlier model. The RS2 is now becoming relatively rare. But the problems caused by the fire meant Ekco had to put the two leading models in the 1933 range into the previous year's cabinets, and sales slumped, large quantities of unsold receivers were stockpiled, and the company was plunged into financial crisis.

Things looked bleak for the future, especially after two top directors resigned, but Cole and Verrells mortgaged their own properties in order to gain sufficient overdraft to keep the company solvent. Their risky strategy paid off, and by the end of 1933 things were back on track, with a range of new models designed with the aid of talented architectural designers – and most sets now used superhet circuitry. The receivers of the following years established Ekco's reputation for reliability and advanced design.

By 1935, the *Essex Weekly News* tells us that 'more than 3,000 girls were employed in the enormous factory'. The paper comments:

> Raw Bakelite powder is poured into moulds and electrically treated (sic, read 'heated') dies bring terrific pressure and force on the powder, resolving it into a plastic substance. For a few minutes the pressure is applied – the workmen use an egg timer to judge the time – and the dies are released, and a highly polished cabinet results. Chromium fittings are moulded into place, and in a few minutes powder has become polished perfection. The dies, tools and mould weigh upwards of 15 tons each... cut from solid blocks of chromium nickel steel... (they) involve an expenditure of several thousand pounds before the first finished cabinet can be made.

The Seemingly Inevitable Decline

It is fair to say the Ekco's real heyday was in the decade preceding World War II. After the war, quality production restarted, but the innovation that in earlier years had so popularized the marque seemed in short supply. It was as though everything worth doing had been done, and the new designs were really little more than improvements on these established features (revised and modernized valve line-ups, simplified cabinet detailing). Although the firm branched out into non-domestic electronics and other plastic production work, gradually but inexorably Ekco went the way of the rest of the British radio manufacturers, and the depressing and ever-decreasing circle of takeovers and downsizing finally finished off the once-pre-eminent radio company. Only the brand name lives on, albeit in a sadly emasculated form.

HMV (His Master's Voice)

HMV was a trademark of The Gramophone Company, a British organization that was an offshoot of the Victor Talking Machine Co., based in New Jersey, USA. Their business was, historically, the production of good quality mechanical phonographs – wind-up acoustic gramophones, in other words. The growth and development of radio was seen by the company as a threat, but despite their misgivings they were dragged into making provision for electrical reproduction when, in 1925, records themselves began to be produced by electrical means; finally, in 1929, they entered the arena of radio manufacturing with the acquisition of the 'Marconiphone' brand and assets from the Marconi company who saw their radio-manufacturing arm as unprofitable. The Victor Company had by this time been taken over by the Radio Corporation of America (RCA), and David Sarnoff, the RCA chief, developed plans for HMV to become a major player in both radio and record production.

What the determined Sarnoff wanted, he got. Careful marketing ensured that the HMV brand became associated with quality in the minds of the buying public, and the HMV radios that began to appear in the early 1930s were certainly well built and designed. Chassis fitted to both HMV and Marconiphone radios were generally identical in most or all respects; only the cabinet, and of course the brand name on it, differed. The HMV cabinets were in themselves fine pieces of cabinet making, and this was especially true of their radiograms, huge, heavy items of furniture with record-playing units married to standard or slightly modified radio chassis. With the top of the company entrenched in such a very traditional approach, it is small wonder that they declined the offer for the production of Bakelite cabinets from the German AEG Group, the same company that subsequently offered Bakelite cabinet production facilities

to Ekco, with a very different outcome (*see* 'Ekco', above).

HMV's main competitor in the record and gramophone production field was undoubtedly the Columbia Graphophone Company – and yes, 'Graphophone' is the way they chose to spell their brand name – broadly, it means 'written sound'. Columbia was a British organization with strong world-wide distribution facilities and a number of overseas manufacturing subsidiary companies. They did not manufacture radio chassis themselves, but they had arranged for the British Plessey Company to make sets for them. But the depression hit record and gramophone sales hard, and profits for both Columbia and HMV – along with many others – plummeted. The two companies merged, and EMI (Electrical and Musical Industries) was created.

HMV had been slow to change from their traditional acoustic gramophones to the newer radiograms, but by the early 1930s, the public were showing such a marked reluctance to purchase the obviously inferior mechanical gramophones that EMI quite quickly expanded radio production. The company did have a renowned research staff, headed by Isaac Shoenberg of notable merit, including the ex-Columbia A.D. Blumlein, the inventor of stereophonic recording on gramophone records and a main contributor in the development of all-electronic television. The beam-tetrode output valve was developed by them as a very successful answer to Philip's patent on the production of the pentode valve. The brilliant Blumlein was also part of the EMI-Marconi team that brought the world's first high definition television into operation at Alexandra Palace in 1936. Tragically, he died in 1942 when his plane crashed during the testing of an airborne radar mapping system.

The Marconiphone brand was given a lower status, even though the actual product differed little from the 'superior' HMV-branded radiograms other than in cabinet details or styling terms. Marconiphone products were available by the general trade through wholesale sources, whereas HMV-branded goods were restricted to a registered dealership. This type of arrangement came to be standard for many other companies.

ABOVE: **AD31, Lissen advertisement, 1933.**

LEFT: **Marconiphone advertisement, 1951.**

Lissen

Lissen Ltd was founded in 1923 as a maker of radio parts components, and by 1934 Lissen Ltd of Edmonton, London and Isleworth, Middlesex had become a popular name both for the production of factory-built sets and for their range of kits for home construction. The company had been bought in 1928 by the Ever-Ready battery company, in fact, but retained its founder, T.N. Cole, as managing director. Cole later left and set up the Vidor battery company, in direct and damaging competition with Lissen/Ever-Ready. In fact, home construction was for a time at least quite a big hobby activity, and although it is probably the case that any savings made by such home building were more apparent than real, the fact is that thousands of enthusiastic amateurs built these Lissen kits – and kits by other makers, such as Cossor – on their kitchen tables.

Others avidly read the radio magazines of the day, preferring to learn at the same time as construct from articles in *Wireless World*, *Practical Wireless*, *Amateur Wireless* and others, and thereby becoming true enthusiasts to whom building a kit would be seen as cheating

A Lissen advertising leaflet tentatively dated to around 1934 offers a choice of four different kits, three of which were battery operated and one AC mains powered. As usual with such material, no date is actually given for the sets depicted, and in fact they cover more than one year of production, so we can presume that a Lissen policy was to retain a successful design for more than one year. There is only one superhet kit, and that must have been quite something in its time as it is battery powered but uses no fewer than seven valves. One can only speculate on the speed at which HT batteries would have needed replacement and accumulators required charging. It is probable that to legitimize the claim of seven valves,

Early 1930s Lissen kits advertisement.

no multi-valves would have been employed; for example, a separate diode valve for detection and a separate oscillator valve may have been used. The kit was offered complete for £11 10s (£11 50p), a great deal of money in those days, so it is understandable that there was the offer of 'convenient gradual payment terms' for the purchase of the kit.

The 'Skyscraper 4' battery receiver kit is on offer as a 'kit of parts', or a 'kit of parts plus cabinet', or a 'kit of parts plus cabinet and PM loudspeaker'. By the time this leaflet was published, however, kit sets were beginning to fall from favour with potential purchasers, one contributory reason being, perhaps, that it had by then become readily apparent to the purchasing public that the savings to be made over a ready-built commercial radio were modest in the extreme. Ever-Ready kept the Lissen name alive during the 1930s, but it seems that the brand name became moribund after World War II.

McMichael

Leslie McMichael was an electrical engineer and a founder member of the London Wireless Club, 1913. Renamed the Wireless Society of London, in 1922 the club merged with others and became the Radio Society of Great Britain (RSGB). After serving in the Flying Corps during World War I, McMichael went into business in 1920 as L. McMichael Ltd, and sold war-surplus equipment from, of all unlikely places, a stall outside his home. Before long he joined forces with one of his suppliers, Benjamin Hesketh, to make receivers under the initials 'MH'. When in 1922 the first all-British wireless exhibition opened in London, L. McMichael Ltd was able to display a range of receivers. The company had a policy of selling quality, and they progressed steadily, if unspectacularly, until in 1932 they became a public company, sticking to their policy of selling only through accredited dealers because they had no wish to see their product sold alongside other radios that were only able to offer low cost as an incentive to purchase.

The 1930 'Mains 3' featured an illuminated full-vision scale marked in metres and complete with a cord-controlled dial pointer – but no integral loudspeaker. The 'Duplex 4' series produced in the early 1930s were suitcase TRF portables. The 'Duplex Super 5' of 1933 was a battery-powered five-valve transportable. The 'Twin Supervox' of 1933 was a four-valve (plus rectifier) AC mains-powered TRF receiver featuring twin loudspeakers, Osram 'catkin' valves and a simple switched 'top-cut' tone control.

After a trading loss during the 1934–35 period, Hesketh left. One cause of the crisis was the rather old-fashioned appearance of 'Twin Speaker Superhet', which, as its name implied, featured two loudspeakers to provide, McMichael claimed, better sound quality. Unfortunately the loudspeakers resided behind a single grille, and the small curved dial aperture, already becoming dated, did little to enhance the rather plain appearance of what was an expensive receiver. It seems that the company's slogan 'Costs a little more – so much the better' became ironic under the circumstances. At 18 guineas it was certainly costly, and did not persuade sufficient members of the public to part with their cash.

The next season's models were redesigned to make them visually more up to date, and they were keenly priced to sell. Model 135 shows the different approach, with its curved cabinet front boasting twin octagonal loudspeaker apertures, an optional stand with cabriole legs, and a large dial accessed by lifting a lid on the cabinet. At £15 it presented a far better bargain than the previous year's models. Externally this set is similar to model 137, released in 1937. The latter has short waveband coverage and a tuning indicator, both features absent from the earlier 135. Other interesting receivers were marketed; model 235 offered an unusual lozenge-shaped cabinet containing a three-valve AC superhet. Model 435 was a five-valve transportable receiver (plus valve rectifier) for AC mains housed in an elegant cabinet. Model 361 is another set that is unusual yet elegant in appearance. A three-valve AC superhet, it is contained in a walnut cabinet with pronounced angles where the top meets the sides, in effect giving it something of the 'tombstone' appearance. The angular cabinet is complemented by the escutcheon design surrounding the dial and the loudspeaker grille.

Model 808 is a truly unusual receiver. It was first released in 1938, in either a blue or maroon leatherette-covered cabinet with a rear-mounted two-position tone switch, although later cabinet versions from 1939 were walnut veneered with a side-mounted variable tone control. The really eye-catching thing is, however, the so-called 'rotabar' tuning, also used in their 'Bijou' battery portable presented in the same leatherette case. To tune the set, the horizontal bar across the dial aperture is moved through an arc. It seems that, once they had started with oddities, they were loathe to stop; model 380, a four-valve AC superhet, had three separate tuning dials.

Post World War II, McMichael's products were solid but fairly uninspiring in visual terms. The company was taken over in the 1950s by Radio and Allied Industries, previously known as Sobell.

Murphy

At the end of his service career, Frank Murphy returned to his former civilian job with the Post Office, but like so many before him, his experience in World War I had opened his mind to other things and he became discontented with humdrum normality. He decided to use his demobilization gratuity of £450 to set up a publicity firm, along with another similarly inclined ex-officer, Rupert Casson. Although by the late 1920s Murphy was making a good living, he was frustrated at not being able to use his technical skill. He was critical of the radio receivers of the time as being far too complicated and unreliable, and he was sure he could do better. The Murphy Radio Company was set up when he convinced E.J. Power, a young but talented radio engineer, to join him as chief engineer.

Power was an ideal acquisition for Murphy; he already had experience of radio manufacture. Their first receiver from the new factory in Welwyn Garden City was a four-valve portable that gained considerable praise from the trade press for its ease of use and good performance. It was carefully priced to undercut rival products. A long-running advertising campaign began, featuring Murphy himself as 'the man with the pipe'. The adverts were sensible, well thought out and convincingly persuasive. The apparent common sense of these won many customers.

Frank Murphy –
The Man with
the Pipe.

Murphy remained astute in his hiring of staff, and obtained technically excellent people to further his product ranges. He also involved Gordon Russell, the famous furniture designer, to some extent, although it is not clear precisely what his input was. What is known is that Russell's designer brother, Richard, produced many designs for Murphy cabinets that were, to say the least, uncompromisingly Art Deco influenced and certainly far from safe conventionality. Whether the sets sold because, or in spite of the cabinet styling is a matter for conjecture. Certainly the chassis contained within them continued to be well built and reliable, as well as easy to operate.

Problems began to surface in the later 1930s, reaching a crisis when Murphy tried to insist on making all decisions for the firm personally. He could not persuade his board of directors to accept that ultimatum, so Frank Murphy resigned and left the company, never to return. Despite the loss of their founder, the Murphy Radio Company continued to produce excellent products until the outbreak of World War II. Postwar activities included the innovative range of 'Baffle' radios. These featured large front panels for good quality reproduction, especially of the bass register; often they were in 'console' form. After trading losses in the early 1960s, the company was taken over by the burgeoning Rank Organisation, who had already acquired Bush.

Pilot

Beacon Electrical were established in 1908 in New York. Initially a battery manufacturer, the rise of radio presented an irresistible challenge, and they diversified into the manufacture of radios and radio components for the booming home construction market. When the Beacon company combined with a small company named Pilot Electrical Manufacturing, they dispensed with the Beacon name (although it was the Beacon company that were by far the major player in the takeover) and were then able to lay claim to possessing the world's largest radio parts plant. By the end of the 1920s, Pilot were manufacturing almost everything 'in house' including valves, cabinets, components, Bakelite mouldings and parts.

By the middle of the 1930s, Pilot receivers were being exported to Britain. Soon a British factory was established, and some British designs were marketed. Arguably their most successful product – at least in volume-of-sales terms – the 'Little Maestro' series of small table radios started life in 1939 and continued through a series of cabinet and chassis variations into the early 1950s; then, in common with so many other makers, Pilot slowly lost ground, until finally it succumbed to the take-over of the British 'Pilot' brand by Ultra in 1959.

Pye

Pye were founded originally as a company for the manufacture of scientific instruments, and were exceptionally successful in that field during World War I. The cessation of hostilities was a setback for the company, and the loss of lucrative war department contracts could have spelt disaster, so they chose to diversify into radio receiver production, at first producing interconnecting valve panels for the educational market. When broadcasting proper began, a series of domestic receivers was produced, and after some initial sales and production problems, Pye's investment in wireless began to prove worthwhile. By 1928, wireless-set production was the major and most valuable part of the firm's output. Pye's advertising agent, C.O. Stanley, took a calculated but astute gamble when he bought Pye's radio business in that year, and a year later Pye Radio Ltd was registered as a limited company.

In the late 1920s there was a national vogue for fretwork. This was a harmless but rather odd hobby activity where the man (or boy) of the house would construct wooden items in endless variety to use as gifts or birthday presents, such as pipe racks for the dedicated smoker, handy walking stick/umbrella stands for the hall, letter racks to keep those important seaside postcards or chatty epistles from favourite aunts, and sewing boxes for home seamstresses. Fretwork was ubiquitous. Amidst all the variations, one thing remained constant: there would be decoration in the form of intricate patterns laboriously pierced (fretted) in thin wooden panels by means of a fine and very thin-bladed 'fret'-saw – laborious, that is, unless the woodworker was the fortunate owner of the latest Hobbies' treadle-operated fretsaw. One aim of *Hobbies Weekly* magazine seems to have been the fostering of interest in fretwork, perhaps understandably since Hobbies, the manufacturers of the aforementioned fretworking machines, plus handsaws and tools, regularly advertised their wares within the magazine. Whether there was any actual business connection isn't clear, but the magazine was a Newnes publication, edited by none other than F.J. Camm. One regular feature it contained was a popular radio construction section, believed, of course, to have been the work of Mr Camm.

It thus became quite the norm to see fretted patterns, often based upon Art Nouveau, Art Deco and Rennie Mackintosh-influenced motifs, adorning the fronts of loudspeaker cabinets of the time, so it was not surprising that when casting around for a suitable design for radio cabinet grilles, a member of Pye's staff suggested a fretted pattern based upon a design he'd seen adorning a friend's cigarette case. This proved to be enormously successful for the company: the 'Rising Sun' motif was used for many years, probably beginning with the model 25 of 1927, a five-valve 'portable' (portable in truth only because it sported a carrying handle). Adorning the front of the wooden cabinets of many of their most popular receivers, the motif became an easily recognized trademark and seems to have contributed to the success of the firm; it was certainly as recognizable to the public at large as Ekco's 'round' series of Bakelite radios.

In point of fact, Pye were far from alone in their use of intricate fretted panels. A few examples among very many during the early 1930s are the Classic 'Super Two' of 1931 by Hustler; Simpson and Webb Ltd (later to be named the Aerodyne Radio Company), which used a boldly complex geometric design; the Ferranti Model 32, which sported a fleur-de-lis pattern; and the Marconiphone model 66, which boasted a sinuously curving pattern that seems to belong to the earlier Art Nouveau era. Despite the plethora of fretwork, no other maker seemed quite to hit the spot with consumers in the way that Pye did with their 'Rising Sun', and it can be seen that as the decade progressed and grille designs became more 'streamlined' Deco and less complex, Pye remained reluctant to relinquish the design that had succeeded so well for them. After 1933, however, they produced many sets without their trademark grille, and when it did appear again it was in muted form, adorning the circular loudspeaker opening of their Baby 'Q' portable.

Free to amateur constructors

With every HOBBIES WEEKLY for Nov. 18th now on sale, there is a large free design chart with complete instructions and patterns for making this modern radio cabinet. Details of cost of wood are also given. The design is No. 1987 and copies will cost 4d. each after this week. Hobbies Weekly is full of interesting and helpful articles for the handyman, and is obtainable from any newsagent for 2d. each Wednesday.

This week only

If your newsagent has sold out send 3d. in stamps for a copy to Hobbies Weekly, Dept. 16, Dereham, Norfolk

The link between the hobbies of fretwork and radio construction is evident from this November 1933 advertisement in *Wireless World*.

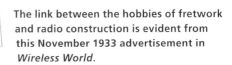

After World War II they attempted to revive the design and, presumably in an effort to modernize, they simplified it by dispensing with the clouds when they produced their Model M78F portable in 1948. This showed a truly amazing lack of foresight. With no clouds, the pattern closely resembled the then hated Japanese national flag, Japan being a wartime enemy

of Britain. After public protestation the receiver was withdrawn from sale, and remaining stocks destroyed. Paradoxically, despite this unfortunate gaffe signalling the end for Pye's beloved Rising Sun, the effect has been to make the M78F a much sought-after radio entirely because of its scarcity and, of course, the story behind it.

The 1951 Festival of Britain made the public more aware of functional styling. Pye engaged Robin Day, at that time a young and promising industrial designer, to produce cabinets that were typically simple in line and essentially modernistic. Apparently Day had trouble convincing some of the Pye board of directors that the high-gloss finishes and gilt decorations characterizing their product needed updating – but convince them he finally did, and stayed as a designer for the company, winning awards and inspiring others over the period during which Pye remained autonomous. His Pye PE60 cabinet design is a good example of his logical, intelligent approach.

ABOVE: A sad end to an illustrious trade mark, this Pye portable was the last to use the 'Rising Sun' fret design. Pye brought this receiver to the market not long after the war with Japan had ceased, and compounded the error by removing the clouds from the fret, making it look even more like the Japanese flag. The vast majority of these sets were unsold and scrapped. Consequently, they are now prized by collectors.

RIGHT: Pye PE60, c. 1950. Six valves including rectifier AC S/H, eleven wave-band coverage. Large table model.

Roberts

Roberts Radio has its beginnings in 1932. Harry Roberts had been employed by two firms specializing in portable radio construction, but at the age of just

1038 (Advt.) THE WIRELESS AND ELECTRICAL TRADER November 26, 1949

The
Finest
of ALL
Portables

MODEL P.4D. PRICE 14 gns. PLUS P. TAX £3.3.3.

ROBERTS RADIO CO. LTD.
CREEK ROAD, EAST MOLESEY, SURREY.

1949, and the message to the trade carried in this Roberts advertisement is clear: a big claim, but perhaps one not without merit.

seventeen he found himself out of work when the second of the firms he worked for closed. He found employment as a freelance radio salesman, collecting sets from suppliers and demonstrating in the homes of possible purchasers, before teaming up with Leslie Bidmead. With the latter's technical know-how, they opened a very basic radio factory in two rented rooms in London. Roberts set his sights high from the beginning, intending to sell top quality sets to affluent purchasers. By means of personal demonstration to their buyer, he persuaded Harrods to take his sets. The company grew only very slowly during the 1930s, but that growth was secure, and financed from profits. Roberts Radio became a limited company in 1937. They worked hard to live up to their claim of 'the finest of all portables'. Princess Margaret took delivery of a Roberts portable in 1939, the first sale by the company to the royal family.

Roberts Radio Ltd moved to larger premises during World War II and made ready for the commencement of civilian production in 1946. Harrods valued their P4D portable above any other, and the same set was selected for the 1946 'Britain Can Make It' exhibition. Always in the forefront, the 1949 Roberts 'Junior' portable featured a compact and efficient layer-type HT battery and miniature all-glass valves. The royal family continued to purchase Roberts receivers, and in 1955 Roberts were awarded the first of their four royal warrants. Although ownership of the brand has changed, the 'Roberts' name remains in business today.

Ultra

Edward 'Teddy' Rosen founded his company in 1920. Based in London, his principal product was an improved type of headphone of his own devising. His firm was soon producing horn loudspeakers, to which they gave the name 'Ultra'. He converted his business into a limited company in 1925, renaming it Ultra Electric Co. Ltd. For the remainder of the 1920s the company gained ground steadily, producing a small range of items as well as the horn loudspeaker until, in 1930, the first mains-powered Ultra receiver appeared. By this time, Rosen had developed his factory through expansion-forced changes of location and reached a point where almost all components were made in house.

The early 1930s saw the Ultra factory in production of a range of well built but conventional TRF receivers such as the 'Tiger' and the 'Lynx', and the company made well founded claims as to ease of service and reliability. By 1935, Ultra products were being manufactured in a large new and splendidly Art Deco factory on Western Avenue, London. Rosen, however, had little interest in cabinet design, and this aspect of Ultra receivers began to cause concern regarding a perceived lack of market appeal as the 1930s progressed.

After World War II, Rosen made an effort to redress the situation, and Ultra receivers began to take on a stylish appearance that complemented the reliability they were known for. Ultra's series of late 1940s–early 1950s Bakelite-cased 'Twin' receivers are always popular with collectors. Several variations of basically similar battery-mains receivers were produced by the company, probably the most sought-after being the 'Coronation Twin' R786 of 1953, displaying a coat of arms centrally on the grille. A De Luxe version was also produced, but looked very different as it was supplied with a simulated crocodile-skin cabinet with sliding doors to the front.

In the late 1950s, Ultra took on the Pilot brand as television receiver sales boomed. This proved disastrous. The company was engaged in the production of 'special products' (that is non-domestic radio) and the success of these activities concealed temporarily a poor domestic product sales performance. Ultra struggled on for a while but was taken over by Thorn in 1961, ending the business career of Teddy Rosen.

CHAPTER ELEVEN

SAFETY

So you've bought your first vintage valve radio and you can't wait to plug it in, switch on and hear that lovely warm valve sound. Wait a moment, though: how long do you think the set has been idle? How long since music or speech issued from its venerable loudspeaker? Why should that matter, you may question. Unfortunately, it does. Just like modern-day electrical and electronic equipment, radio receivers were built with a finite life expectancy, and it's a fair bet that few, if any, set makers expected their receivers to be in use after ten years, and surely not as many as seventy years or more.

Age takes its toll, even in receivers that have been lovingly cared for. Components and wiring suffer from insulation breakdown, and, in particular, old receiver mains leads – usually rubber-sleeved wire covered over with cloth – are almost always dangerous because of the tendency for rubber, a natural product, to decay and crumble, leaving exposed the electrical conductors within. The insulation of all capacitors is prone to gradual leakage, and electrolytic capacitors in particular leak heavily after periods of non-use. Mechanical problems may have arisen, too: the knobs may not be securely fixed to the control spindles, the rear cover may be damaged or missing.

The advice must be: never, ever connect a newly obtained vintage radio directly to the mains. Power applied to a damp-damaged transformer winding or via the rectifier valve to age-compromised components can lead to sudden catastrophic failure.

If (*and only if*) you have some electronic experience and are confident of your ability to proceed at this point, the first thing to do is to carry out a visual check that all valves are present. Examine the mains lead and replace it if the insulation is impaired through damage

or age – which in all likelihood it will be. Mechanical problems may have arisen, too: for example, the knobs may not be securely fixed to the control spindles. With any mains-powered receiver – and especially those with 'live' chassis, where the metalwork is connected directly to one side of the mains supply – such problems must be noted and corrected before the radio can be deemed fairly safe to connect to the power supply.

Replacing mains leads is not always as straightforward as it ought to be. With AC/DC receivers using live chassis technology, it is essential that no earth connection is made – the mains lead should have only live and neutral wires. With AC-only receivers employing a fully isolating transformer, an earth connection via a three-core mains lead is generally advisable, even though many were not fitted with one. A further difficulty arises with sets that use either an autotransformer or a heater transformer. The transformers make them AC only, yet the chassis will be 'live', so again, no earth should be fitted.

In the author's opinion it is always prudent to obtain service data for any unknown radio, whether or not any electronic restoration work is envisaged. The data will help you decide the best way forward, as it will show the power supply arrangements for your radio. These vary considerably, some small sets using a 'line cord' to drop the mains voltage to suit the valves used. These cords consist of resistance wire wrapped in asbestos fibre and sheathed with woven cotton. They are designed to run warm in use, and must never be shortened or the valves in the radio will be overrun. Apart from the obviously unfortunate presence of potentially injurious asbestos fibres, the insulation in these cords is often suspect because of their age. Such cords were often fitted to American imports to allow radios designed to work at 110 volts to be operated from our higher 240-volt supplies, the line cord dissipating the waste power as heat. A few British-made sets also used the cords, as they represented a cheap and simple answer to the problem of supplying valve heaters.

Even if you have no intention of working on a set yourself, the data may be useful to a restorer – but here, yet another warning is needed: do not entrust your precious vintage radio to just anyone. Satisfy yourself that you have someone with the requisite knowledge and experience of vintage electronics as even the best of today's technicians may be completely out of his or her depth with yesteryear's technology and can, sometimes, do more harm than good.

Once any obvious problem, such as a dangerous mains lead, has been corrected, an easy way to check a receiver for working condition is to use a test lamp, connected to the mains via the protection of either an RCB (residual current device) or an earth leakage circuit breaker (ELCB). Either of these plug-in adapters will offer some measure of protection against severe electric shock. The test lamp is a simple device that places an ordinary lamp in series with the radio's power supply. If the lamp lights up, and then dims, and no smell of burning or other untoward effect is noted – no crackling, no smoke issuing from the radio – after thirty seconds or so, the set may begin to work. If it does, the volume and sensitivity will not be at maximum due to the lowered power level, but at least you will have proved that the set is safe enough to apply full power to. If you do, be prepared to switch off in an instant should anything happen unexpectedly (for example, that burning smell or smoke mentioned earlier).

It will be apparent now that mains-powered radios fall into a number of groups, but all use potentially lethal high voltages. Transformer-equipped sets can offer a slightly greater degree of protection, but whether the set is designed for AC mains only and possesses an isolating transformer, or is designed for AC/DC operation and is linked directly to the mains supply, there will be points within the chassis assembly that carry 'raw' mains. It is therefore essential for the novice restorer to bear these points in mind whenever working on an exposed chassis. It is worth keeping in mind that a radio that once might

have been safe could now be compromised by time or by inexpert modification. Never, ever assume or take things for granted, but *ensure*, regardless of the type of set, that the chassis can never become live to full mains potential, only neutral.

Whether or not the chassis is live is a situation that can be checked easily by the use of a mains neon screwdriver/tester. Touching the chassis with the tester probe when the power is connected should *not* result in the neon lighting. Also, ensure that mains connections are the correct way round, and that where the chassis should be earthed, as in *fully isolated* transformer-fed power supplies, it actually *is*. Always check the chassis of transformerless AC/DC types for neutral connection. Never leave exposed grub-screw heads in the knobs of live-chassis sets. Where such knobs are standard for the set (many AC/DC types use spring-grip push-on knobs, to avoid the use of grub screws) the screw should be sealed with hard wax melted into the hole. It would have been quite possible to produce AC/DC sets without making the chassis live, but few if any makers bothered to do so. As an aside, it might be thought that knobs using a spring grip instead of a grub screw are safer because there cannot be finger contact with a screw top; certainly that was the thinking of most commercial set makers. In reality, spring-held knobs are today, if anything, less safe – in this writer's opinion – because with age the springs often either work loose or snap, allowing the knob to either drop off or at least be easily removed from the metal shaft of the control. As the latter will almost certainly be in contact with a metal chassis, the risk of shock from live mains present there due to incorrect mains wiring is a clear and obvious hazard, whereas the grub screws of knobs can easily be insulated by recessing and filling with hard wax. Note that certain Philips receivers use twin grub screws for each knob.

To minimize problems when earthed-case test equipment is connected to a mains receiver, ensure that these are powered through the circuit-breaker. If working with a live-chassis receiver, ensure correctness of polarity. Whenever possible, connect test equipment, such as signal generators, through series isolation capacitors.

Treat all valve-type mains radios with great respect. Ensure that your work, when completed, cannot pose a danger to any subsequent user. If you are inexperienced, consider seriously whether it would be better – and safer – to have your receiver checked over or restored by an expert (*see* Appendix). Even if you have experience of modern electronic equipment, you should not assume that you are competent to work with valve technology. There are many textbooks on the subject, some of which are mentioned in the bibliography, and you are strongly advised to read and learn as much as possible before you attempt to work on a vintage receiver.

If, after reading the above, you feel able to proceed, here are some important general points to note:

- A multi-test meter will prove very useful; low cost ones can be obtained easily.
- Bear in mind that digital meters present far less loading on circuits under measurement, and this can, under certain circumstances, give rise to readings that appear considerably higher than those quoted in elderly service data, so allowance must be made for this.
- Your working area should have good illumination.
- The floor should be made of, or covered with, well insulated, dry material such as thick linoleum or carpet. On concrete, a wooden 'duckboard' is a good idea.
- The workbench or table should be of wooden construction, with a wooden, plastic (Melamine), thick linoleum or cork surface – *definitely NOT metal.*
- The use of a mains isolating transformer (1:1) gives a good measure of personal protection to the restorer and is a worthwhile investment, especially if you plan to make many restorations.
- A residual current circuit breaker, fitted to your mains outlet, also gives protection but must not be used together with an isolation transformer, or its safety function may be compromised.
- *Always* check the polarity of any fitted mains plug; do *not* assume that an already fitted plug is sure to be correctly wired; it is safest to assume the opposite.
- If a chassis-mounted mains transformer has exposed connections, tape over them, if only temporarily, to avoid inadvertent contact. Be especially careful if you wear a metal ring, bracelet or 'dangly' necklace.
- Valves, especially output and rectifier types, can become extremely hot in use, as can power resistors.
- When working on a receiver under power, *NEVER, NEVER, EVER* put both hands into or on the chassis of a working set. *Work with one hand only, and put the other in your pocket. Memorize this as a mantra: single-handed for safety.*

Build a Series-Type Test Lamp

This is a simple device, but very useful to the restorer because it allows power to be fed to an 'unknown' radio in order to test for potential problems with mains transformers, smoothing capacitors or rectifier short-circuits without the danger of explosion or fire, should anything be amiss within the chassis. The device works like this: the power is applied to the set under test in series with a 60W lamp. If the lamp lights brightly, then quite quickly dims to a dull glow, the radio is probably safe to apply full power to. If it fails to light at all, there is an open-circuit problem as no current is flowing. This means there is a break in the electrical path into the set, perhaps due to a faulty on-set mains switch – generally part of the volume or tone control. Other common causes are a damaged mains transformer or a faulty dropping resistor. Should the lamp light brightly and remain so, there is a short-circuit on the mains input to the receiver.

Once satisfied that no danger of burn-out or catastrophic failure is likely, the switch is thrown to short out the lamp and apply power directly. It's that simple – and that useful. Before using a test lamp for the first time on an unknown receiver, cold checks – resistance checks without any power connected – should be made from the HT+ line to chassis. A convenient point for this is the tags of the reservoir/smoothing capacitor. A test meter set to ohms × 1 is best for this. Any reading much below about 10,000 ohms should lead to further cold investigation before connecting the lamp.

Bear in mind that the test lamp only checks the mains input circuitry, and you should satisfy yourself

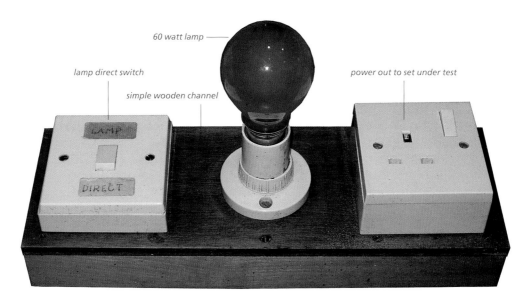

60 watt lamp

lamp direct switch

simple wooden channel

power out to set under test

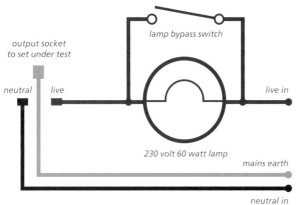

lamp bypass switch

output socket
to set under test

neutral   live

live in

230 volt 60 watt lamp

mains earth

neutral in

ABOVE: **The author's well-used test lamp.**

LEFT: **The schematic of the test lamp.**

using the cold resistance method described earlier that no other obvious problem exists, such as a shorted HT (high voltage) line, caused perhaps by faulty reservoir or smoothing capacitors, or a faulty rectifier valve, before applying full power. With the lamp in circuit, leave the set switched on for a couple of minutes to allow it to warm up, then try to receive a station or two by switching wavebands and rotating the tuning across the bands. A short length of wire in the aerial socket may be needed for this. If signals are heard, no matter how faint, then HT must be present and therefore no short exists. If no signals are heard, is there a faint hum from the loudspeaker? (place your ear close to it to check). If there is, rotate the volume control and listen for a slight rustling or crackling, the

presence of which tells you that the AF stages are working and are being supplied with HT. If there are gram sockets, advance the volume to its maximum setting and touch the tip of a screwdriver on the sockets, one of which should provide some crackling or hum in the loudspeaker – but make sure that any switch position provided is set to 'gram' for this test. Any hum or rustling from these simple checks indicates that it should be safe to apply full power.

It may be that no actual transmission signals are heard when the lamp is in series as the set will be working under reduced power. Often, bypassing the lamp and running under full power will immediately correct this, and often, especially in the case of super-hets, the local oscillator valve will start to work and bring in stations where none were available before. *If, however, you are in any doubt about your knowledge and ability to construct the device safely, you are advised not to attempt the work.*

Safety Guidelines

ESSENTIAL: Never connect to the mains until the mains input and HT lines have been checked for short-circuits. Power the set-up using either a test lamp (preferable) or a variac (variable voltage source), and watch for signs of trouble.

ESSENTIAL: Use an ELCB or RCD mains adapter when powering a radio.

ESSENTIAL: Always disconnect completely before taking resistance measurements or touching exposed parts of the chassis.

ESSENTIAL: Always work with only one hand inside the set, never by holding the chassis with one hand when working on the set with the other.

ESSENTIAL: Ensure electrical safety (properly connected and secure mains cable, secure rear panel, correct knob types) before allowing others to use the set.

ESSENTIAL: Avoid damp conditions. If the set has been stored in a damp area, allow sufficient time for moisture to evaporate before testing.

ESSENTIAL: Check the chassis for 'live' with a neon indicator screwdriver.

HIGHLY RECOMMENDED: Stand on insulating material such as dry carpet.

HIGHLY RECOMMENDED: Obtain proper data whenever possible.

HIGHLY RECOMMENDED: Work with good bench illumination.

If you decide you'd like to learn more, read and discover the technology for yourself, *see* the appendix for a list of textbooks and magazines. However, good as vintage technology books were in their time – and still are, in truth – safety issues were never treated with the rigour that we expect today. For this reason alone, read and enjoy vintage books and magazines, but keep in mind the essential need to contrast the book's contents with modern standards. Unfortunately there are only a few newly produced books available presently that deal with the subject, and it is to be hoped that others will become available, because the written word is virtually the sole way that any aspiring vintage radio restorer can access knowledge about the subject.

THE BEST SAFETY MEASURES

These pointers are provided in good faith, but no responsibility can be accepted for accidents or injury. The best safety measures are common sense and a careful, considered plan of work. Take your time, do not hurry. Respect electricity – work safely – and you can only do that if you know what you are doing. Remember that although vintage radio may be yesterday's technology, it is far from crude or simple, and learning about it is not something that can be achieved in a short period of time.

OBTAINING VINTAGE RECEIVERS

There seems to be a commonly held but mistaken belief that vintage radios in the UK are very scarce. Whilst it is true that certain models are now rare and coveted by dedicated and wealthy collectors, so raising their purchase costs far beyond the pocket of the average aspiring collector, it is also the case that millions of valve radio receivers were produced between the years 1930–60, and large quantities of transistor radios were marketed from the early 1960s onwards; so whatever your interest, you can be assured that the products are out there just waiting for you to unearth them. There are numerous ways in which sets can be obtained, each with advantages and disadvantages, and some of these are discussed below.

Advertise

An advertisement in the local newspaper classifieds might pay dividends: draft something along the lines of 'Vintage radio enthusiast seeks valve radio sets in need of a good home, cash waiting'; or more specifically 'Wanted, transistor radios of XXX make'. General statements such as the former may produce more replies but also lots of time-wasting and unsuitable radios. After all, what you have in mind when you advertise may not be the way others read your request, so you may end up fending off sellers of enormous radiograms when what you really wanted were shelf-sized Bakelite radios. Don't be too specific, however: try to strike a balance – and never accept the description a vendor supplies over the telephone. Never answer a 'What's it worth, roughly?'

type of question, because you need to see the radio first-hand before you mention fixed amounts of money.

You might like to specify how anyone might easily contact you: email or telephone, for example – but think very carefully before giving your home address away. It is best to remain cautious when advertising, being no more specific than stating your general area – not that any person selling a vintage radio is sure to be less than honest – it is simply that you have no control over who reads your advert, and an opportunist thief might decide that your home could just be a lucrative source of presumably valuable vintage radios.

Join a Society

The British Vintage Wireless Society (see Sources) is effectively alone in this respect in the UK. You really do get value for money here. The Bulletin is a high-quality quarterly publication and carries a members' adverts sheet – sales and wants – with each issue. There are other useful and interesting items on offer or freely provided from time to time, and the BVWS also arranges meetings where sets may be bought and sold.

Subscribe

A magazine subscription will allow you to advertise your needs, often free with the subscription. Also, one magazine in particular holds regular events where you

Meetings and auctions provide an enjoyable way to obtain vintage receivers, books and magazines, and other radio-related items. *(Photo courtesy 'The Radiophile')*

can buy and sell from stalls, and also organize well-attended auctions selling receivers, test equipment, vintage magazines and books, and spares. At the time of writing there are no specialist vintage radio magazines to be found on the shelves of British newsagents. It seems likely to be the case elsewhere.

Auctions

Twentieth-century (general goods) auction sales often have a radio or two on their listings. If you don't like the idea of standing around for two hours or more until the one radio you've spotted is put up, simply fill out a bid form with your maximum bid amount. You may be lucky, although this method can cost you more: it depends upon the individual auction system. Another alternative is to ask an auction room employee to bid in your stead, for a small fee, hopefully.

Collectors' auctions are also held by many auction houses, and these often include vintage radios along with collections of *Rupert* and *Eagle* annuals, assorted memorabilia, cameras and Corgi toy lots. Radios appearing in these sales are usually in a better condition than those in general goods (attic and house clearance) sales. Quite often, vintage magazines such as *Radio Times* and radio makers' advertising leaflets turn up in boxes of general interest papers.

Car Boot Sales

Buying from these is always rather risky. They vary enormously, but at some it seems that for every honest trader there's one not so honest, and you have no idea of the provenance of goods bought this way – no trader's home address or any means of contact after your purchase. That said, providing you follow the guidelines on what to watch out for, and you feel secure in the transaction, go ahead. But just remember: it is rare for anyone to offer a radio known to be valuable at a car boot sale, so that Ekco AD65 you've just spotted on offer for a few tens of pounds, though actually worth far more, ask yourself why. Car booters are mostly – though not always – wise in the ways of the world, and usually their prices are at the top end of the range. So, to reverse the old adage, look any potential gift horse in the mouth before parting with your cash.

Antiques Fairs

Occasionally good radios crop up at these, though strictly speaking, few if any radios have reached the 100-year age that qualifies them for the accolade 'antique' in Britain, although in America it seems that any valve radio is automatically considered to be an antique – another example of two countries divided by a common language. Antiques fairs always have a good selection of goods that are far from true antiques, in any case. You should be prepared to bargain, and do not pay the asking price as it will almost certainly be inflated.

Antiques Shops

Genuine antiques shops may sometimes have a radio or two, usually in good unrestored order. Bargain shops – the ones once known as junk shops, that is – will generally have, hidden away amidst piles of old furniture and clutter, an odd radio or two, especially of the transistorized variety. Bargain again. Walk away rather than pay the asking price. It needs to be remembered that in today's safety-conscious world, many dealers are put off selling electrical items for fear of subsequent legal claims for accident or injury. Few valve radios can hope to reach the standard required for the electrical safety tests now carried out routinely, so it must be expected that fewer and fewer shops will be offering old radios of the mains-powered type.

Internet Auctions

These have become extremely popular recently. The most famous of these is, of course, ebay. I have both bought and sold through such auction sites for a number of years, and I offer here a few suggestions for guidance to the newcomer, based entirely upon my own experience.

It is a surprising phenomenon, the internet auction. Where else could buyers be persuaded to part with their money – and sometimes, large amounts of it – without actually seeing the object they are purchasing? True, there is usually a photograph or two, but even the best photo is a poor substitute for seeing and handling the real thing. Remember the danger of buying, as the old phrase has it, 'a pig in a

poke'. Another apt phrase *caveat emptor* (buyer beware) also comes readily to mind in respect of these auctions.

There's more to say about photographs and what they might – and might not – show, a little later; for the moment, let's start at the point when you find a radio you'd consider bidding for on an auction site. The very first thing to check is the accuracy of the auction statement as provided by the seller. Is the radio *really* a 1930s model? You will often find that accuracy is lacking when manufacturing dates are mentioned; often it may simply be an error on the seller's part, but the point is that there exists a world of difference in terms of value between a good 1930s set and a good 1950s set. It is a simplification of the situation, but generally true, that the older a set is, the more attractive it is to the collector, all things being equal in other respects. Learn to recognize the tricks of the trade – terms such as 'Art Deco' do not truly apply to radios manufactured after World War II, although this is a benign error and some Bakelite models display attractive echoes of the Deco past in their presentation.

'Stunning' and 'Wow!' along with other general superlatives, really are meaningless and are there only to attract your attention. 'Rare' is a matter of opinion, usually. 'Found in my Grandfather's house.' So what? Take notice of what is *not* said, rather than what is. More to the point might be a comment explaining exactly where in Grandad's house (the chicken shed, perhaps?) but such frank honesty is rare. Some of the sales pages are highly decorated with colour, large text and fancy graphics, but you are bidding on a radio, not clever display technique, so don't be taken in. It is also surprising how many 'collectors' are seemingly disposing of their collections because their wives are threatening to leave them otherwise. Is this perhaps just a cunning way of avoiding giving the real reason why the set is up for auction?

Often, in truth too often for comfort, the seller cannot supply any background for the radio he has put up for auction. Common statements are 'found in a loft' and 'Part of a house clearance', both of which are non-specific and both of which absolve the vendor from any link with, or prior knowledge of, the radio in question.

Consider whether the vendor who claims not to know anything about radios is totally truthful. Take a look at his history. How many sets has he sold? Whilst it is true that you can do no better than make an informed guess by reading feedback comments, it can be enough to indicate whether or not the claim to radio ignorance is likely to be true. Certainly some who sell vintage radios on the internet are being honest when they say that, but others can and do use it as a 'blind', pretending not to know that the loudspeaker, valves, dial glass or mains transformer is missing. Check the availability of pictures of the set you are interested in. No pictures should mean no bid, at least until you have made contact with the seller and obtained pictures via email. If you don't get them, for whatever reason, reconsider your position.

If pictures exist, what story do they tell? Do the control knobs match, is one broken or missing, is that a hole where a control should be? Take as an actual example the auction listing of an attractive-looking Pye set from the 1930s. The seller (obviously a trader – a quick look at his sales feedback record confirmed this) claimed to know nothing, not even the make of the set, though the rising sun motif should have given a huge clue in that respect. The pictures, of which there were two, were not very distinct. One showed the front of the set, the other one of the sides – but interestingly the blank one, not the side where the control panel was. I therefore emailed him to ask pertinent questions (in a polite manner, of course – I did not simply assume the worst). No answer of any kind was received, so I did not bid; the set finally sold for over £70. I'd be inclined to bet that something was adrift with it – perhaps no control panel or knobs, otherwise why no answer? As an aside, it is worth noting that missing knobs, a very common problem with these very early Pye transportable sets, are virtually impossible to replace as the control shafts are non-standard in diameter.

Before placing a bid, you can and should check the seller's feedback (comments both good and bad left by previous purchasers); this is helpful, although it is not a cast-iron guarantee.

Finally, there are now lots of commercial traders plugging their goods in these auctions. Nothing wrong there, but it is always good to know from whom you are buying. Another old saying has occurred to me: 'A fool and his money are soon parted.' Don't rush to give it away. When paying, I originally preferred to send a cheque directly to the seller, although I find now that Paypal, an easy-to-use paying system available on ebay, simplifies and speeds matters. There have been instances where the escrow service (where they hold the money as a third party until both parties are satisfied) has been hacked into, and false escrow addresses used to rob people who send their payment in good faith. If you send directly to the seller and you don't get the goods, at least you know who has your money.

Remember – these are only the author's personal opinions. You must decide for yourself and accept the fact that the business of online auction buying has its attendant risks whatever steps you take to minimize them. Having said all that, there are some absolutely genuine folk selling regularly on internet auction sites, and they are an interesting resource.

Internet Auction Scams

A number of vintage radio enthusiasts have found what appear to be identical goods on more than one auction advertised on the same site. The obvious inference is that one of the 'sellers' is attempting to sell something he or she does not own, having 'found' a photograph elsewhere, sometimes from enthusiast internet sites. This has proved to be the case, several people losing their money and, as the objects they thought they had purchased never existed in the first place, nothing is received in return. When, and if, any monies can be recovered, it appears that auction sites levy a fairly steep 'processing charge' of some kind; in other words, it costs you to get your money back. It is quite possible that this kind of heartless scam is widespread throughout online auction categories. There are warning signs: alarm bells should sound when goods of obvious high value are being offered at a figure, perhaps a buy-it-now figure, considerably below the likely trading value. If in doubt, email the seller, ask pertinent and preferably technical questions, and for more pictures to be supplied. Base any further actions on the answers. Do not rely completely on a good feedback record: fraudsters have found ways around feedback problems, so these are not a foolproof indicator of a seller's honesty.

Auction sites tend to claim that the vast majority of traders are decent, honest folk and this is very likely true; but by inference it means there are some who are not. Here's another scam: suppose you bid on an object but someone outbids you. So you've lost the auction. But wait, there's an email from someone offering to sell you the same item as a 'second chance' offer. This applies if the winning bidder reneges on his bid! Great, you think, and send off your cheque. What could be wrong with that? Nothing, unless the vendor has been sending 'second chance' offers to all who bid originally on the item concerned. It may well be the case that he doesn't own such an item in the first place and has no intention of honouring any deal. All he wants is your money.

In case you think this is far-fetched, think again. In truth it is yet another example of just how resourceful these heartless spoof merchants and thieves are. You'd think with the intelligence they must possess in order to dream up these novel methods of robbery they could as easily take up gainful and honest employment, but obviously such a course holds little fascination for them and it would seem their pleasure comes from defrauding innocent people, at a safe and anonymous distance. Of course, not all second chance offers are scams – far from it – but it is up to you, the prospective purchaser, to check thoroughly before parting with cash or cheque. Be aware: there will be other ingenious scams masquerading as honest deals. Take care.

Is It Genuine?

Vintage radios are no different from any other vintage or antique item. There are many ways to 'improve' a radio, some much worse than others, and it is far better to spot a fraudulent offering before you part with your money. Here are a few points to watch out for.

Woodworm

Too often, old radios have spent a good part of their lives in less than perfect storage, such as attics and sheds. One unfortunate result of this is that the effects of woodworm are commonly seen on wooden cabinets. Look for tiny circular holes, often in little bunches. These are the flight holes of the adult fly, the larvae of which will have spent a good length of time munching away below the surface. The effects vary wildly from mild, localized damage to total destruction. I have seen sets where the plywood loudspeaker baffle panel was totally destroyed and yet the rest of the cabinet remained untouched. It is more often found, however, that the worm has attacked large areas. There are things to watch for: test the cabinet for softness by pressing with the fingers – if it yields, the outer veneer sheet might be all that is left of the original ply. Tap near the holes. If fine wood dust comes out, the holes are relatively recent and the cabinet may not have been treated with insecticide.

Can't see any holes? Tilt the set into the light at an acute angle to examine the veneer surface. Filled holes are likely to reflect incident light differently from the surrounding wood, and should show their presence by this method. Holes are often filled with Beaumontage (cabinetmaker's tinted wax) in an attempt to hide them from view. Look underneath the cabinet and around any wooden feet for signs of holes. Be wary about bringing any wooden cabinet radio into your home if you have any doubts about the presence of woodworm. Get the set into the garage or shed and treat it with proprietary woodworm killer. Any holes you find can be injected with aerosol versions of the same type of fluid. The author's preferred approach is to remove the chassis from the cabinet, clean out the wooden shell, and treat liberally with 'Five Star Wood Treatment' – a thorough soaking on the inside surfaces, which are usually bare wood, which allows the fluid to sink in. Although this procedure is time-consuming and adds to the cost of purchase, it should be measured against exposing your home to woodworm infestation. If you are short of time, at least put the untreated set in a large bin liner and tape it securely closed until you have the opportunity to work on it.

Bakelite. Or Is It?

Originally, the term 'Bakelite' referred only to phenol formaldehyde, but over the years the reference has widened to accommodate other forms of thermosetting plastics, most notably urea formaldehyde. The author has seen celluloid and other thermoplastic materials misleadingly placed alongside Bakelite objects in books on the subject, the inference being that they were forms of Bakelite.

Bakelite is a thermosetting plastic compound, and as such, the long chain molecules bonded together permanently when the granulated material was exposed to the heat and pressure of the moulding process during cabinet manufacture. It cannot, therefore, melt again, regardless of the amount of heat applied (within reason – it will crack and burn if subjected to excess heat). If you can do it, a good test is to heat a pin then attempt to insert it somewhere out of sight on the cabinet under test, perhaps along a back edge or underneath. The pin should not sink in. If it does, the cabinet is made from a thermoplastic material, not Bakelite (or urea formaldehyde). What if you can't use the hot pin? Lick your finger, rub the cabinet and sniff. Wetted phenolic resin has a faint smell not unlike cat pee: once you've smelled it, you won't forget!

Painted Bakelite sets – commercially sprayed, not brushed – were popular for a time, post-war. They tend to be in less-than-attractive pastel shades, and few have escaped the ravages of time. Paint rubs off on corners and especially from control knobs, and all surfaces are prone to becoming scuffed and scratched. Brown Bakelite should show through. If the paint appears perfect, it is overwhelmingly likely to have been resprayed. This may or may not matter in itself, depending upon your point of view; would you prefer a scratched and tired-looking original, or one that looks smart and fresh? Would that it were so simple, however. Some people spray paint sets to hide damage such as cracks and repaired areas. This again is perfectly acceptable practice – as long as the seller is honest about it. You can sometimes spot where repairs have been done by the 'acute angle to the light' examination technique as outlined above under 'woodworm'. This is not infallible, but if you remove the back panel, you should be able to see evidence of any repair inside, either as a visible crack or a resin/fibreglass mat patch.

Grilles and Grille Fabric

One thing that almost always suffers the ravages of time and circumstance is, understandably, the decorative material covering the loudspeaker opening. Few original weave materials are obtainable today, which means that any replacement fabric is likely to be 'wrong' in that it will be dissimilar in appearance to the original. Unfortunately, there is little that any restorer can do about this situation in Britain. In America there are a couple of sources who specialize in producing new runs of authentic pattern, but of course, only for American vintage radios. It is likely therefore that a British restored radio, whilst genuine in other respects, may fall short of full originality because of the grille material. I personally feel this is a small price to pay for a neat restoration. Unrestored sets should, conversely, have the original material in place – albeit rotted, in all likelihood. *See* the appendix for a supplier of grille cloth.

Back Covers

For some reason completely unfathomable to most collectors, the back covers of vintage radios are often missing. One restorer once commented that somewhere on our planet there must be a veritable mountain of receiver back panels. For safety in use, such covers are essential and that means making a replacement by hand, either from hardboard (use picture framer's hardboard if you can persuade one such craftsman to supply you, as it is appreciably thinner than the standard $\frac{1}{8}$in board and much easier to work with saw and knife) or 'millboard', 'greyboard' or other type of thick, tough card, usually obtainable from arts and crafts suppliers. Such board can be painted with water-based matt paint of the PVA type. Emulsion paint works, too. Paint both sides, and if you can't find a suitable brown, mix from black, red and yellow! Add air vents, covered for safety with fine hessian or other 'breathable' material. Use the absence of a rear panel as a bargaining tool.

Bakelite phenolic resin was invented in 1907 by the Belgian chemist Leo Baekeland whilst working in New York. He patented it under the name 'Bakelite'. From this it would seem that Bakelite was a product of the early twentieth century, and in terms of its success, this is true; however, many experimenters had contributed to its creation, albeit perhaps unwittingly. It had long been known that plastics existed in natural form – the natural resin of amber being a good example.

Essentially, there are only two forms of plastic, by far the most common today being the thermoplastic variety, partly because of economies in production – it can be re-melted and re-used. Examples are styrene, vinyl, ABS and acrylic; these are relatively modern creations. The other form of plastic is the thermosetting variety – this can only be used once. The application of heat first softens the plastic, but the polymers then cross-link and harden permanently. In the hardened state, the plastic produced is generally heavy, rigid, tough but rather brittle. Bakelite (phenol formaldehyde) is the most famous example of thermosetting plastic, and was arguably the first successful fully synthetic plastic.

Bakelite production begins by combining carbolic acid (phenol) and formaldehyde (methanol), derived from coal or timber. The brittle resin compound that is the product of this combination is allowed to cool before being ground into powder form and, usually, mixed with fillers such as wood flour (effectively, fine sawdust) or cotton or other fibres. Pigments for colouring, catalysts and other modifying chemicals are added at this stage. A further stage of heating starts, but does not complete the chemical reaction process. Finally the powdered resin compound is used as is, or pressed into accurately measured blocks known as pre-forms for use in moulding presses (the Ekco Radio Company used 500+ ton hydraulic machines).

Inserts such as brass screw retainers may be added to the mould along with the pre-forms before the moulding process begins, then, under great pressure and considerable heat, the powder or the pre-forms melt to become a viscous liquid that fills the steel cabinet mould. The polymer material completes the chemical reactions to form cross-links between the long-chain polymers, which cause it to set permanently and retain the exact contours of the mould.

Removed from the mould, any 'flash' (excess plastic around the mould extremities) is trimmed or ground away and another cabinet shell is completed. Because the original pattern or mould must be extremely well made and finished, and must also be capable of withstanding the great pressures involved, the work of the mould maker was – and still is – highly skilled. The moulds themselves represent a high financial investment, and it is only mass production that makes their use economical.

Eden Minn's uncompromising cabinet design for the 1940 Murphy AD94 demonstrates the versatility of Bakelite.

Control Knobs

No apology for repeating this as it is so important. Are they all present, and if they are, are they original? Unfortunately only experience can help in the latter assessment, and you will need to decide whether they look 'right' or not. On most sets they have a similar size and style, differing occasionally by lettering to identify the control function, for instance L.M.S for wave-change, VOL for volume and so on. Some early 1930s receivers did use a different, larger knob for tuning. Be warned – missing knobs can be a problem to source, despite the air of confidence exuded by the seller, who may tell you that they are easy to obtain on the internet, or some such tale. If it were that easy, he would in all probability already have done it.

Dials

Broken glass dials or dials with missing lettering greatly reduce the visual value of a receiver, the former rendering a set virtually unsaleable unless it is something very special. Although it is possible to reproduce a fair copy of a dial using a computer graphics program and printing on clear film, the finished effect is rarely completely satisfactory. Dials were screenprinted onto glass – or sometimes clear acrylic sheet (perspex). When fitted in sets, such dials were usually edge-lit, producing that characteristic glowing lettering effect that is so much the signature of vintage radio. Home-produced dials cannot reproduce that. It is possible to have a dial screenprinted as long as you provide a good original – or a good scan via computer of one – but the processing of a single dial is likely to be very expensive.

Dial Drives

The drive system used on the great majority of valved receivers was a spring-tensioned cord. This thin cord, often stronger-than-cotton flaxen twine, typically is arranged to pass over pulleys, around a grooved drum attached to the spindle of the tuning capacitor, and perhaps passing through holes or gaps in the chassis to reach the tuning control knob spindle. After two or three turns around that spindle, the cord returns to the drum where it is anchored to a lug. The dial pointer is fastened to the cord at a suitable horizontal or vertical point between two pulleys, and traverses the dial as the cord is moved. Most receivers from the late 1930s onwards will be found to use this type of cord drive, but there are many variations to be found. In particular, receivers from the early 1930s may be found to have friction drives that are cordless and entirely mechanical. Others use drum-type drives, sometimes with mechanical gearing. Some, mainly transistor radios, use an 'epicyclic' drive which is mounted directly on the tuning capacitor spindle and controlled by a large circular tuning knob/dial.

Philips radios, so often quirky regardless of period, are well known for what is sometimes rather disparagingly called 'string engineering'. The cord drive arrangements on some of these can be complex indeed, sometimes combining Bowden cables (similar to cycle brake cables), wire and cord.

Finishes

Wooden cabinets were finished with a variety of methods over the years, and any still with their original finish intact will have been very well cared for. It is more often the case that an unrestored set looks tired, showing at least some evidence of flaking shellac or cellulose. Restored cabinets should have been refinished in a way that is sympathetic to the original. Sprayed shellac is unlikely today, but sprayed cellulose lacquer is a fair alternative, especially if used along with toning lacquers, tinted to match the original wood colour and any shading effects used on the original reproduced. Toning added visual variety, apparent shape and 'quality' to what might originally have been a rather plainly veneered square or oblong box.

Chassis Condition

Most chassis were made from plated or painted sheet steel, and even when the cabinet looks externally sound, the chassis inside may sometimes be found to have suffered quite severe rust. This is generally limited to the upper surface, leaving the more protected underchassis area reasonably clear of corrosion. If you are interested in the technical side, a spot or two of rust shouldn't be enough to deter you. Components such as capacitors were never meant to last forever and, by and large, they don't. Most British radios use wax-coated paper dielectric components that almost always become leaky, which means they can pass current. This can lead to a shortening of valve life but also to the leaky capacitor itself becoming either short-circuited or overheating, resulting in all kinds of unwanted problems. Restored receivers should therefore have had many or all of the larger capacitors replaced, sometimes disguised as original, either by fitting new miniature components inside the emptied shells of the old ones or by new outer cases with printed period-style labels.

Wiring is often suspect due to the insulated sleeving crumbling and the (possibly) tin-plated copper conductors corroding. Especially prone to insulation failure is the wiring to the resistive dropper (with AC/DC receivers) and the mains transformer (AC receivers). Mains leads are usually unsafe and should be checked carefully before use. With some small American and British table models – sometimes called 'shelf radios' because of their size – there was no room within their diminutive cabinets either for a mains transformer or a dropper resistor, and so these sets used a device known as a 'line cord' mains lead. This is a deceptively normal-looking lead that has a built-in resistive-wire mains dropper. The cords run warm in use and should never be shortened. As they also contain asbestos fibre, they are best left alone, but unfortunately they too, can, and usually do, suffer from age-related insulation failure. Although it is possible occasionally to find sources for replacement cords, a better bet is to have the receiver converted to a safer type of power supply, either from an external transformer or an internally fitted capacitive or diode dropper arrangement. This must be carried out by a competent restorer, and is definitely not a procedure recommended for the beginner to attempt.

In the mid-1930s, a broad market still existed for battery receivers, as this 'Broadcaster' trade advertisement shows.

What to Buy – and What Not To

The first thing on the list of most collectors to avoid is any floor-standing radio-gramophone (radiogram), for the simple reason of size. Few people have space in their home for even one of these, let alone a collection. This is a shame, because the better quality items were expensively constructed to a very high standard and do sound superb. The silver lining to the cloud is, of course, the fact that because they are unpopular, they are generally easily affordable. In their day they were considered to be the epitome of quality radio, with luxury console cabinets veneered in attractive hardwoods such as walnut, with inlaid contrasting veneers or lacquer toning. There was generally space for record storage, closed off by doors or shutters. Access to the radio controls and the record decks, which varied from single players to auto changers, was most often via a large lift-up lid, and the chassis units fitted were generally of a high quality,

sometimes with push-pull output stages (two output valves working together), comprehensive tone controls and three waveband coverage.

Battery-operated radios can be difficult to bring to working order, especially those earlier ones using a 2V wet cell for filament supplies and, with some really early or homebuilt examples, a separate 9V battery for grid bias. For this reason, unless you are prepared to buy or build a mains adapter or, in the case of the latter all-dry battery receiver, make up your own HT battery by assembling, say, sufficient 9V PP3 batteries in series, they may be best left alone.

The heyday of the large radiogram seems to have been over by the mid-1950s, though FM broadcasts and, towards the end of the decade, stereo recordings gave them a partial resurrection. Cabinet styles varied from vertical consoles – more common in the late 1930s and early 1940s – to horizontal consoles in the late 1940s and early 1950s, with slim-line, splay-legged stereo radiograms appearing in the later 1950s. Cabinet style alone is, unfortunately, not a completely reliable guide to age.

Judging the Approximate Age of Receivers

Any estimation of age without prior knowledge of, or data for, the set concerned is bound to be subjective, as so often manufacturers produced the old alongside the new. A case in point is the battery-powered radio. It might be thought that once all-dry miniature valves had arrived in the post-war years, any set using the old 2-volt types that needed an accumulator to power their filaments was perforce pre-World War II. Not so, however, because some makers kept such sets in production after the war, presumably to satisfy the demand. With caution in mind, here are some points to look for, starting with the types of valve fitted: British five- and seven-pin = earlier 1930s. Octal and side-contact = late 1930s, 1940s. All-glass miniatures = approximately 1950 onwards. Waveband names on the dial: Long and Short = late 1920s, very early 1930s (note that the term 'short wave' referred to what was

later to be called the medium wave). Long, Medium, Short = 1930s onwards. British receivers with VHF/FM band will be post 1954 (the first BBC FM transmitter opened at Wrotham, Kent, in May 1955).

Radio station names on dials are also a good guide to age. For example, a dial displaying the Third Programme has to be post-war, because the programme did not exist until that time. The Third Programme was renamed Radio 3 in 1967. Any dial displaying Home Service must be post-September 1939. Before that, Droitwich National appears on dials from October 1934, having replaced the old 1930 Daventry National transmitter. Cabinet size and shape can also offer an approximate guide when noted along with other clues, as already mentioned. Large 'upright' sets tend to be prior to 1950. Many small Bakelite all-dry battery/mains AM models date from the post-war/early 1950s period. Wooden-cased miniature-valve receivers were fairly rare pre-World War II in Britain, but quite common in the USA and Canada.

With radiograms, the type of record player unit gives a good clue: 78rpm only with replaceable needle = before 1952. Three-speed with turnover cartridge = mid to later 1950s. Stereo (or stereo compatible) cartridge = 1958 onwards. The term 'compatible' means that although possessing only a mono output, the cartridge has a stylus mounting that is compliant – free to move in both horizontal and vertical directions. Non-compatible cartridges tend to be stiff in the vertical direction.

Kit Radios

There was a demand for kits for home assembly well into the 1950s. These often used surplus manufacturer's stocks of parts and cabinets, which generally gave the kit set at least the appearance of quality, though often the circuitry employed, whether superhet for the more advanced constructor or TRF to simplify home assembly, was designed to utilize low-cost or surplus components and therefore left something to be desired in terms of quality. Also, valve line-ups tended to be 'exotic', odd mixtures of differing types, again probably to use war-surplus valves or cheap ranges.

Because so many kit radios of all kinds were sold, they crop up in sales quite regularly and it can be difficult to judge their age and origin, or even whether they actually are a kit or a genuine radio. Take the example of the Pilot 'Little Maestro', which first appeared housed in both a Bakelite cabinet with Art Deco overtones and an alternative wooden cabinet with neat walnut veneering. The wooden version case first appeared in 1939 and was followed by the Bakelite one in 1940. Pilot went on for a few years with variations of the dial and the chassis within, but by 1950 had reviewed the range and brought out new cases for their 'Little Maestro' receivers.

At that point, or fairly soon after, the Bakelite shells and the neat little wooden cabinets that had been good sellers for Pilot appeared on the market containing not Pilot chassis but a variety of receivers, typical of which were the offerings from firms such as

Premier Radio, Concord Electronics, Clyne Radio and the Radio Supply Company of Leeds. Kits using the cabinet were still widely advertised in 1958 and after in magazines such as *Wireless World*, which probably makes the cabinet a 'longest cabinet life' contender for the *Guinness Book of Records*.

The way to judge whether a putative 'Little Maestro' really is the genuine article is to look for the 'Pilot' name moulded into the front, occupying the space between the dial and the centre tuning knob. This was absent on the kits. Another check is the dial itself, which should carry the Pilot name and a rather impish little maestro in a circular design, which is illuminated by the dial lamp. Without one or other of these indications, the receiver is home-built. One other rather odd point to note about the 'Little Maestro' Bakelite cabinets concerns the louvres that are so much a part of the design. On all the original Pilot receivers seen by

ABOVE: Another of the numerous kit offerings utilizing the ubiquitous 'Pilot' Bakelite cabinet, this time by the Radio Supply Company in a 1958 *Practical Wireless*. The veneered ply Pilot cabinet is offered as an alternative housing.

LEFT: 1954, and the original Pilot 'Little Maestro' Bakelite cabinet shells, slightly modified, are on sale from several sources, either as kits or as empty cabinets for those wishing to build their own chassis. This Norman H. Field advert is typical for its time.

the author, those louvres run around the edges at left and right of the front panel but stop after about 35mm to leave the side panels plain; yet on at least some, if not all, of the cabinets supplied with the kit sets, they continue along the sides to reach the back edge of the cabinet, with a slight but evident 'join' where the original louvres meet the added ones.

It is less easy to spot most other home-built sets other than by the alternative names they were given, an example of which is the Perdio PR25 of 1961. The case was a decidedly unpleasant polystyrene moulding in two-tone blue. In 1965, long after production of the set had stopped, the receiver was offered as a kit, renamed the 'Realistic 7' and sold by Laskys Radio. A Perdio in all but name? When well constructed, perhaps; but as home construction quality varies greatly, dependent as it is on the skill and patience of the constructor, there's no guarantee. To be truthful, even the original Perdio product wasn't anything special, particularly in regard to that rather style-less textured case.

Magic Eyes and Other Selling Points

Many true advances were made, especially during the 1930s. To begin with the most obvious one, superhet receivers were inherently more sensitive than their TRF counterparts, although some makers were, in retrospect surprisingly, slow to accept that fact. Philips and Cossor, among others, continued to produce TRF designs in the mid-1930s alongside their superhet offerings. In fairness, Cossor's battery receivers were often TRF for economy of operation.

A potentially troublesome problem that might have beset both TRF and superhet receivers concerned powerful stations blasting out loudly as the receiver was tuned across the bands, especially if the volume control had been turned well up to listen to a distant or weak station. This was neatly counteracted by the use of 'vari-μ' valves (variable gain). These were valves with grid wires wound with a non-regular spacing, the gain of which could be controlled by means of a varying voltage. They were at first often used in TRF designs with a variable resistor in the cathode circuit of the first (i.e. HF) valve, which acted as an effective volume control. Superhet design utilized the property of the vari-μ valve to create an automatic volume control system (AVC). Simply put, the voltage level of the received and amplified signal is fed back to one or more controlled valves to moderate the gain of the valves, effectively limiting the blasting effect and also compensating for signal 'fade' (short-term variations in signal strength).

Good in principle as the early AVC system was, it was greatly improved by setting a delay level below which the gain of a receiver remained full. This prevented AVC operating to partially reduce gain even on the weakest signal. Delayed AVC remained an important feature of superhet design. It became known more accurately as 'delayed AGC', the 'G' representing the gain of a receiver.

One problem sorted – another created. AVC caused the sensitivity of the receiver to rise to maximum when tuning between stations, which allowed a good deal of hiss and noise caused by electrical interference to make its presence felt. This led to the development of 'QAVC', the 'Q' representing quiet. When signal level dropped to a very low level, as it does between stations, a suppression circuit comes into action to mute or limit the gain until an acceptably powerful station is tuned in. The total silence experienced between stations is quite eerie. These systems, usually found on quality sets, were often switchable for convenience.

The AVC voltage was also used to control the display of various types of so-called 'magic eye' tuning indicators. These were commonly valve-like devices with a windowed end or side where a fluorescent display could be seen, usually in the form of green 'leaves' or bars. As the required station is tuned in manually, the leaves broaden and close together, the maximum closeness or overlap representing the optimum tuning point. Their display should be bright and clear, but unfortunately magic eyes seem in general to have short lives and often the only way to check if an eye is working at all is in a darkened room or by cupping hands around the window to exclude external light. Forms of neon tuning indicators had been used on a few receivers for a couple of years before the first true valve types appeared in British models from 1936 onwards.

Who Needs a Chassis?

Philips – again – produced some oddities, one of the strangest of which was the set without a chassis. This was the 1936 model V5A, where all the components were attached to mounting lugs moulded into the Bakelite surrounding the loudspeaker opening. It was probably an attempt to save costs, but as the idea was discontinued it seems it failed in that respect!

Motor Tuning

As an alternative to the supposedly tedious task of manual tuning, some makers offered a variety of tuning aids, one of which was motor tuning. In its simplest form, this consisted of an electric motor driving the main tuning capacitor, and was operated by a press button which the listener held down until the desired spot on the dial was reached. Better systems provided preset buttons for favourite stations. Bush offered 'Teleflic' tuning, Ultra offered 'Teledial', both systems presenting a front tuning control with the appearance of an old-style rotary telephone dial.

Push Buttons

Push-button station selection became popular in the later 1930s, and receivers continued to be made with buttons or, latterly, piano-key controls throughout the valve era and early transistor radio era. The buttons allowed for waveband and/or individual station selection, either complimenting or sometimes entirely replacing manual tuning.

Vidor's 'Lido' portable certainly was large – and although it was true that larger batteries were more economical because they lasted longer, the added weight, plus the heavy steel leathercloth-covered case, made this receiver less than convenient in portable terms. The mains lead and battery access is via the hinged base.

Aeroplane Dials

This was a term given to any dial of circular or oval form that possessed a double-ended pointer. Dials of that style were popular in the early to mid-1930s, and some makers used variations of the type for many years. The term 'aeroplane' relates to the shape, typical of indicator dials found in the cockpit of an aeroplane.

Mains/Battery Operation

This offered flexibility in use and allowed sets to be either portable or at least transportable into, say, the garden on a summer evening. Many makers offered receivers of this type from around 1950 onwards. Usually they had the appearance of a standard portable radio – rexine

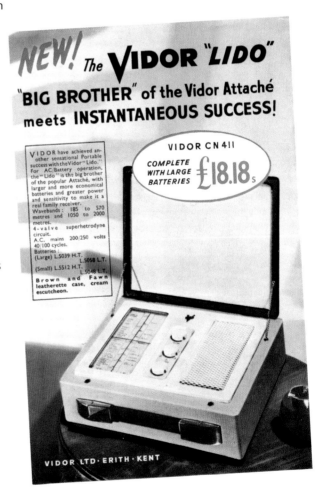

case, handle on top – but some retained the table, model styling that was still popular at the time.

Gram Sockets

Fitted to almost all but the cheapest radios from the early 1930s, these sockets allowed the audio amplifier section of the radio to be used to reproduce records. All that was needed was a turntable and a pick-up arm and the radio became, in effect, a radiogram. Unfortunately it was not always as easy as the adverts for add-on record-player units implied, especially with TRF designs where the volume control operated on the first (HF) vari-μ valve cathode voltage, which meant in most cases that the signal supplied to the pick-up or gram sockets went directly into the amplifier without benefit of moderation in strength by the set's internal volume control. Some, but not all makers of players fitted integral volume controls. (*See* below, page 158, under 'Radio to Radiogram' for more on this topic.)

Tone Controls

Simple tone control by means of limiting the higher frequencies (top cut) became popular once good quality moving-coil loudspeakers had extended the frequency range. Some more costly sets were fitted with individual treble and bass controls, others had a switched tone system, sometimes marked as 'mellow', 'bright' and 'speech'. Still others had compensated volume controls, better known today as loudness controls. These allow for the characteristic response of the human ear that causes an apparent reduction on bass frequencies at low volume settings.

Reverbeo

This device was another fairly rare Philips oddity. Fitted to at least one Philips radio of the early 1960s, it consisted of a spring-type mechanical delay line which gave an unearthly echoing effect to music and rendered speech very hard to follow. Quite why Philips thought this was a good idea is difficult to imagine.

Single Control (Philips Again)

Was this simplified operation brought to its ultimate? Possibly, until it goes wrong – which it does. Used on their model 795A and also on equivalent Mullard receivers MAS5 (AC only) and MUS5 (AC/DC), the solitary control knob, operating in both rotary and joystick mode, replaces the usual separate knob features such as volume, tuning and wave-change.

Full-Vision Dials

These became popular early in the 1930s, a precursor of which was the Ekco RS3 with its illuminated dial with a range of station names, this at a time when most other makers were supplying dials marked in degrees or metres, usually visible as they rotated behind a segmented aperture. Although a little slow in take-up, the full-vision illuminated dial became virtually standard despite problems with station frequency reallocations during the 1930s, which meant that replaceable dial panels were needed.

PCBs

In the 1950s, receivers began to be constructed using printed circuit boards. These replaced the old and labour-intensive hand-wired chassis, and brought the benefits of greater speed and uniformity of production, although they did suffer from localized heat damage around output and rectifier valve holders and wire-wound resistors. Good design minimized these problems.

COLLECTING RADIO-RELATED EQUIPMENT AND EPHEMERA

Another unsubstantiated claim by a major battery manufacturer in this 1949 *Trader* advertisement.

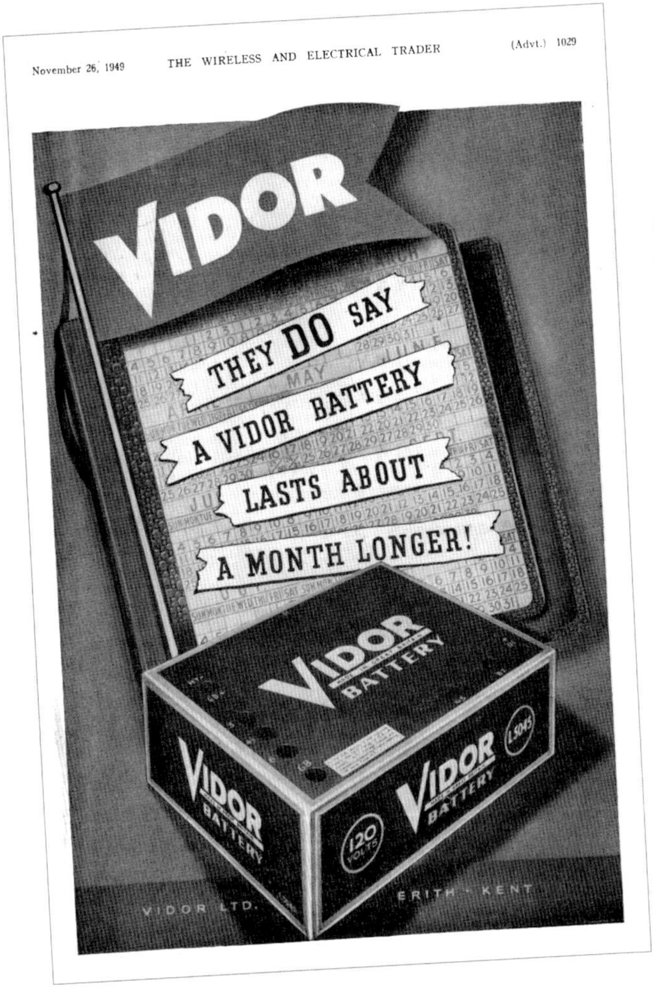

November 26, 1949   THE WIRELESS AND ELECTRICAL TRADER   (Advt.) 1029

VIDOR

THEY DO SAY A VIDOR BATTERY LASTS ABOUT A MONTH LONGER!

VIDOR BATTERY

VIDOR BATTERY

VIDOR BATTERY

120 VOLTS

VIDOR LTD.   ERITH · KENT

and these are just a few examples among a plethora of other weird and wonderful radio-concealing objects. But why stop at radios? There's a host of related ephemera, from retail shop advertising boards, emblems and signs, illuminated signage, literature and books, all of which find homes with radio collectors. Technical and design-oriented books and magazines are a specialized subject in their own right, and there is a suggested list in the appendix. 'Point-of-sale' advertising material makes for fascinating and nostalgic reading, and adds interest to home displays of related receivers. Often the claims are truly outrageous; in the early days of radio there was no advertising standards authority to oversee truthful and honest claims. Leaflets showing a given radio company's range (usually but not exclusively one year at a time) offer an insight into the state of the art at a given point in time, though allowance must be made for the more conservative approach of some makers. For example, some HMV receivers have the 'traditional' external appearance of products ten or more years older than they actually are. Philips continued to trumpet their so-called 'Superinductance' designs, which were TRF when almost all other makers had abandoned the TRF principle and adopted superior superhet circuitry.

Radio receivers do not have to be in containers of plastic or wood: there was, and still is, a market for the 'novelty' radio, sometimes produced as a marketing tool for other products, for example disguised perhaps as a soft drinks can. Others take on the form of a book, a world globe or a Chinese Buddha figurine –

Some collectors search for valves, especially early examples for their rarity and appearance. Others go in for ex-military communication equipment, or for vintage radio test gear. The choice is yours!

Radio to Radiogram

Over the years makers had commonly fitted 'gram' sockets to their sets, and some enterprising companies, two of which were Columbia and Plus-a-Gram (later Dansette), marketed add-on gramophone units fitted with electric motors and magnetic pick-ups, devices which allowed a radio owner to convert, in effect, his set into a radiogram without going to the high expense of purchasing one complete. Although this idea was really of the 1930s, as late as the early 1950s the Philips Company brought out a companion to their Disc Jockey self-contained record player. They named the little unit, which had no amplification of its own, the Disc Jockey Minor. These are neat little units, but as they use a lightweight crystal 'rock-over' pick-up unique in design to Philips, it is a problem to source a replacement should one be needed (and it probably will). The original styli were sapphire rather than much longer-lasting diamond.

Battery Substitutes

Eliminators (so named because they eliminate the need for a battery) designed to convert battery-only receivers into mains sets, were steady sellers for companies such as Amplion and Ekco. If you are tempted to purchase one of these units, be aware that they never would have passed today's electrical safety regulations even when they were new. Age will be sure to have worsened the situation, and such mains add-on devices cannot be trusted for use without being thoroughly checked by a competent technician. That said, they can and often do replace the impossible-to-obtain batteries used by valve receivers,

BELOW: Having bought your radio at great cost, it could be used as an amplifier and would play records by converting your old wind-up acoustic gramophone using a magnetic pick-up such as this 1933 example from Belling-Lee.

BOTTOM: Convert your radio into a radiogramophone – the easy, low cost way. This 'Plus-a-Gram' unit has a shelf on top large enough to support most radios, and contains an autochange record deck (78rpm only). Date unknown, but probably immediately post-World War II.

valve radio battery production having ceased in the early 1970s.

Additional Speakers

Extension loudspeakers can be an art form in themselves, and during the late 1920s and early 1930s, a host of different types appeared, from straightforward designs in Bakelite to ornate mantel-clock-style wooden cabinets adorned with fretted patterns or flowery woven silk grille fabrics. The horns on some rare early units were occasionally made from exotic materials such as china, solid hardwood or electrodeposited copper. The loudspeaker units within vary from early dynamic cone types to good permanent magnet moving-coil units. Which you choose depends upon the radio you use to drive the extension loudspeaker with – but remember, moving-coil loudspeakers require greater output power than the dynamic cone and horn speakers, and receivers designed to work with the latter may not have the power to provide adequate volume with the former. There is also a potential problem with impedance matching, in that dynamic units often were driven directly from the output valve, their high impedance matching the valve without need for a transformer. Moving-coil units usually have a very low impedance, and connecting these directly into the anode circuit of an output valve without the protection of a transformer will almost certainly cause immediate burn-out of the delicate speech coil.

Look for the Signs

Enamel on metal radio signs of various kinds are sometimes offered on internet auction sites. Sometimes it is made clear that they are modern creations,* sometimes it is not. They vary from the kind of maker's brand sign that you might suppose would have been part of a retailer's display to BBC emblems claiming to have been attached to radio microphones. Whilst it is true that some of these are going to be genuine, the onus is on the purchaser to be satisfied that this is truly the case. Heavy cardboard period point-of-sale display material is more likely to be genuine. Framed adverts appear from time to time; these are usually pages taken from original magazines of the period concerned, and if that kind of thing appeals to you, consider the possibility of buying such magazines and framing your own.

'Modern' Vintage

Some modern radios have been deliberately designed to look as if they are vintage – at least, that seems to have been the intention; but if so, the makers rarely succeed. The giveaway – apart from the fact that the kitsch design and generally crude execution of cabinetwork leaves a great deal to be desired – is physical size: they are almost always much smaller than any original vintage radio of an approximately similar style, consequently destroying the elegant proportions. At best they are a weak pastiche of the real thing. The modern 'reproductions' do often claim the advantage, if that's what it is, of being able to play CDs, but as most working vintage radios will happily accept CD input via the gram/pickup sockets, even that is to some extent spurious.

A Final Word of Caution

Because so many millions of receivers were produced there remains a vast reservoir of sets, and buyers can afford to be selective. Unless you really are gripped by the desire to own a particular radio, think twice and check for other sources and comparable prices before buying, especially if it is a post-World War II set made by a well known manufacturer. There will always be another DAC90A or 'Coronation Twin' if you wait long enough. Damage of any kind will greatly affect the value of a receiver.

---

* In the sense that no such sign originally existed, meaning that the things are a pretence.

The Ekco company was one of the first British radio manufacturers to recognize the importance of the thermosetting plastic material Bakelite. They took full advantage of its seemingly unlimited potential for innovation in radio cabinet design by employing several brilliant designers of the 1930s to produce some outstanding and modernistic radios.

SERGE CHERMAYEFF (1900–96)

Chermayeff was one of Britain's foremost architects and designers of the inter-war period. From a rich Russian–Jewish family, he was educated at Harrow. When the Russian Revolution of 1917 caused the family to lose their wealth, Chermayeff's search for work took him through Britain, Europe and as far as Latin America.

By 1924 he was established in Britain as an interior designer and became a leader in this respect, so much so that by the 1930s he was in demand for both product design and architectural design. His designs for Ekco include models AC64 and AC74. He was modernist in his approach, and was a member of organizations such as MARS and the Twentieth Century Group. He formed a partnership with Erich Mendelssohn, the German architect. At the start of World War II he became bankrupt once again, prompting him to emigrate to America to work as a professor of architecture at Yale University.

TOP: **Jesse Collins produced this startlingly original design for the AC97 in 1936.**

LEFT: **Model AC74, Serge Chermayeff's uncompromisingly modernist design for Ekco, 1933.**

MISCHA BLACK (1910–77)

Another famous Russian émigré, Mischa Black moved to Britain in his childhood. He received training as an architect and, in the early 1930s, like Chermayeff, joined the Modern Architecture Research group (MARS). He designed cabinets for Ekco, one example being the UAW78. He advanced his career in the early 1940s, when, together with the designer Milner Gray, he set up the Design Research Unit, a highly successful international design service. He ended his career as Professor of Industrial Design at the Royal College of Art. He was knighted in 1972.

WELLS COATES (1895–1958)

Wells Coates was born in Japan of Canadian parents. He became influenced by Japanese architecture, and also by his mother, herself a successful architect. In Canada, he studied engineering at the University of British Columbia. After fighting in the trenches of France and Belgium with a division of the Canadian Gunners, he became a fully trained pilot with the RAF. He completed his studies at London University and then during the 1920s began work as a science correspondent in Vancouver, Paris and London, for the *Daily Express* newspaper.

His career as an architect began in 1928. Always a leading modernist, his contribution to British architecture in the 1930s included Embassy Court in Brighton and Lawn Road Flats in Hampstead, London. He became a key member of the influential group of architects and designers who effectively founded the Modern Movement in British design. This included the Modern Architecture Research Group (MARS) and Unit One.

Possibly because of his wider background training in engineering, he was always ready to experiment with new materials. In 1931, together with Jack Pritchard of the Venesta Plywood Company, he formed Isokon, a company with the aim of designing functional modern buildings and furniture. The furniture, designed by Coates and other highly distinguished modernist designers, was largely in plywood, favoured because of its sculptural qualities. His Lawn Road Flats in Hampstead, London, completed in 1934, became home to some of the leading designers in the modern movement, including Walter Gropius. The flats were innovative because they were fully fitted – not simply empty rooms – and used 'new' materials such as concrete, steel and plywood. Coates also designed a studio for the BBC's prestigious new Broadcasting House.

J.K. White designed this 1931/2 cabinet for Ekco. It was used in adapted form for the RS series and the M23. The 'cathedral' form displays Art Deco influences.

BELOW: Wells Coates.

continued overleaf

Princess Christmas 1948 advert, trade magazine.

His design, originally in 1932, of a circular cabinet radio in Bakelite, won a competition organized by the Ekco Radio Company. The AD65, marketed in 1934, was followed by years of other successful designs for the company, including other radio cabinets, fires, alarm clocks and television. He designed the Ekco P63 'Princess' portable (1948), using then novel thermoplastic materials. This compact portable radio must have seemed futuristic at the time. He went on to work in the aircraft industry, designing cabin interiors for passenger airliners; also, back in Vancouver during the final year of his life, he designed an electric monorail system said to be of great merit which, sadly, was not taken up by companies already committed to existing transport methods.

Of course, as far as knowledgeable vintage radio enthusiasts are concerned, he will be best remembered for his series of 'round cabinet' radios, designed for Ekco and beginning with the AD65. This radio, with its chrome grille, circular form and large dial, broke all the conventions of the time, its strong visual appeal setting a precedent for the future. Other variations on the theme followed with continuing success. The A22 of 1945 was the last in the line of these striking designs.

These radios command a high price today, being highly collectable – and highly prized. An idealist who believed that architecture and design could be used to create solutions for many of the world's problems, and that the future had to be planned anew rather than attempt to shore up the failures of the past, Coates' farsightedness and his personal high standards led him to offer guidance on modern design that had a characteristically strong functional ethic. He did not simply design: he showed an innate understanding of, and ability to employ the qualities of the materials in use, whether Bakelite, thermoplastic, plywood or concrete. His designs are proof of his mastery: they stand the hardest test of all, that of time.

Others who produced outstanding design work for the Ekco company include J.K. White (RS3/M23 series) and Jesse Collins (AC97).

The Ekco A22, a post-war version of Coates' round series, 1945.

EXTERNAL CARE AND RESTORATION OF VINTAGE RADIOS

The ravages of time. The cabinet of this HMV 1122 needs a full restoration.

The usual approach taken by museums when dealing with the preservation of antique or vintage artefacts is to do nothing that cannot be reversed – and this is as it should be; after all, the function of a museum is surely to display the things of the past as far as possible in their found state. Preservation, in terms of the prevention of further deterioration, is often the limit of their involvement. Most private collectors do not own museums and want their collections to look as attractive as possible, and this is when restoration rather than simply preservation becomes important. Of course, if you are fortunate enough to come by an example of an extremely rare receiver, you would be well advised to take the attitude of the museum and do as little as possible to alter its condition; but the vast majority of receivers are far from rare, and with these, restoration is often advisable because, despite some radios being in good overall condition and showing

only minimal wear when presented for sale, the majority will be found to be in a well worn or rough state when offered.

The unfortunate truth is that receivers in general tend to have suffered a rather hard life in their latter, unwanted years, and this can show itself by various forms of cabinet damage: typically, wood cabinets may have scuffs and stains to the finished surfaces, or water marks and damaged veneer; or joints may have worked loose, and evidence of old or recent woodworm attack may be found. The wise collector should ensure that any wooden-cased receiver entering his home will first have been thoroughly treated with woodworm-eradicating chemicals.

Years of neglect take their toll. Bakelite cabinets, tough though they are, will often be found scratched, cracked or broken, perhaps to an extent where there are missing sections of Bakelite. Sometimes the surface of the Bakelite is dull, and fillers may be exposed; the former may be due to sunlight damage and the latter to prolonged exposure to dampness. In neither case can much be done to improve matters. Portable radios, essentially contained in lightweight cases covered with fabric, textured plastic film or paper-backed leather-effect material, can look very tired, and the thin sections of timber used in case construction seem especially prone to woodworm attack. Rexine fabric coverings can usually be cleaned with care, but paper-based materials are less easy to restore.

All sets with grille fabrics may show signs of staining or tears in the cloth. Metal grilles may be corroded or discoloured. Knobs may be broken, or one or more may be of an incorrect type. Surrounds (escutcheons) may be cracked, corroded, discoloured or missing altogether. The first thing to do when confronted with a sorry-looking set is to take careful stock of the situation. Firstly, is the set something special, to the extent that you may not see another for a very long time – if ever? Rarity may be an acceptable reason to take on a wreck! Secondly, have you the resources – in terms of skill, equipment, space, funds, time – either to make a successful restoration yourself or alternatively to pay an expert to do it for you? Thirdly, if not, are you prepared to accept the set 'as is' in the full knowledge that it will likely as not stay that way?

Assuming you've answered one or more of these points and you accept the set and decide that you wish to restore the cabinet, here are a few suggestions, beginning with an important point that applies in equal measure to any cabinet regardless of its construction

material: first of all you have to dismantle it. Simply stated, the chassis should be removed from the cabinet before any practical stripping or renovation work starts. Remove everything that can be removed – the knobs, the loudspeaker (possibly complete with its wooden 'baffle' board) and any ancillary fittings such as metal or Bakelite dial surrounds (these are known as escutcheons), maker's metal or plastic emblems and so on. If the grille cloth or metal grille mesh comes away with the baffle board, so much the better. If not and you wish to preserve it, cloth should be very carefully protected but left bonded to the baffle panel – it is extremely likely that damage will occur during removal, and in any case it will prove difficult to replace it as tightly as it was fitted originally. Metal mesh should be easier to remove and replace as it won't be glued but pinned, stapled or screwed into place. All this preparation is essential when using paint stripper, otherwise you run the risk of irreparable damage to delicate parts. Dismantling should be done in a careful sequence and notes made as you progress, or you may end up with a left-over collection of little plates, clips and bolts.

If you can, obtain service information, as this usually contains a basic chassis removal guide for the model concerned. An obvious point, but essential: disconnect the radio completely from any power source before removing its back cover. Generally speaking, most

General view of a cabinet before restoration. This early 1930s Aerodyne 'Drake' was in poor condition. The top was severely cracked, probably due to exposure to an external fire.

The damaged top panel removed. It was surprisingly easy to remove the top without damage to the sides. The blackened surfaces support the fire theory.

receiver chassis are held in place in the cabinet with metal screws either from beneath the cabinet or from the rear chassis runner. Knobs may be held on control spindles by clips – in which case, they may pull off – or with one, or occasionally two small headless 'grub' screws in holes on the sides of the knobs. These screws can be slackened with a fine screwdriver, but if they have rusted, a drop of freeing agent such as WD40 plus patience should help loosen them. Never apply leverage, such as a screwdriver, to one side of a knob or you will almost certainly break either the knob or the cabinet beneath it. It is possible to apply leverage

– gently – from two opposing sides of a resistant knob, but take steps to protect the cabinet by spreading the leverage pressure through thick packing such as hardboard strip. The golden rule is: take your time, apply pressure gently, and watch and listen for anything untoward. With luck and the obligatory patience, you'll get the control knobs free. Just remember – Rome wasn't built in a day, and those knobs may have been in place since long before you were born.

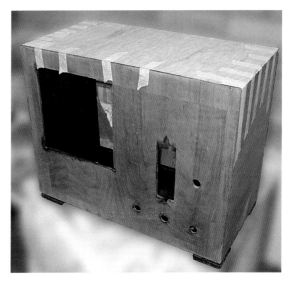

Testing the new top panel for fit. With allowance made for veneer (added later), a matching panel of ply was prepared, using the original top as a template.

The replacement top secured. The new top panel is shown pinned and glued into place, with masking tape 'hinges' pulling the top edges into place.

Selecting veneer for the new top. A suitable veneer sheet was obtained and the pieces trimmed to approximate fit.

Veneering completed. A good match to the existing veneer was made.

Wood Cabinets

Most radio cabinets will probably have been spray lacquered when manufactured. The choice you have to make is whether to attempt to emulate the original finish, or to use a simpler alternative requiring less skill. Such decisions must be made in the light of your own experience, and to some extent on the treatment the veneered cabinet received in the first place. Some makers tended to use dark stains and/or contrasting veneer inlays to emphasize certain areas and to deflect the eye from the basic cabinet 'boxiness'. Successfully repeating some of these visual decorations can prove taxing. Before any stripping of the surfaces begins, it is wise to take photographs showing the extent of added toning and colouring, and for this task a digital camera is convenient. Masking, as an aid to localized toning or staining and shown in some of the photographs, may be needed to bring life back to the inlays.

Working Conditions

When paint stripping and respraying, it is best to work whenever possible in an open environment, perhaps on a bench set near the open door of the workplace. This minimizes the ingestion of paint stripper or spray aerosol lacquer fumes, but you should always use a face mask, something that is doubly important if you are prone to chest problems or asthma. Use one when sanding, too. A dust-free environment is essential for a good, smooth lacquer finish. Refill with water an empty trigger-spray bottle of the type used for glass cleaning, and use it to damp the floor area around your work site. When applying finish either by spray equipment or aerosols, cover anywhere and everywhere except the cabinet parts you are refinishing, as overspray seems to get into the smallest gaps. Keep all chemical compounds, thinners, varnishes and strippers well out of the reach of children and animals.

Paint stripper is unpleasant stuff when it comes into contact with skin, and much worse if it enters the eyes, so wear protective clothing or old clothes when using paint stripper, as even the gel types are almost certain to splash a little. For the same reason eye protection is sensible. It does tend to throw off fumes, so read the instructions carefully before you start, and wear a face mask if needed. Protect your hands with gloves, preferably of the long-sleeve variety. You can expect the fingers to wear through quite quickly, especially if you are using – as will be suggested – wire wool with paint stripper. If you do get stripper on your hands, wash it off immediately, don't wait: white spirit is quick to neutralize its effects, but a good wash in warm soapy water works equally well, and though the hot water will accentuate any burn already caused by the stripper, you must persevere and remove all trace of the solution. When paint stripper comes into contact with skin, its effects are not always immediate but soon develop into a burning pain.

Stripping

Whatever final refinishing technique you decide on, to get a really good result it is always necessary to remove the old finish completely and get down to bare wood. Sanding alone can accomplish this, but great care is needed as it is all too easy to cut through the very thin veneers, especially on corners. A far better method – though much messier initially – is to use paint stripper. Some are presented in liquid form, others are a gel type; both have their advantages and disadvantages in use, and either can be used successfully. Some are described as water-soluble, the implication being that you can wash off stripper with water. This is hardly easy to do in practice, and in any case you should not expose your radio cabinet to water; it is better to use turps substitute – white spirit – where you use a water-soluble or spirit-soluble stripper.

Apply stripper to one surface at a time, never to an entire cabinet, or you run the very real risk of finding that the stripper has dried into a hard-ridged and immovable mess which is incredibly difficult to move, as adding further stripper at that point is useless: stripper does not dissolve stripper. Work quickly, using a paintbrush of perhaps 1in (2.5cm) in size. Put plenty on, stippling and agitating with the brush. Finishes vary in their resistance to stripper attack, but most yield fairly easily. Scrape off the first layer and recoat where necessary with stripper. A plastic scraper is safer than a metal one as it will not dig in or scratch the surface. Remember that the veneers used on cabinets are extremely thin. In difficult cases, wire wool soaked in stripper may be used along the grain.

Grain Filling

If you have occasion to re-veneer part of a cabinet – and this is usually the top where the greatest damage is found – then you must be aware of open grain. This is a characteristic of some hardwood timbers, and it shows itself as gaps between and parallel to the grain direction. These slight voids create an uneven surface, and if they are not corrected before refinishing there will be a distinct difference in the glossiness between the old and the new. One way to correct the problem is to apply several – many, even – layers of finish, rubbing each one down until you arrive at a point where the grain is level and no voids are apparent. This is labour-intensive, however. Another and quicker way is to use a ready-made grain-filling compound, and these are readily available in a variety of timber shades. Rubbed across – not along – the grain, they fill the surface effectively and are easy to use. After sanding level with fine sandpaper and a cork block (not with glasspaper held in the fingers), they will accept any finish. Note that grain filling is unlikely to be needed on stripped surfaces.

When selecting grain filler it is essential to choose colour as near as possible to the timber you are finishing, otherwise the filler will show through any applied finish. Some proprietory types may be mixed to create intermediate tones. Experimentation may be needed as grain filler will not change or darken when coated with lacquer to the same extent as natural wood does. Slight tonal variations can be covered easily if you are using toner spray, but with French polish any marked difference in shade will be difficult to hide completely. When using Danish oil, it may be preferable not to use grain filler at all as the oil provides a finish that is simply too transparent, allowing the slightest variation in tone to show. Unless, that is, you intend to stain the timber, as most grain fillers will either take stain after application, or can be thinned with stain beforehand – but again you are strongly advised to check before using, and the best way to do that is to try the filling and staining process on a piece of similar scrap timber.

French polish will do duty as a grain filler where the openness isn't excessive, and if you decide to use it, a variation of French polish called shellac sanding sealer is preferable, as its consistency is such that fewer coats are required. French polish as a finish can look superb, but it does require some skill in application, the process of which is briefly described below. Bear in mind, however, that once hardened off, French polish can usually be oversprayed with cellulose or other forms of lacquer without an adverse reaction taking place, so whatever finish you choose, surface preparation with sanding sealer is likely to be acceptable.

French Polishing

After the surface has been thoroughly prepared and cleared of all dust using a tack cloth (slightly sticky cloths, obtainable from good general finish suppliers), a piece of clean lint-free cloth is folded around a pad of cotton waste or cotton wool to form a shape called a 'shoe' or a rubber. The waste is charged with sufficient French polish to allow it to penetrate through the base of the rubber as you apply it to the wood. Practice on scrap is infinitely better than diving straight in on a cabinet. Most authorities suggest that the rubber should be moved about the surfaces in a figure-of-eight motion, but you might find this tricky due to the rapid drying of the polish. Whether you work in a figure-of-eight movement or in straight bands, application must be continuous until the particular surface being treated is covered. Stopping, even for a second, may result in pick-up and 'tearing' of the partially dried finish. The slightest drop of linseed oil applied to the foot of the rubber will help minimize tackiness. After a couple of coats, leave to harden off, then lightly sand or wire wool along the grain; clear the dust completely before continuing.

It is important never to use French polish at full strength, even for the first coats, or you will end up with rather obvious and unsightly ridges on the surface. Dilute with methylated spirits – nothing else will do – in a clean container such as an old mug or jam jar. Each coat should be diluted further until the last coat is almost pure meths. If you make a slip or you are not satisfied with your work, neat meths will remove all your coats and leave you free to start again. A word of warning: French polish seems to get under the fingernails and it can be very difficult to get your hands completely clean. Always wear rubber gloves.

French polish (shellac) comes ready mixed in a range of tints, so-called 'button' polish being a good choice for general use as it warms and tones wood into a golden brown and helps blend slightly different timber colour by obscuring. Black French polish is ideal for ebonized finishes that are found on early receiver front panels, and Garnet polish is useful for dark timbers such as walnut. You can also mix your own polish from shellac flakes and methylated spirits.

Plastic Coatings

The late 1950s and early 1960s saw a vogue for mirror-polished cabinets, and it might be thought that obtaining such a finish would be beyond the resources of the amateur. Not so: Rustin's Plastic Coating is a two-part cold-curing plastic finish which is applied by brush or short-haired or sponge roller. After curing, it can be burnished to a brilliant gloss using burnishing cream or a car-cutting compound such as T-Cut or, if preferred, it can be rubbed down with wire wool to provide a semi-matt finish. Although perfect for the type of radios mentioned, plastic coating does not look quite 'right' on 1930s receivers as it is just too hard and bright a gloss.

Spraying and Toning

There has long been a tradition within the furniture industry of toning spray-lacquered timber surfaces. This is usually done in one operation, the lacquer having suitable wood-shade pigment matter added before spraying. This builds up as the spraying progresses until an adequate depth of toning has been achieved, sufficient to have obscured any variation on the base timber colour. A few coats of clear lacquer are then applied to seal in and protect the toning.

After World War II, the shortage of materials meant that inferior grades of timber had to be used for radio cabinets, and this made toning necessary to camouflage

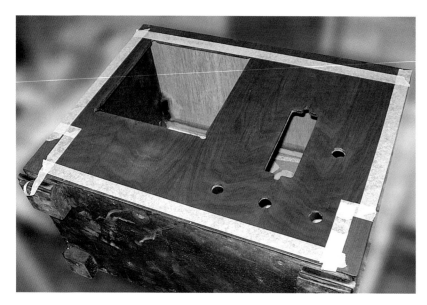

Masking the front for localised staining. The original two-tone finish was carefully recreated.

The chassis before work began. Rust and soot – an unusual combination.

BELOW: Front view of the completed set. A worthwhile improvement.

Rear view of the cleaned chassis. With the dirt washed off carefully and the rust neutralized, the chassis condition was acceptable.

ABOVE: Aerodyne 301 preparation. Another two-tone finish. Masking is shown here for first spray coats.

RIGHT: Aerodyne 301 finished. The finished cabinet recreates the day the receiver left the shop.

the less attractive grain patterns of the available wood. By this means a presentable radio cabinet was created from less than ideal materials. Cabinets finished in this way are all well and good when new, but knocks and scratches received in general wear and tear show all too clearly the inferior, usually lighter timber beneath. Such damage is well nigh impossible to disguise, and beyond a few light scuffs, a stage is quickly reached where refinishing is essential on such receivers.

Working in a warm, dry atmosphere, follow the working procedure described above. Strip, clean and prepare. If you have used white spirit to clean the cabinet, either leave it to dry thoroughly – I recommend at least a twenty-four-hour period – or go over the cabinet with cellulose thinner, allowing this to dry, which it will, rapidly. Unless you have replaced a panel or a section of veneer, grain filling should not be required.

A suggested spraying procedure is as follows: using aerosol or HVLP spray equipment and working from the back of the cabinet towards the front, spray lightly on only the surface that is horizontal; this prevents 'curtaining' or sagging in the finish due to gravity. Reposition the cabinet so as to bring each side in turn to the horizontal. Always spray from a position that places the already coated surfaces in the 'shadow' of the spray to prevent overspray. For the same reason, when spraying the front, lie the cabinet on its back and spray with the bottom of the cabinet nearest you. Patience is needed – do not stand a cabinet on a coated end until the coating is hard dry. Most lacquers are highly volatile, so this can be a matter of a ten to fifteen minutes or less. The volatility is a very good reason to wear a protective face mask.

Once you have applied a couple of clear coats, allow to harden off before flatting with very fine paper – wet-and-dry used wet with a little solid soap as a lubricant works well. Check after drying for voids such as grain cavities by sighting with the light at an acute angle on the surfaces. If you intend to use a toner spray, now is the time to do so, as the first couple of coats will act as a sealer and prevent variations in toner take-up that otherwise may cause unsightly variations in toner intensity. The number of coats depends upon how deep you wish the toning to be, but it is worth

remembering that sometimes 'less is more', and it is very easy to overdo the process and end up with an overly dark and grain-obscured cabinet. In the extreme case, it might just as well have been painted! Always finish with at least a couple of clear gloss coats.

Allow to harden thoroughly – for a few days, ideally – before finishing to your taste either with a cutting compound for a smooth gloss finish, or fine wire wool and wax polish for a matt/semi-matt/eggshell gleam. Take great care not to overdo cutting along edges and corners or you may cut through the toner and ruin all your careful work.

Spraying Lacquer

The summer is the best time to spray near an open door, ideally within an hour before noon to two hours afterwards, the reason being the possibility of 'bloom', which is moisture from the air trapped in the lacquer surface, which shows itself as greyish white opaque patches. If this happens, prompt use of a warm-air setting on a hairdryer can sometimes drive the moisture out. This must be done quickly, before the lacquer surface hardens off.

Aerosols are very affected by temperature, and success or failure may be a matter of a few degrees. If your aerosols feel cold, stand them in warm water for a while. You will be rewarded with a fine, high-pressure spray pattern with minimal spatter. Spray between 6–9in (15–22cm) from the surface.

Never finish with toner. A couple of clear gloss coats protect the applied tint, and also provide a higher gloss than the pigmented toner is capable of. Rub down with wet-and-dry paper, used wet with soap, perhaps after the first three or four light coats. Don't leave all cutting back until the final coat. Dry with *gentle* heat from a hairdryer.

If for any reason you use T-Cut or other cutting compounds between applications of lacquer, remove all traces with white spirit, *not* cellulose thinner, which will strip off your existing coats. White spirit must, however, be allowed to dry completely or it will interact with the next lacquer coat.

Danish Oil

This is a simple-to-use alternative finish and can give pleasing results with the minimum of skill and at a low cost. The gloss achieved does not rival lacquer but comes quite close to French polish by the time several coats have been applied. Toning Danish oil by adding pigments is possible, but results are unpredictable and it is probably best reserved for cabinets that require no toning.

The procedure is as follows: after stripping and cleaning the cabinet of all existing finish, wash down with white spirit. When dry, apply a couple of coats of Danish oil by brush, working along the grain. Spread it well to avoid curtaining or pooling, and leave for fifteen to twenty minutes before wiping down with a lint-free cloth. Several further coats can be applied, each building the gloss, but it may be advisable to rub down lightly with fine wet/dry paper, used wet, to prevent ridging. Then the last coat or two can be applied using a soft rag rather than a brush. The finished surface can be maintained or buffed to a higher shine with a good paste wax polish.

Bakelite Problems and Solutions

Bakelite can look beautiful, but not all cabinets can be restored to original high-gloss glory. The worst effects of ageing occur when sets have been stored for long periods in damp conditions; the surface of the Bakelite tends to absorb moisture, and slowly but surely what was once smooth and glossy becomes slightly roughened and dull. One certain cause of this intractable problem is the swelling of the inert filler, used to bulk out the Bakelite at the moulding stage. A variety of fillers were used, one of the most common being wood flour (finely powdered sawdust); this expands as it takes up moisture, damaging the smooth Bakelite surface. Attempts to polish out or cut back with Brasso or other compound are usually unsuccessful, and may make the problem worse by producing lighter spots and patches. Also, when a receiver has been exposed for long periods to the bleaching effect of the ultra-violet in sunlight, the colour of the dyestuffs used in the Bakelite will fade. This may be improved slightly by cutting with T-Cut or Brasso, but it is unlikely to result in a return to full-depth colour.

Some restorers advocate the use of Bakelite filings to mix with resin-based filler compounds such as Araldite when filling missing areas in a cabinet. This cannot be a sensible idea, for two reasons: firstly, the filings are going to be a different shade and possess a differing light reflectivity from an intact Bakelite cabinet surface, and so any patch made by this method cannot help but show; and secondly, and perhaps more importantly, it is said that one of the filling agents used from time to time was asbestos. Therefore filing Bakelite could at least in theory release very fine asbestos dust into the air, a potentially dangerous thing to do. For safety, a face mask should be worn if filing is carried out to clean up the edges of a break. Furthermore, the surface to be filed should be wetted with white spirit to limit dust formation, and the area cleaned with a vacuum cleaner after filing work is completed.

So far, intractable problems have been described, and when purchasing, such faults should be looked for to avoid later discovery and disappointment. Fortunately, there is quite a lot that can be done to improve most Bakelite cabinets.

Cleaning and Polishing

Cabinets are often found intact with no cracks or broken sections but with a dead-looking surface due to coatings of nicotine tar, coal-fire smoke, dirty wax and so on. Antique dealers call this muck 'patina'. To clean this off effectively it is easiest to strip out all fittings, especially any glass dial – remember that wetting the screen-printed side of such a dial is almost inevitably going to result in the loss of some, or all of the markings – to leave the empty cabinet shell. Foam cleanser can then be sprayed liberally on the shell; it should be left to stand for a few seconds, then rinsed off with warm water, mopped down with an absorbent cloth, and dried thoroughly inside and out with warm air –

Ferguson 'Flight' cabinet before restoration. The black Bakelite cabinet had been sprayed at the time of manufacture but had suffered badly – not just scratches, but actual missing sections of the protruding front edge.

Ferguson 'Flight', cabinet corner rebuild. After all the paint was stripped from the cabinet, repairs were undertaken. Here, Milliput epoxy putty is being used to replace the missing corner.

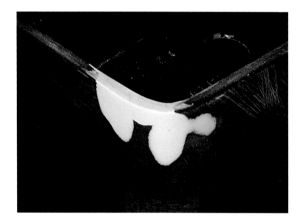

ABOVE LEFT: Ferguson 'Flight' corner. The repair is almost complete.

ABOVE: Ferguson cabinet, primed. The cabinet is shown here after several coats of grey primer paint.

Ferguson 'Flight' completed. After flatting the primer with fine wet/dry paper, several top coats of cream paint were sprayed, then cut back to achieve this high gloss.

an old hairdryer is ideal for the purpose. Hot-air guns as used for paint stripping may produce excess heat, and although thermosetting plastics won't melt, they can crack and will blister under excess heat. An alternative and quite adequate, though slightly less efficient cleaning agent, is ordinary washing-up liquid.

Slight Scratches and Surface Marks

The clean, dull cabinet can be brought up to a good gloss in several ways, the most well known of which are using Brasso metal polish, T-Cut car-body restorer or proprietary Bakelite polish (Bake-O-Brite). A really 'dead' cabinet might need the use of a more abrasive compound such as Farecla cutting paste, as used in the automotive body repair trade. Slight scratches may disappear when filled with tinted wax filler stick. To do this, first warm the area with your hairdryer then, using a soldering iron (carefully cleaned of residual solder) or a match or lighter flame, melt the stick and allow the molten wax to drip on to the scratched area. It will quickly set and can be carefully scraped and pared down level. A safe way to do this is to use a Stanley knife blade held in the fingers. Run short lengths of clear adhesive tape on either side of the repair area, spaced so as to carry the blade corners as this prevents dig-in and additional scratching. Scrape at a slight angle to the surface, with the top edge of the blade tilted towards the direction of travel. Patience and care is needed. A very gentle buffing with a soft cloth completes the job.

If there are many very light surface marks, consider the use of 1000 grade wet-and-dry paper, used wet with soap lubricant. Don't overdo this treatment or the cure may make things worse by showing up lighter patches. It will be necessary to buff energetically with a cutting compound and, ideally, a power tool fitted with a buffing wheel or pad to save effort – but take care on corners and edges with buffing machines, and remember to allow the cabinet time to cool, as power buffing creates frictional heat, which if unchecked could cause cracking. If uncertain of the possible result, test on the underside or the inside of the cabinet in an area that will not be on show.

This Bush receiver had seen better days. Dull, damaged Bakelite and rotted grille cloth combine to present a ruined appearance.

Repairing Deeper Faults

Small nicks and notches that are too deep to polish out can usually be corrected by a mix of Araldite and gloss paint. Adding a very small quantity of paint to the adhesive/hardener mix will give a dense colour. Note that although Araldite may have the advantage of possessing sufficient viscosity to remain – more or less – where it is placed, it is always preferable to have the surface under repair horizontal. When hard, the same blade-scraping process may be used as suggested for wax levelling, though the hardness of fully set Araldite may need you to cut with fine wet-and-dry paper to achieve a good finish. A Swann-Morton scalpel is a convenient tool in combination with a Stanley blade as it is more easily controlled for fine work. Newly set Araldite will scrape down fairly readily.

To complete the repair, buff with compound on a soft cloth. To keep the shine, furniture wax polish can be used, but it does tend to stay on the surface and remain slightly sticky. A better alternative is a silicon spray furniture polish or a car interior aerosol polish.

The Bush after exterior restoration. Bakelite gleams and freshened grille cloth and restored paint lines have transformed its appearance.

Bakelite Damage Repair

If there is one unfortunate property that Bakelite possesses in common with all thermosetting plastics, it is brittleness. In this respect the phenol formaldehyde cabinets, moulded in dark Bakelite, brown, black or 'walnut' mottled, tend to be rather less fragile and less prone to stress or heat cracking than the creamy-white urea formaldehyde cabinet varieties; but Bakelite in any form will shatter under impact, for example, if it is dropped. Remedial work is made much easier if a damaged cabinet was originally spray-painted, as this can be refinished to cover all work after repairs are complete. It is easier to disguise repairs to non-painted but 'mottled' Bakelite than to attempt the same with plain black or brown.

To deal first with painted sets, epoxy fillers such as 'Milliput' can be used. The superfine white version of this useful material provides a very smooth finish, but the standard reddish brown version works well enough and has the advantage that the distinct colour difference between the resin and the hardener means that mixing is easier to carry out. The material comes in two sticks, resin and hardener. The sticks are wrapped to keep air

out and should be re-wrapped carefully to exclude air after use. Slice off an equal amount from each stick and knead together in the fingers to mix the two. If using the superfine, mixing is something of a guess, so overdo it, rather than risk an inadequate mix. You have plenty of time as the material is very slow in hardening. Kneading it is rather like using cold, stiff and slightly crumbly clay, but it has an annoying tendency to stick to the fingers. It helps to dip your fingers in warm water as you knead. Water is also useful to prevent the stuff sticking to tool surfaces when applying the filling material, but don't over-wet the edges to be filled.

Press the kneaded compound firmly into the gap and shape it roughly with the fingers. The wetted blade of a table knife or metal scalpel handle is a useful tool for smoothing and pressing the filler. Milliput is very unlikely to need support unless the hole is extremely wide, in which case it can be backed with thick card, oddments of timber or shaped wood; but cover any surface that comes into contact with the Milliput with plastic tape to limit adherence. After some hours the filler will have hardened sufficiently to allow further trimming and shaping, and here again the scalpel comes in useful for scraping and slicing until almost, but not quite, level with the surface being filled. When set hard, a day or so later depending upon temperature and the age of the Milliput, further very careful scraping and slicing will level it to a point where it can be finished with 400 grade wet/dry paper, used wet with soap lubricant.

After drying, a thin coat of cellulose filler will take care of any small voids that might remain, although additional Milliput can be used instead. Working with a strongly directional light source such as a desk lamp assists in spotting imperfections and hollows. Place the repair to one side for a few days if you have used cellulose filler, as it has an annoying habit of shrinking as it hardens. Any additional filling should be levelled with the wet and dry paper, and the cabinet may be keyed all over by the same method in order to create a surface for the sprayed paint to grip. Several coats of primer should be applied and allowed to harden, then three or four good finishing coats of suitable colour aerosol paint. Car accessory shops are a handy source of colour sprays, and some will mix you an aerosol to your colour sample. Again after waiting for the paint to harden, the cabinet should be gently rubbed down with wet and dry, used wet as always, before the final couple of coats of paint are added. Finish with fine 800-grade wet-and-dry, then cut back to a good gloss with T-Cut or cutting compound, taking care along edges and at corners.

Dealing with Large Voids and Cracks

Cracks can be sealed with good quality superglue. You need a watery type, not a viscous one, as a lasting repair relies upon the phenomenon that liquids possess, that of capillary action where the liquid will 'wick' up the closely fitting crack. Help this process by placing the cabinet so as to allow the glue to run downwards into the fault. Where the crack has reached an edge, open it slightly with a craft knife blade before applying the glue. Placing a blob of liquid glue at the open end should ensure that, as you release the blade and the crack closes, the glue will follow the course of the crack. You need to work quickly with most makes of superglue as the 'open' time is very limited.

Where cracks have developed in the centre of panels, use fingers or wood sticks to press the sides of the crack outwards from within the cabinet, in such a way as to open the gap slightly. This should assist the penetration of the glue. Remove the sticks and pull a few strips of masking tape tightly across the crack to help keep it together. Once the glue has hardened it can be scraped down with a Stanley knife blade.

Internal reinforcement may be needed in cases where the crack reaches the edge of a cabinet; this can be done before or after sealing with superglue. Aluminium mesh, obtainable from model shops and automotive accessory suppliers where it is used as a body repair base material, can be bonded into place within the cabinet using resin of the type used for fibreglass repairs. This has a high viscosity and short working time once mixed, so the repair area should be placed horizontally to prevent the liquid migrating under gravity. Old scissors are useful in cutting the mesh. Despite the aluminium feeling weak and flexible, once it is bonded into a resin and the repair hardens, it possesses considerable strength. Using coarse emery or glasspaper, abrade the inside surface of the Bakelite to help adhesion of the resin. Thin, flexible strips of timber can be cut and placed so as to act as simple springs to wedge the mesh in place once a good coat of resin has been applied thickly enough to squeeze through the mesh. This repair method can also be used from inside to bridge larger holes in the Bakelite, to be subsequently filled with Milliput or some other two-part resin filler.

Repairing Holes in 'Walnut'-Effect Bakelite

Milliput can still be used in the manner described, but for best results it should be carefully scraped to a point below the surrounding surface, then filled with a thin layer of either fibreglass lay-up resin or Araldite, either of which may have colour mixed in to create a close match. To provide the best chance of an invisible repair, mix two separate small quantities of resin and hardener, one with a very small amount of brown paint added, and another with black. Pour a little of each into the depressed surface of the Milliput, and gently swirl to imitate the mottling of the Bakelite. After setting, the repair may be rubbed level with very fine wet-and-dry paper, used wet with soap lubricant, before polishing as already described. Be sure to add as little paint as possible, and mix very thoroughly as this avoids the development of 'soft' paint areas. Any form of gloss paint should work, including aerosol types. You need a minimum of three basic colours: red, black and yellow. These should be pre-mixed on, for example, an old saucer or a scrap of card before adding to the resin. Like most tasks, experience is a good teacher: if your first attempts are less than successful, you have lost nothing but time. Try again!

Sometimes, despite your best efforts, repairs refuse to 'disappear'. Very fine touching-in with a watercolour paintbrush and suitable gloss enamel paint mix can help, but it is important not to *paint* it on in the conventional sense: rather, with the brush almost dry, stipple the colour along the repair. If you work carefully, cracks will be virtually invisible unless closely inspected. Again, it is rather easier to disguise cracks in mottled walnut-effect Bakelite than in plain brown or black mouldings, as the stippling can use touches of darker colour to blend in with the mottle, in the manner of camouflage.

Alternatives

Another method for crack repair, useful when the edges of a crack have crumbled and lost Bakelite in places, is to use Isopon plastic metal. This two-part compound sets much faster than Milliput – in minutes, in fact – but is not quite so easy to form into shape, and it is not nice stuff to handle in the fingers, so a plastic spatula should be used. The parts must be mixed before the grey paste can be buttered along the edges of the opened crack. Pull together with tape, fill holes proud of the surface, and allow the filler a short time to set, after which it can be scraped back quite easily and finished by the painting methods described above. More than one application may be needed before a good surface free from blemishes or porosity is obtained.

For safety, you must ensure that any metal mesh used as reinforcement to a repair cannot be touched when the set is in use, nor come into contact with the metalwork of the chassis.

Re-Covering Portable Radio Cases

Valve portable radio cabinets of the early 1950s pose particular restoration problems when compared with the usually more robust construction of the average table radio cabinet. They tend to be built with lightness of weight in mind – often with thin ply panels with internal softwood stiffeners – and are therefore rather fragile. Then there is the fact that they may be covered in imitation snakeskin or some similar plastic material, often paper backed. This material is flimsy and very prone to tears and scuffs. Inevitably, few portable receivers remain in pristine condition, and little can be done to remedy this once the damage has reached eyesore proportions; in this case re-covering may be the only option.

All fittings and the chassis should be removed to leave an empty cabinet shell. Strip off the old covering as best you can, and if possible keep any complete pieces to use as patterns for the new covering. A careful examination of the existing cover and the location of seams and folds will be of great assistance in this respect. Finding matching material is not an easy task, and you may have to compromise.

Rub down the wood surfaces with abrasive to smooth out any rough parts. Lay any recovered old pieces on your new covering material with both 'back uppermost'. Use a fine-tipped felt pen to mark around the shapes. Good sharp scissors will cut Rexine and plasticized paper covering material quite well, but you get a better and straighter edge by the use of a steel rule and a scalpel or craft knife, backed with a self-healing cutting pad. An A3 size is convenient, obtainable from art shops. Try your pieces for size before sticking them in place. If in doubt, cut the shape from paper and test-fit it to the cabinet before you commit yourself.

A suitable adhesive is good quality white PVA woodwork glue. Copydex latex adhesive works well, too, but is rather trickier to spread evenly over a large surface area. Once covering is complete, leave the cabinet to harden off for a few hours before reassembly, and the reattachment of fittings such as handles and hinges. Finally, treat bare surfaces to a dose of woodworm killer/preservative.

AMERICAN AND CANADIAN RECEIVERS

In general, receivers originating from Canada or the United States were built for operation on a lower mains voltage supply of 110–120 volts, and need adapting, or must be used with a transformer or an autotransformer before they can be operated safely in areas where higher mains voltages are standard. This does not – or should not – apply to sets that have been commercially imported, as they will already have been so adapted, perhaps by the use of a line-cord mains dropper (in itself a possible problem).

Despite the possible voltage compatibility problem, some American sets are popular and demand very high prices, especially those with 'Catalin' cast resin cabinets. It is therefore essential that when purchasing an American radio with the intention of using it, that checks are carried out to see if and how it has been modified to work on the local mains supply. The fitting of line cords is no longer considered safe practice,

but step-down transformers are readily available in the UK and elsewhere. The reverse holds true, also: importing British-made radios into the USA may require the use of a step-up transformer in order to work on 110–120V, though some AC/DC models have suitable mains tapping settings.

Early American design (late 1920s–early 1930s) was often ornate, to say the least, featuring elaborate carving of quality hardwood. Radios were prized pieces of furniture. By comparison with the design of the typical British receiver, understated they were not; no British 'reserve' here! Another big difference between the early American and the British or European product concerns the number of valves. Large American sets often had more, sometimes many more, than similar British products – at times there were as many as eighteen valves in the former compared with the typical five of the latter; but then, valves were far less expensive in the USA.

RCA 'Radiola' 111A, 1924.
Four-valve battery receiver.

Crosley 'Showbox', 1928. Eight-valve broadcast band TRF, AC at 110V.

RCA Victor 121, 1931. Six-valve AC S/H, long- and short-wave bands (short = medium wave, American broadcast band).

ABOVE: Emerson 'tombstone' 5E, 1931.

RIGHT: Majestic, c. 1932. Marketed in the USA but made in France.

Pilot 'Liberty', 1932. Medium table model, rounded 'tombstone' cabinet top, grille pattern reflecting Art Nouveau influence.

Silvertone 114, 1932. Classic American 'tombstone' styling.

G-E K52, *c.* 1933. M/S. Nothing more known.

G.E. K60P, 1934. Unusual 'mantel clock' cabinet styling.

Majestic 55, *c.* 1934. No details known.

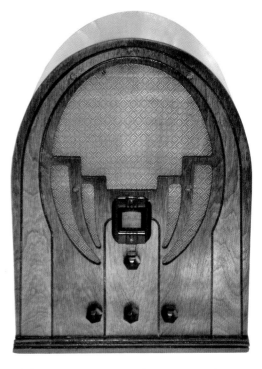

Philco 60, *c.* 1934. Four valves plus rectifier valve AC (115V) S/H, M/S. Wooden 'tombstone'-style cabinet (Canada).

LEFT: Philco 37-60, 1937. Four valves plus rectifier valve AC (115V nominal) S/H, M/S. Wooden cabinet.

RIGHT: Emerson Catalin AU190, *c.* 1937. An example of a Catalin cast cabinet.

BELOW: Philco 37-62, 1937. Four valves plus valve rectifier S/H, AC/DC (117V), L/M.

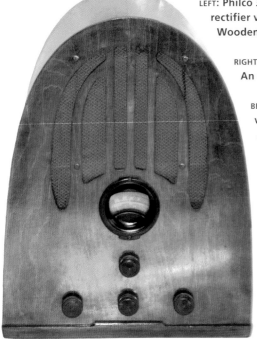

Philco 38-12, *c.* 1937. Four valves plus valve rectifier AC/DC (110V nominal) S/H, broadcast band. Small table model, veneered ply cabinet.

ABOVE: Ultradyne, 1937. Small table model.

LEFT: Arvin model 444, *c.* 1938. Metal case. Three valves plus rectifier valve AC/DC S/H, broadcast band. A true miniature table model, shown with a standard audio cassette for size comparison.

BELOW LEFT: Philco 38-15 'Transitone', *c.* 1938. Four valves plus rectifier valve AC/DC (110V nominal) S/H, broadcast band. Small table model, veneered ply cabinet.

BELOW: Emerson Midget, *c.* 1939. Extremely small receiver, little over half the size of the small Pilot 'Little Maestro', yet packed into its cabinet is a four-valve plus valve rectifier AC/DC TRF chassis. The line-cord resistive dropper and the addition of long-wave reception indicates the likelihood of the set having been an export model.

Beginning immediately prior to the onset of World War II and getting into full production in the post-war period, many American manufacturers produced smaller Bakelite-housed models, and some very attractive and unusual designs can be found from this era. Paradoxically, when they were small they were often very small. This was possible, at the cost of simplification and a considerable amount of cramming, because with AC/DC operation the valves used in such sets had high voltage heaters that were wired in series to approach the 110V level, thereby dispensing with the essential British requirement of a mains dropper resistor or line cord, both of which generate heat – especially the former, essentially housed within the cabinet. With no sizeable and hot-spot-producing mains dropper needed, cabinet sizes could be reduced to a minimum; the result is often an appealing, discreetly ornate cabinet in the 'moderne' style, although the cabinet top immediately above the rectifier and output valves might have developed stress-cracking from the heat generated by them, and this is a point to watch for when considering purchase.

Some American and Canadian designers didn't stop at 'discreet', however, and truly outlandish styling can be found, realized in both Bakelite and wood and even, on occasion, metal. The variety is quite amazing, yet within the cabinets is a more or less standard design of the five-valve superhet type. Note that the majority of these small and miniature sets usually have just the one waveband: 'broadcast' (medium wave in the UK).

LEFT: **RCA Victor 14X, 1941. Four valves plus valve rectifier AC/DC (117V) S/H, short and broadcast bands. Bakelite 'walnut'-effect cabinet. Small table model.**

BELOW LEFT: **Emerson 520B,** *c.* **1946. Four valves plus rectifier valve AC/DC (110V nominal) S/H, broadcast band. Bakelite. Miniature table model.**

BELOW: **Motorola HS-50,** *c.* **1947. Four valves plus rectifier valve AC/DC (110V nominal) S/H. Broadcast band, Bakelite cabinet. Small table model. Similar receivers are 55X11, 55X11A, 55X12, 55X12A, 55X13, 55X13A. The blue colour would seem to be non-standard, possibly applied by an owner.**

RIGHT: Stromberg-Carlson 11011 'Dynatomic', *c.* 1947. Five valves plus rectifier AC/DC S/H, broadcast band. Small table model. Suffix 'B' = brown Bakelite. Suffix 'I' = ivory.

BELOW: Bendix 110W, 1949. Four valves plus valve rectifier AC/DC S/H, broadcast band. Bakelite, the suffix 'W' indicating white (or off-white!). Similar cabinet design spanned several models and years. Small table model.

ABOVE: Bendix 110, 1949. Brown (Bendix call this 'walnut') Bakelite with gold trim. Small table model.

LEFT: Emerson Bakelite 5UB1, *c.* 1949. Small table model, broadcast band.

RIGHT: Philco 48-200, c. 1949. Four valves plus valve rectifier AC/DC (110V nominal) S/H, broadcast band. Three variants available: brown Bakelite; suffix 'I', ivory Bakelite; suffix 'W', wood.

BELOW: General Electric 408, 1950. Seven valves plus metal rectifier AC/DC (110V nominal) S/H, broadcast and FM bands. Plastic (Bakelite?) cabinet. Small table model.

BELOW LEFT: Admiral c. 1951. Miniature receiver in plastic cabinet. No information available.

BELOW: Monarch RE51, 1951. Four valves plus rectifier AC/DC S/H, broadcast band. Bakelite cabinet. Miniature table model.

RIGHT: Northern Electric 'Midge'. Sprayed Bakelite case. Miniature table radio. Canadian company name, but no other details found.

BELOW: Silvania 910, c. 1950. Miniature table model.

ABOVE: Silvertone, c. 1952. Miniature Bakelite table model.

LEFT. Stewart Warner 9160, 1951. Four valves plus rectifier valve AC/DC S/H, broadcast band. Miniature Bakelite table model.

Westinghouse H-648T4, 1955. No details known. Miniature table radio, with tape cassette alongside for size comparison.

ABOVE LEFT: Packard Bell 5R1, *c.* 1956. Broadcast band. Miniature Bakelite table model, various sprayed colours.

ABOVE: Zenith Transoceanic 'Royal' 3000-1, 1964. Ten transistors, FM, L/M/S plus 6 S/W bands. Battery operated, facility for auxiliary 12V power input. One of a long series of Oceanics, starting in 1942. Zenith Radio Corporation, Chicago, Illinois, USA.

LEFT: Zenith Transoceanic, cover open to show world map and controls.

RIGHT: Zenith emblem.

One reason why Catalin-cased radios are expensive is the unique semi-translucent quality that many of them possess. Catalin was a thermosetting plastic that was cold-poured into moulds and left to cure, after which much hand finishing was needed to bring the surfaces to the smooth glossy brilliance so characteristic of the material. There was considerable skill required in the pouring of cabinets with 'swirled' colour, and as each was done by hand, every one is individual. Unfortunately, Catalin poses a problem due to the casting process being a 'cold' one. Without heat to accelerate it, the curing process of the plastic never quite completed at the making stage. In fact, exhaustive curing may take many years, during which time an apparently rock-solid cabinet may shrink noticeably. Colours, too, may, and often do, fade or change over the years due to the use of non-lightfast dyestuffs.

ABOVE: **Addison 5A Catalin, 1940. The Addison company built radios in Toronto and Ontario, Canada.**

RIGHT: **Fada 'Bullet' 1000, late 1940s. Five valves plus rectifier, 117V AC/DC S/H, broadcast band. Catalin case in a variety of colour effects.**

ABOVE: **Addison 2A 'Catalin', 1940s. The bright, clear colours of the Catalin casting make this Addison popular with collectors.**

Airline 93BR 462A. Broadcast S/H, four-valve, all-dry battery receiver, c. 1939.

Olympic 6501U, late 1940s. Five-valve S/H, broadcast band, 105–125V AC/DC.

Emerson 652B, c. 1950. Five-valve broadcast S/H, 117V AC/DC.

Emerson 518, 1947. Five-valve broadcast S/H, AC/DC.

Emerson 659, 1949. Eight valves plus metal rectifier broadcast/FM S/H receiver, 115V AC/DC.

Pricing

This is particularly difficult, and I can only offer a general guide, as follows:

1930s cathedral-style wooden-cased receivers: ***
1950s wooden-cased receivers, and Bakelite small or miniature sets: **
Catalin types in perfect order: ****

Importing receivers can be done personally, but there will be additional costs to consider, for example import duty and not inconsiderable carriage charges. A personal buying trip to the USA or Canada could be made, but sources should be located first, possibly via the internet, or precious time may be wasted. In fact, unless you intend to import in quantity, it may be preferable to obtain a set via a specialist dealer in your own country.

EUROPEAN AND IMPORTED RECEIVERS

Post World War II, the typical radio imported into Britain by the larger continental makers was often a bulky, high quality item. Many featured piano-key switching, multiple tone controls and two or more loudspeakers, and these types of set produce a most impressive sound. The styling, a generalization across the continent* but especially true for sets of German origin, tends to be rather '1950s' bland, characterized by ultra-glossy finishes and rounded cabinet sides and corners. Some very good receivers come from other continental countries, too; Philips imported some of their range from the Netherlands. Relative rarity means a premium has to be expected when such sets are purchased – though remember that, if you are tempted to import one for yourself, carriage costs can be high, especially by air.

Siera, c. 1956. Typical of continental receivers, this Belgian Siera from 1956 is based upon the Philips B4X61A chassis, with a transformerless series push-pull output stage and capacitor-coupled loudspeaker. No phase inverter stage is used with this system. A total of nine valves including the rectifier and tuning indicator, the superhet L/M/S/FM set features separate treble and bass controls and piano-key band selection. Brown Bakelite cabinet. Medium table model. **

* Except the French, that is. French receivers are more often than not rather ornate, even looking back to the organic forms and embellishment more typical of Art Nouveau. Of course, as with any generalization, there will be exceptions, and many sets from European countries are interestingly designed and presented, even those originating from former 'Iron Curtain' areas.

RIGHT: Philips, French, c. 1938. No information on this receiver.

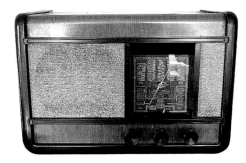

LEFT: Phenix 'Alsace', 1940s. Five valves AC S/H, internal aerial with external rotational positioning, L/M/S, tone, Tl. Ornately fitted wooden cabinet. Medium table model. *

RIGHT: Philips BX685U, 1949, the Netherlands. Six valves, AC/DC S/H, L/M plus six short-wave bands and 'tropical' band. Large table model. **

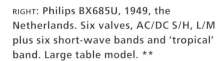

LEFT: Radialva 'Superclips', 1952, France. The cabinet is made from three separate Plascon (Bakelite) mouldings plus a metal top grille. Four valves plus rectifier AC/DC; the valve heater voltages suggest that the set was intended to operate on 120V input. At only 210mm wide by 130mm high, this is a very compact valve receiver. **/***

LEFT: Tesla 'Talisman', *c.* 1953, Czech Republic. Three valves plus rectifier valve AC/DC S/H, L/M/S. The 1946 Czech Philips factory was nationalized to become part of the Tesla group. The (basically pre-World War II) designs started by Philips were continued for a number of years, with at least four differing cabinets using the same 'Talisman' title and near-identical chassis. Bakelite, medium table model. **

ABOVE: Blaupunkt 2340 'Barcelona', *c.* 1956. Six valves plus TI AC S/H, L/M/S/FM. Piano key selection, tone controls. Large table model. ***

LEFT: Braun 99UKW, 1956. Six valves, two metal rectifiers plus TI. AC S/H, L/M/S/FM. Export version of Braun RC61. Large table model. **

Oceanic 'Surcouf' *c.* 1956. Seven valves, metal rectifier, L/M/S plus VHF. Wooden cabinet with plastic front, the turquoise parts of which illuminate. French. Styling perhaps to the point of excess. The glass scale-plate on the set pictured has slipped to one side. **

Orion AR612, 1959, Hungary. Seven valves including rectifier and TI, L/M plus two short-wave bands and FM. AC S/H, piano key selection. Large table model. **

Blaupunkt 'Salvador', c. 1960. AC S/H, medium-wave plus four short-wave bands, piano key selectors. Three loudspeakers, bass and treble controls. Large table model. ***

VEF Spidola, Latvia, Soviet Union, 1961. Ten transistors and two diodes are used in this superhet circuit. Wave change is, unusually for a radio, by means of a turret switch (turrets were typical of television tuning systems). The western European model had six wave-band coverage, but the USSR version only featured five bands. **

ABOVE: VEF Spidola, Latvia, Soviet Union, 1961, view showing dial.

ABOVE RIGHT: VEF Transistor, 1962, Latvia. This is an export model with five short-wave bands plus M/L. **

ABOVE: Grundig 'Concert Boy', 1966. This twelve transistor S/H receiver has a mechanical timer facility. Two short-wave bands plus the usual M/L and VHF. An optional mains adapter was available. West Germany. **

LEFT: Graetz 'Super Page', c. 1967. Westphalen, Germany. Twelve-transistor battery portable S/H, M/L/S/FM. **

Grundig 'Yacht Boy', *c.* 1969. Ten transistors, West Germany. L/M/FM. **

Kriesler, Australia. No information available, but this attractive Bakelite set is most likely of 1940s vintage. The Kriesler Corporation was one of Australia's largest radio manufacturers.

Pricing

Import costs again add to the difficulties faced by the collector with these types of radios. Importing a single radio is hardly worthwhile unless the particular receiver possesses significant value. Typically, expect **/***. Remember that even when buying in your home country, at some point the set is likely to have been imported, and if this was recent, it will be reflected in the price asked. There are always exceptions and bargains to be had, whatever the source of a radio, so if you like the look but not the price of a given set, remember that radios were mass-produced and there is always the possibility of another of the same turning up before too long, unless the receiver in question is a Catalin-cased model in perfect order.

POSTSCRIPT

Radios began as technical instruments that were adapted for ease of use by the public at large, and certainly receivers from the early days of radio give every indication of their heritage by their appearance and complexity of operation: marvellous instruments for their time that were created by the efforts of some of the greatest scientists and technical designers of the twentieth century. During the later 1920s and into the 1930s, radio valve technology developed and, driven by a surprisingly rapid process created both by public demand and commercial forces, the early so-called 'wireless set', a kit of interconnected radio receiving units consisting of a receiver (possibly a crystal or single-valve unit), an amplifier (possibly a two-valve unit), a loudspeaker (an exponential horn) and a power supply (often consisting of high tension, low tension and grid bias batteries – three individual dry cell batteries – plus a wet cell accumulator for low tension), metamorphosed into a single item as the domestic market for radio underwent a rapid expansion. Receivers became much more user friendly, often combining internal technical wizardry and innovation with great flair for external styling, especially in the Art Deco idiom.

Adapting to Change

The rate of progress in those early years was astounding. Almost all the obstacles that blocked the way to the perfection of radio had been surmounted by the mid-1930s, and from then on, rapid development and improvement work built on the early creativity. It also became obvious to a few far-sighted individuals that the days of large, ornate radios could not last for ever, and in the years following World War II, as radio broadcasting gradually began to lose ground to the inevitable advance of its arch rival, television, the market slowly evolved into smaller and more economical receivers to meet the demand created by the perceived need for 'second sets' to be used in the kitchen or bedroom.

The Transistor Revolution

By 1960 the transistor portable had ousted the relatively heavy and power-hungry battery valve receiver; despite the considerable efforts, some more successful than others, to design a lightweight and easily carried valve radio, it was the development of the transistor that finally made available truly portable radios. These compact receivers with their low running costs renewed public interest in radio listening 'on the move', and although mains-powered radios still used valves, it wasn't long before the transistor began to appear more generally in mains-powered radios.

Since then progress, that relentless force, has brought about great changes, and as digital broadcasting revolutionizes transmission and reception systems, valve and early transistor receivers with their 'quaint' analogue circuitry are now no more than relics of a bygone era; nevertheless they are important ones, and there remains a need to preserve the history and artefacts of radio, not simply to feed nostalgia for days long gone, but to demonstrate appreciation both for the technology and the design styling of yesteryear.

But whatever the reason, it must be right that the technology is kept alive for future generations to marvel at. Outmoded, certainly, but far from being crude, the development of twentieth-century radio was, and remains, in hindsight, as complex a technical system as ever was devised by some of the great technical and scientific minds of the nineteenth and twentieth centuries, coupled with sometimes extravagant and quite brilliant visual design in wood, metal and Bakelite.

SOURCES FOR RADIOS AND RADIO-RELATED MATERIALS

Useful Websites

There are very many websites devoted to vintage radio and related subjects. A few of the best are mentioned here, but a search for others is a rewarding if time-consuming experience. Most sites have a 'links' list for convenience.

www.bakeliteman.com
This is Jools Zauscinski's site, and it is packed with fascinating details and photographs of Bakelite products. Great fun and very informative, a must for anyone with the slightest interest in Bakelite or product design. Jools also offers a popular and useful talk on Bakelite.

www.dundeecoll.ac.uk/sections/cs/staff/al_radio
This is Alan Lord's website and there is much of use here for anyone interested in the technical side of vintage radio, all presented in Alan's intelligent but easy-to-read style, complemented by good photographs and clear descriptions of some of his many restorations.

www.vintage-radio-resources.com
A very useful site, offering lots of spares and other items. Well organized too, with much to interest the enthusiast.

www.vintage-radio.com
This is a truly superb site with lots of useful features. There's a forum for all to join, regardless of experience, plus constructional articles, examples of servicing and restoring, and a useful range of service sheet CDs. A big site, full of valuable information.

www.vintageradioworld.co.uk
This is the author's own site.

www.pasttimesradio.co.uk
A full restoration service is on offer, plus restored and unrestored sets for sale.

www.bushradio.co.uk
This is another excellent site. As the name implies, the major focus is on Bush radios, and extremely well written and presented it is, too, making a fascinating and enlightening journey into the background of one of the great names in radio.

www.radio-memories.co.uk
A wide range of interesting and evocative material here, especially about Radio Rentals receivers.

www.nostalgicvintageradio.com
Lots of American receivers for sale on this fine British website.

web.tiscali.it/leradiodisophie
Here's a site full of vintage radio ephemera, with a schematic service among its many offerings. In Italian, but there's a British flag for limited text conversion.

www.bvws.org.uk
The site of the British Vintage Wireless Society, an organization that promotes vintage radio. Well worth taking up membership; a regular and well produced bulletin

magazine is complemented by other yearly offerings, a variety of meetings and other facilities. Open to all.

www.antiqueradio.org

Phil's Old Radios is a superb American site packed with information and images.

www.classicradiogallery.com

Classic Radio Gallery has photographs of vintage receivers from around the world. Another fine website, this one is best viewed with a broadband connection due to the image file sizes. American.

www.antiqueradios.com

Antique Radios – the American collector's resource.

Auctions and Shows

www.ebay.co.uk

The popular auction site. Search from the site guide to reach Collectables/radio/television/telephony/radio/tube/valve.

The Radiophile

This magazine holds regular meetings at set locations around the country, where stalls display vintage receivers and other radio-related items, books, magazines and spares for sale, plus auctions. For details *see* Further Reading page 198

BVWS

The British Vintage Wireless Society holds a yearly Vintage Radio Show (the National Vintage Communications Fair) as well as a variety of other meetings at times throughout the year. *See* their website (above) for details.

Useful Addresses

Geoff Davies (radio)

13 Bowen Road, Rugby CV22 5LF.
Tel: 01788 574774.
Email: geoffdavies@fsmail.net
Valves and components suitable for vintage radio restoration. A telephone call or an email will bring the latest lists.

Sid Chaplin Traditional Radio Grilles

Sid Chaplin, 43 Lime Street,
Leigh-on-Sea, Essex SS9 3PA.
Tel: 01702 473740.
Email: sidney@tradradgrilles.freeserve.co.uk
Large variety in stock of materials suitable as replacement grille cloth, plus other useful spares such as carrying handles and cabinet clips for portables. Samples of cloths are always available.

Savoy Hill Publications

Fir View, Rabys Row, Scorrier,
Redruth, Cornwall TR16 5AW.
Tel: 01209 820771.
Email: sales@savoy-hill.co.uk
A vast stock of vintage service data, plus vintage receivers, components and other items for sale. Publishers of a regular newsletter.

The British Vintage Wireless and Television Museum

23 Rosendale Road, West Dulwich,
London SE21 8DS.
Tel: 020 8670 3667.
For an appointment to view,
please contact Gerald Wells, curator.

FURTHER READING

Including in-print, out-of-print and vintage books, and also magazines.

Current Magazines

The Radiophile
A subscription magazine devoted to vintage British domestic radio, with articles concerning repairs and restoration, technical matters, history and nostalgia. It is intentionally presented in a manner reminiscent of the 1930s heyday of radio magazines. However, good as it is, *The Radiophile* is far more than just a magazine. There are regular 'swapmeets', auctions and events in various parts of the country. Bakelite polish – 'Bake-O-Brite' – can be obtained from their offices, as can service data.

Radio Bygones
A well presented magazine covering vintage radio in all its forms, but with especial focus on all forms of radio-based wartime communications. Published bi-monthly, it is available on subscription only.

The Bulletin
The title of the British Vintage Wireless Society. A very high quality standard of presentation is always evident. The magazine carries articles by, and for, BVWS members, and membership of the BVWS is essential to receive *The Bulletin*, published quarterly.

Books

Bakelite Radios
Much of this material has appeared in at least two different publications with the same title, one being *Bakelite Radios* written by Robert Hawes and published by Eagle Editions, ISBN 1-86160-523-4. Another is a 'Collector's Corner' edition, *Bakelite Radios* published by Quantum Books, ISBN 1-84013-293-0.

Cook and Slessor, *Bakelite Collectables*
This large-format book has a number of impressive colour plates of Bakelite radio and TV from the golden years, including some American models. The text is reasonably informative but, typically for this type of book, the strength lies in the very attractive illustrations. Well worth a look. ISBN 1-86160-212-X.

Cullingham, Gordon G., *F.J. Camm – The Practical Man*
This is a biography that sticks to the facts – the late Gordon Cullingham was the honorary archivist of the Royal Borough of Windsor, where FJ and his brother, Sir Sidney Camm (the designer of the Hawker Hurricane of World War II fame) were born and raised. Having recently re-read this book, I was struck by just how broadly skilled Camm was. His graphic ability was first rate, too. I think someone should make a biopic of his life for cinema or TV! Published by Thamesweb, ISBN 0 9528448 0 X.

Geddes, Keith and Bussey, Gordon, *The Setmakers*
The story of British radio from the manufacturer's perspective. Well illustrated with lots of period material, some in colour. Highly recommended! Buying a copy proved to be tricky. I could not find it on the usual websites or in the high-street shops, and although it possesses an ISBN, the same sources could not help with ordering, either. Maybe I was unlucky. If so, I hope you have better luck. The copy I read for this brief review was very kindly loaned to me. Published by BREMA (the British Radio and Electronic Manufacturers' Association), ISBN 0-9517042-0-6.

Hawes, Robert, *Radio Art*

A great looking book, lots of superb photographs of vintage British and American radios. At the time of writing, the book could not be located in Britain, though it is rumoured to have been republished.

Ask for ISBN 1 872532 29 2. It's published by the Green Wood Publishing Company of London.

Hill, Jonathan, *Radio! Radio!*

published by Sunrise Press ISBN 0 9511448 71.
A large book, packed with details of radios from the very earliest efforts through to the transistor era.

Hill, Jonathan, *The Cat's Whisker – 50 Years of Wireless Design*

Published by Oresko Books, London, in the 1980s (ISBN 0 905368 46 9) but may be out of print or republished by others by now. Well worth searching for.

Julier, Guy, *20th Century Design and Designers*

Published by Thames and Hudson, this is a dictionary in a modest-sized format and is very comprehensive. ISBN 0-500-20269-9.

Kamm, Anthony and Baird, Malcolm, *John Logie Baird: A Life*

Baird has come to be thought of in the public imagination as a slightly potty old-fashioned inventor who spent his life working on a hopeless cause, namely mechanical television. This book redresses this great injustice and places Baird in his rightful position as a far-sighted and inventive near-genius. It is a story of one man's hardship, determination and bravery against incalculable odds. The text concentrates on Baird the man, rather than his inventions and developments, though of course to a great extent the two are one. Well written and researched.
Hardback. NMS Publishing, ISBN 1 901663 76 0.

Twentieth-Century Designers

This is described – accurately – as an illustrated dictionary. Full of facts, mini-biographies and pictures, covering exponents of the wider aspects of Art and Design. Published by Quantum Books, London. ISBN 0-86288-178-1.

Wells, Gerald, *Obsession: A Life in Wireless*

Well known as the founder of the Vintage Wireless Museum, Gerry Wells has led a colourful and active life, driven by his obsession: vintage radio. At first glance, it might not seem that such a life would make for interesting reading, but make no mistake, this is one of those rarities that, once you open its pages, you will be unable to close them. It is by turns fascinating, funny, sad, but always well written and totally absorbing. The only minor criticism I can make is that although the book is well produced, the quality of the photographs leaves quite a lot to be desired; but then the book is not about photos, rather it is about the life and times of a unique character. All old-hand radio and TV engineers will recognize something of themselves here. I certainly did. Verdict, overall: quite brilliant. Read it, or miss out on something very special.

Published by BVWS, free to members and a bargain £6 to others. Check the BVWS website for ordering details.

Vintage Technical Books

These may be as interesting to read as much for the quaintness of content and presentation as they are for their technical value. This is especially true of the 1920s and early 1930s. Here is a small selection:

Audel's Radioman's Guide An American publication with lots of technical information, presented in the style of the USA. Many editions, but look for early red covers.

Wireless Servicing Manual by Cocking, published by Iliffe. W.T. Cocking was a member of the staff of *Wireless World* magazine and this useful and well-written book ran to many editions from the start in 1936. Packed with practical information on testing and servicing receivers.

Foundations of Wireless A famous book with many reprints and still available today as a paperback, though now entitled *Foundations of Wireless and Electronics*. The 1936 first edition was written by A.L. Sowerby. M.G. Scroggie revised and enlarged the book when the 1941 third edition was published. The 1951 fifth edition saw a complete re-write. Any edition is well worth reading, remembering, of course, that it will be 'of its time' so the work should be considered as at least a semi-historical report on radio (sorry, wireless) technology of the time.

Introduction to Valves Hallows and Millward, published by Iliffe, 1953. Contains exactly what its title suggests, a straightforward description of the operation of the radio valve.

Newnes Television and Short-Wave Handbook by F.J. Camm (1934). Little further explanation is needed, except to say that the television content is, as might be expected, based around Baird's thirty-line experiments of the time.

News Chronicle/Newnes Wireless Constructor's Encyclopaedia. The same basic content, but varied via partial updates throughout many editions, written by F.J. Camm. Many line illustrations, containing a wealth of period detail and information with early editions describing the construction of a Baird thirty-line televisor. (1934 on.) In subsequent years the *News Chronicle* tag was dropped and *Newnes* substituted)

Radio and Television Servicing: a series of technical books originally published by Newnes
If your interest is technical, then the Newnes 'red' books should be useful. This series was published for many years, starting out in 1952 as the now rare *Radio Engineer's Service Manual* by Molloy and Poole – although this first effort had blue covers – followed by the *Radio and Television Servicing* series over many years and volumes. Packed with the schematics of sets marketed year-on-year, together with well written and comprehensive descriptions of the 'latest' developments.

The *Radio Servicing* series, published by Norman Price. Main contributors: G.N. Patchett and B. Fozard. This softback series of books was published during the 1960s and became required reading for the radio and television engineer of the time, as an aid to passing examinations. Well written, with clear diagrams.

Vintage Magazines

A lot can be learned from the perusal of magazines from the halcyon days of radio. They are a useful resource for restorers in their own right, but are also interesting, often quirky, and full of vintage adverts to take you back to a bygone era. Pre-eminent among the amateur magazines across the decades has to be *Practical Wireless*, but this is not the only publication; it is worth seeking copies of *The Radio Constructor*, a popular and practical magazine in the post-war period. *The Wireless World* of the 1930s evolved into *Wireless World* in the post-war years, changing from being a broad mix of content appealing to amateur and professional alike, into a distinctive and serious professional magazine.

Popular Wireless was published weekly from 1922 and ran until 1937 with a total of 812 editions. It certainly had an impressive line-up of contributors, but in terms of practical designs for home construction, at least in the 1930s, pride of place went to John Scott Taggart, the designer of the 'ST' series of receivers for home building. Even today there are proponents of Scott Taggart's approach, and books written by him find a ready market, though it seems that after his 1920s–30s output, little more about radio construction was heard from him. What is known is that he served in both World Wars. Highly qualified, he rose to the rank of Wing Commander in the RAF, and became the senior technical officer in charge of all radar stations in the UK from 1943 to 1945; after demobilization he worked with the Admiralty for some years before retiring in 1959.

As for the fate of the magazine, it may have been a question of economics that brought about its demise, given the quality of its staff and contributors listed on payroll. A major and ultimately more successful 1930s competitor was *Practical Wireless*, a Newnes publication headed by F.J. Camm, backed by an efficient though less stellar and therefore, presumably, more affordable regular staff.

Also worthy of seeking are copies of *Hobbies Weekly* from the 1920s and 1930s, *Amateur Wireless* and, from the 1920s, *Modern Wireless*. For non-technical aspects of vintage radio, *Radio Times* and *The Listener* make

ABOVE: *Popular Wireless* was a substantial weekly magazine in the 1920s and 1930s. This header from the early 1930s shows an illustrious group of editorial consultants, including P.P. Eckersley (the BBC's chief engineer) and Sir Oliver Lodge. A regular contributor was John Scott Taggart.

RIGHT: Filled with practical construction articles, the *Radio Constructor* magazine offered an alternative to *Practical Wireless* from 1946 to 1981.

Wireless World, very much the professional engineer's paper, never lost the consistent quality of its contents over many years. It is now renamed *Electronics World*.

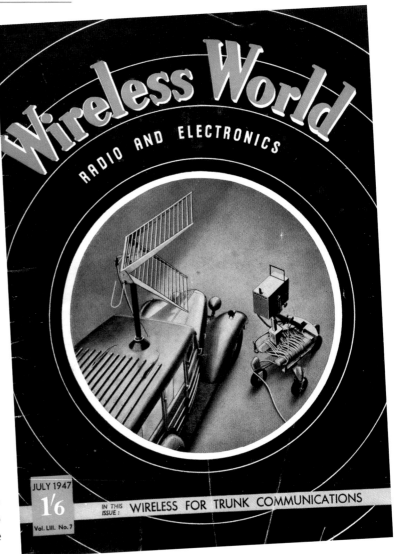

engrossing reading. The limitations of the print processes of the time make some of these publications fascinating to look at, for example the 'thumbnail' scraper-board and line drawings used in the programme columns of the post-war *Radio Times* are marvellous miniatures, tiny works of art used to illustrate plays, talks and music presentations.

Reference Sources

During the compiling of information for this book, all the books and magazines mentioned in Further Reading were used as references for aspects of radio history and technology. In addition, the following sources were consulted:

Clark, T. (editor), *Bakelite Style*, Chartwell Books, New Jersey, USA 1997.

Dowding, G.V. (editor), *Book of Practical Television*, Amalgamated Press, London 1935.

Eckersley, Roger, *BBC and All That*, Sampson, Low, Marston, London, c.1940.

Harmsworth's *Wireless Encyclopaedia*, Amalgamated Press, London. *c.* 1923.

Quarrington, C., A *Modern Practical Radio and Television*, Caxton, London, 1946–50.

Service Man's Manuals, Odhams, London, 1930s.

Williams, Trevor, *A Short History of 20th Century Technology*, Clarendon Press/Oxford University Press, Oxford, England, New York, USA; 1982.

GLOSSARY

All-dry Battery-powered receivers that use dry batteries rather than an accumulator for powering valve filaments.

Antique An object, usually furniture related, of considerable age. In Britain anything older than 100 years is usually considered to be antique, but this is a generalization and the term has become more widely applied. In the USA, the term is used where in Britain we tend to say 'vintage'.

Art Deco Not so much a movement as a 'tendency', which began in France in the early 1920s with small-scale items of jewellery and furniture, spreading in modified form to Britain and the USA in the 1930s. It is characterized by rectilinear forms, often heavy in appearance, with a marked use of chromium and solid black finishes. Art Deco became primarily architectural and was typified in Britain by the 'Odeon' style of architecture (Odeon cinemas). Bakelite lent itself to the somewhat austere and ornament-free styling characteristics of Deco. *See* Modernism and Moderne.

AF Audio Frequency. *See also* LF.

AM Abbreviation of 'amplitude modulation'. Variations in the signal strength of a carrier wave represent the audio signal being transmitted.

Art Nouveau From around 1890 to 1910, the dominant European art style was characterized by sinuous lines and highly stylized foliage-based design elements. Basically two-dimensional, it was typified by illustrators such as Beardsley. Simplified variants of it came to be adapted for ornamental use with radio cabinets, a good example being the grille design used on the Ekco RS3.

Bakelite Originally phenol formaldehyde, the term tends now to be used generically to describe most forms of thermosetting plastic, but particularly phenol and urea formaldehyde.

Balanced armature loudspeaker *See* Cone loudspeaker.

Capacitor A device consisting of conducting materials interleaved with insulating material (the dielectric). Capacitors have the property of storage of electricity for very short time periods, and effectively can pass an AC signal whilst at the same time blocking any DC present. Capacitors are essential components in any vintage radio. The vintage term for capacitor is 'condenser'.

Catkin valve A valve where a metal case replaces the conventional glass tube. Introduced in the early 1930s, but short-lived.

Cat's whisker An early, crude form of diode detector. When a fine wire formed into a coil-spring shape at one end is brought into point-contact with a metallic mineral crystal, the contact between dissimilar metals can create a 'one-way' (rectifying) signal path. *See* Crystal diode.

Catalin Cold-cast thermosetting resin. Lead moulds were used and the liquid resin was poured and left to set. After removal from the moulds, much hand work was needed to bring the surfaces to a high degree of finish. Used in the USA for a wide range of receivers around the mid-twentieth-century point. Catalin cabinets were expensive to produce but each was unique, especially those with vibrant swirled colours created during the casting. Some were deliberately made semi-transparent. One major drawback is that due to the cold pouring, curing of the plastic was never fully completed and the cabinets continued to shrink – very, very slowly – for many years post-production. These factors add up to rarity and expense when collecting. Another problem is the lack of light fastness of the pigments used, and exposure to light can cause colour changes.

Chassis Usually, the metal structure upon which various components are mounted, such as the valves and transformers, of a typical receiver.

Choke *See* Inductor.

Coil *See* Inductor.

Condenser *See* Capacitor.

Cone loudspeaker A simple form of vibrating reed loudspeaker with considerable sensitivity but a limited frequency range. There were several types, each providing minor improvements on the original concept, probably the most successful of which was the balanced armature unit. All provided an improvement on the earlier horn type, but were overtaken by the superior, though less sensitive, moving coil unit.

Crystal diode The crystal diode was a later and enclosed development of the principle of the cat's whisker.

Detector A diode used to convert the alternating transmitted radio signal into a varying but direct form.

Diode A valve with two electrodes. *See* Rectifier, Detector.

Dry cell A single cell with a paste electrolyte, supplying 1.5 volts to 'all-dry' low-consumption battery valves. Often combined with an HT battery.

Egyptiana Stylistic motifs redolent of Egypt, used in furniture and architectural design.

Eliminator A mains-driven power unit designed to replace (hence 'eliminate') the batteries of a battery-only receiver.

Ephemera Material with a short life cycle, such as advertisements, leaflets, advertising matter in general.

Escutcheon The decorative surround fitted to a radio dial scale or loudspeaker grille opening.

FM Abbreviation of 'frequency modulation', a method of radio transmission. Variations in the carrier frequency of a signal replicate changes in the sound being transmitted. *See* VHF.

GB Abbreviation of 'grid bias', a source of low voltage needed to set the operating conditions of a valve. Early receivers used separate tapped 9V batteries, but commercially this practice soon gave way to automatic bias circuits.

HF 'High frequency', vintage term nowadays supplanted by RF ('radio frequency').

Horn loudspeaker Basically, this uses a modified telephone earpiece with an exponential horn attached, similar to the horns used in acoustic gramophones. They were very sensitive, but the frequency range was limited and the reproduction quality mediocre.

Inductor Any conducting material (usually, for convenience, in wire form) that is wound around a former in such a way that each turn lies adjacent to the next, will possess some inductance. This property, simply put, allows a direct current to flow unhindered, but an alternating current will be resisted to a greater or lesser degree.

Integration The history of radio is almost one of continuous component integration. From the discrete components and units of the 'sets' of the 1920s, integration of receiver sections and loudspeakers, combination of capacitors into blocks and combination of valves into multiple units, all in the 1930s, the process still continues up to the present-day complete solid-state (transistorized) circuit integration, along with progressive miniaturization.

LF 'Low frequency', vintage term nowadays supplanted by AF ('audio frequency')

Line cord A simple, low-cost way to convert receivers built for 110 volt supplies for 230V operation. The cord is a mains lead with resistive wire. The dropped power is dissipated as heat – that is, the cord will run warm and is therefore assembled with fire-retardant material in its core. The length determines the resistance, so cords must never be shortened. Often used by importers of American receivers into Britain and Europe. *See also* Mains dropper.

LS Abbreviation of loudspeaker.

Magic eye *See* Tuning indicator.

Mains dropper A large wire-wound resistive element used to drop electrical power to a level suitable for valve heaters. The waste power is converted into heat and removed by convection into the surrounding air. *See also* Line cord.

Moderne A term used in the USA which loosely denoted styling somewhere between Art Deco and Modernism. Lots of chrome brightwork, but with an emphasis on functionality.

Modernism Not to be confused with the church movement! 'Modernism' in the arts is a general term used to describe attempts during the first three-quarters of the twentieth century to break with the traditional approach of earlier times. Effective across all the two- and three-dimensional arts, in radio design its hallmarks were simplification and functionality. There is a rather blurred cross-over between modernism, Art Deco and streamlining.

Ohm The unit of resistance.

Pentode A valve with five electrodes.

Plaskon An American term denoting a form of thermosetting plastic.

PM loudspeaker Permanent magnet. The moving-coil loudspeaker was a great step forwards in terms of quality. The earliest of these used electrically energized field coils to create an electromagnet, but once sufficiently reliable and powerful permanent magnets could be produced, moving-coil loudspeakers began to be used in all situations, including battery receivers.

Rectifier A device designed to convert AC power into DC. All radios require DC. Rectifiers may be diode valves, silicon diodes or metal-oxide types.

Resistor A component that causes a voltage drop whilst allowing an electric current to flow.

RF 'Radio frequency'. *See also* HF.

Rococo A Baroque form of decoration popular in the eighteenth century, characterized by highly ornamental asymmetrical patterns in scroll, flower or shell forms.

Semiconductor A material that is neither a perfect conductor nor a perfect insulator, but can be switched between these states – and to intermediate states – by adjustment of applied voltage. Germanium was an early semiconductor used to make diodes and transistors. Silicon is now widely used. Both of these crystalline materials are specially treated with precise amounts of impurities to create 'P-N' junctions.

Streamlining A term used mainly in the USA to describe a form of styling where aerodynamic forms are employed, whether radio, refrigerator or car. This led to radios styled after cars, cars with fins like aircraft tailplanes, and refrigerators with little wind resistance, seemingly essential in the modern home of the 1940s and early 1950s.

Test lamp A simple, reasonably safe way to check the functionality of a mains radio. *See* the section on Safety for more details (*see* page 140).

Tetrode A valve with four electrodes.

Transformer Simply stated, two separate inductor coils wound either on the same former or core, or on top of each other but not electrically connected. An AC signal passing through one coil will induce a similar signal in the other coil. By adjusting the number of turns and the thickness of the wire, step-ups or step-downs in voltage can be achieved in power transformers.

Transistor *See* Semiconductor.

Triode A valve with three electrodes.

Tuning indicator Often called a 'magic eye' or 'mystic eye', these devices convert received signal strength into a visible display, usually in the form of glowing, overlapping green leaves or bands.

VHF Abbreviation of Very High Frequency, the transmission frequency band used for British FM transmissions. The term 'VHF' has become synonymous with 'FM', although it is perfectly possible to transmit AM at VHF.

Vintage As a generalization, any product made before 1930, though the term is loose.

Watt The unit of power, meaning the rate of expenditure or consumption of energy.

Wet cell A single cell, rechargeable accumulator with a liquid electrolyte, used to supply the filaments of 2-volt battery valves.

INDEX